TODAY'S ISSUES
and Christian Beliefs

For Michael, Norma, Frank and Emma

TODAY'S ISSUES
and Christian Beliefs

SOCIAL & MORAL QUESTIONS
FOR GCSE RELIGIOUS STUDIES

Simon and Christopher Danes

LION EDUCATIONAL

Text copyright © 1994 Simon and Christopher Danes
This edition copyright © 1994 Lion Publishing

The authors assert the moral right
to be identified as the authors of this work

Published by
Lion Publishing plc
Sandy Lane West, Oxford, England
ISBN 0 7459 2521 9
Albatross Books Pty Ltd
PO Box 320, Sutherland, NSW 2232, Australia
ISBN 0 7324 0837 7

First edition 1994
Material updated 1994
10 9 8 7 6 5 4 3

Nihil Obstat: Fr G.C. Stokes, Censor Deputatus,
               Director of Religious Education,
               Diocese of Brentwood

Imprimatur: Rt. Revd. Thomas McMahon,
               Bishop of Brentwood

               8th September 1993

*The granting of an Imprimatur does not mean that the
signatories necessarily agree with the writers' views, only
that the text is free from doctrinal error.*

A catalogue record for this book is available
from the British Library

Printed and bound in Spain

Contents

PART ONE

Making Moral Decisions

1 Good and Bad: Concepts of Morality

Moral language

You are probably quite used to hearing people saying things like these. We all use words like ought, should, must, good, bad, and fair to describe actions, events and people. Words of this kind are examples of what is called **moral language.**

When we talk about moral language in the study of religion we do not mean the opposite of swearing or 'bad language'. We mean words we use which imply that we have made a judgment about something—a judgment based on a set of values.

Everybody uses moral language. Maybe you could think of some examples of your own. But there are two big questions about it:

● Does it really mean anything?

● Where does it come from?

These are very important questions. How we answer them can affect the way we behave and the values we live by. Let us put it another way: if I use the words 'fair' and 'good' about something, does this mean that there really are such things as fairness and goodness?

People who believe in God (*theists*) such as Christians, Jews and Muslims, would all answer 'yes' to this question. For them our moral language is powerful evidence that there is something outside ourselves which decides the things that are good for us. This 'something' they identify with God. By listening to this (to God) we learn to behave in the right way and we know where we have gone wrong. This works even though we have all learned our moral language and values individually from our parents, teachers and friends. After all, we can't be expected to find everything out for ourselves.

Morality without God

Other people who do not believe in God (*atheists*), or who say they cannot tell whether or not God exists (*agnostics*), are not so sure about all this. Try for a moment, if you are not an atheist, to imagine the world as it appears to somebody who is. For the atheist:

● there is no God who created the world for a purpose

● there is nobody to reveal to us what we should do

● but everybody still goes on using the words 'good' and 'bad', 'fair' and 'unfair' to describe things—and people go on expecting us to do good

A lot of people are probably content to go through life without thinking very hard about ideas like these. Many of us are quite happy to let other people do our thinking for us, to bumble along—until something disastrous happens. Do you think that this is a good thing?

Philosophers are men and women whose profession it is to think and write about the sorts of issues raised in this chapter. Are they wasting their time?

Over the years, atheist thinkers have tried to explain and explore moral language without bringing God into it. And because in their view God does not exist, many have tried to suggest rules to live by which do not depend on religion.

History has seen many different types of atheist thinking. Atheism is not just one set of ideas: we cannot talk about 'what atheism teaches' in the same way as we can talk about the teaching of Jesus or the church. We need to know about some of these ideas because they have been very influential.

Some important examples of moral thinking without God (atheist moral systems) are outlined below. (Not all of the thinkers represented here were themselves atheists, but because their moral systems do not refer to God, we can call them 'atheist systems'.)

Hedonism

Hedonism (sometimes called Epicureanism) as an atheist system of moral thinking began with the philosopher Epicurus, who lived between 342 and 270 BC. The name comes from the Greek work *hedone* (pronounced 'haydonnay') meaning 'pleasure'.

Epicurus taught that the universe was purposeless

and that **pleasure** was the highest good. In order to live a morally good life, people should avoid pain and seek pleasure.

This sounds like a recipe for doing exactly what we like, and that is what many of Epicurus' followers did! But Epicurus himself taught that moderation in things like eating and drinking were the key to a good life. Drinking too much was not worth it, because it gave you a hangover! The real pleasures were to be found in friendship, conversation and philosophy.

According to Epicurus we don't need to be told to seek pleasure: it's what we all want anyway. It is a basic part of our psychology.

Every one of us has to make choices and decisions. They can be hard. How can we know what is best, what is right? Where can we turn for help? People have always struggled with questions like these. This chapter looks at some of the answers on offer.

Hedonism has had plenty of supporters down the centuries. But it has problems too.

◆ *Many philosophers do not agree with Epicurus that the universe is without meaning or purpose.*

◆ *Epicurus thought we should do what brings us pleasure, and avoid what brings us pain. This may be sensible advice when we are deciding how much to drink at a party, but it is not always realistic when it comes to bigger things. For instance, most of us would agree that one of the greatest pleasures in life is friendship. Epicurus thought so too. Yet our friends will die and that will make us unhappy. So should we avoid being friends with people in case they die? Hedonism offers no answer to this question.*

◆ *Epicurus taught that people are natural pleasure-seekers. This sounds plausible if we don't think too hard about it. Imagine you have been put on duty at one of the doors of your school. There have been a series of incidents of pushing to get through and one of the pupils has been quite seriously hurt. You are responsible for making sure that it does not happen again. It is a hot day. It would be more pleasant to go off, get a drink, and sit down in the shade. But most people would say that would be wrong. Common sense tells us that it is not always right to pursue pleasure. Hedonism does not allow for the sense of duty and responsibility which reasonable people feel.*

Utilitarianism

Utilitarianism is another scheme of moral laws which does not depend on God. The most important Utilitarian thinkers were Jeremy Bentham (1748–1832) and John Stuart Mill (1808–73). By looking at the consequences of what we do, Utilitarianism claims to provide a rule which tells us whether an action is right or wrong. This is the rule Bentham and Mill proposed:

The right action is the one that produces the greatest happiness or good for the greatest number of people.

(This 'rule' is called the 'Principle of Utility': that is why this philosophy is called Utilitarianism.)

The Utilitarians were political philosophers. They thought this rule would help people govern countries in the best way possible. In their day there was no real democratic rule and government was frequently both cruel and unfair. By concentrating on the effects laws were having on the mass of people, they hoped to change things for the better.

Faced with a moral problem, the Utilitarian thinker asks: 'Will what I am about to do add to or reduce the amount of good in the world?'

The world owes Bentham and Mill a lot. Their thinking helped to further democracy. But that does not mean there are no problems with Utilitarianism. Here are some things to think about:

◆ *Utilitarianism talks about doing the greatest good for the greatest number. Fine! But who decides what is good?*

◆ *Utilitarianism implies that all people are of equal value. Many of us would agree with this (see Chapter 5). But what if somebody comes along and says 'I think that I am more important than everybody else'? Does Utilitarianism have an answer?*

◆ *Suppose the majority of people in a nation decide that killing its immigrant population will lead to greater happiness for the majority. Does Utilitarianism have any means of saying this is wrong?*

◆ *Utilitarianism considers the results of people's actions, not their motives. In Utilitarian theory a politician full of hatred, greed and ambition could do good things for the public and then go home to be spiteful and violent. Most of us would want to say that the politician was morally bad: but Utilitarianism on its own could not.*

◆ *Why should anybody bother working for the good of the greater number of people if he or she is going to be made personally unhappy by it?*

Egoism

The last question we had about Utilitarianism is one which might be asked by a follower of Egoism.

According to this system, we are all firmly at the centre of our own universe and will only do things which help ourselves. 'Egoism' comes from the Greek word *ego* meaning 'I'. Egoism was made popular by the philosopher Thomas Hobbes (1588–1679) who argued that people's lives were 'nasty, brutish and short'. Egoism takes a very negative view of human nature. Hobbes thought that people were wholly selfish. But most people think this is not the whole truth about human beings: Egoism cannot explain self-sacrifice, duty or selfless love.

The twentieth century has seen two significant atheist political systems which tried to build societies based on forms of morality which rejected the idea of God and tried to replace it with different ideas:

Communism

Communism, founded by Karl Marx (1818–83), was born out of the struggle of working people for decent living conditions. In Communism, 'goodness' means being involved in this struggle and so helping to move history forward towards a pure Communist society. This struggle is considered to be more important than the lives of individuals. The Communist ideal captured the minds and determined the government of a great part of our world in the twentieth century. Today we are witnessing its collapse.

Nazism

Nazism was developed by Adolf Hitler (1883–1945) as an answer to Germany's social and political problems following the First World War. In Nazism, as in Communism, the idea of God is replaced by that of a perfect society. Nazi morality saw doing good as taking part in the destiny of the Aryan race and being an obedient and productive citizen. This was regarded as far more important than the lives of individuals, and in Nazi thinking the state had the duty to eliminate—to kill—the unproductive or 'racially impure'. The consequence of this terrible philosophy was the Holocaust, in which millions of Jews lost their lives.

A matter of opinion

A great many people who do not believe in God say that morality is entirely a matter of personal choice and preference. They say that people should be free to decide for themselves how they want to live. This kind of thinking is particularly attractive to people who feel bullied by authority—parents, teachers, the Government—and are tired of it. In Britain and America it is common among those who were young during the 1960s.

The idea that morality is simply a matter of opinion seems very attractive at first sight. However, there are problems with it.

◆ *If it is true, there is little difference between saying 'This is a good game' and 'He is a good man'. We are simply saying 'This is something I happen to like.' But is that really what we mean by 'a good man'? Most people would say it means more.*

◆ *Another problem with the idea is that it is very unrealistic. If you say to me, 'Morality is just a matter of opinion,' I might reply, 'Very well: in my opinion it would be a good idea to steal your wallet and burn your house down.' On what grounds could you object? If morality is purely a matter of opinion, I am entitled to mine!*

Of course, nobody thinks like this when it comes to things done to <u>them</u>. If I really burnt your house down you would call the police and I would be punished—not just because you

Is pleasure the greatest good, as Epicurus taught? For his followers, this meant 'eat, drink and be merry, for tomorrow we die'. But the artist Hogarth did not agree. This picture is one of a series showing a person's road to ruin!

wanted to get your own back, but because society recognizes that such actions are <u>wrong</u>. And nobody would accept that murder, rape, drug-pushing or incest could ever be morally acceptable. If somebody told you that he thought they were, you would think he was mad or having you on. You would not say, 'That is absolutely fine. As long as it is your honest opinion, you can rape and murder as much as you like.'

◆ We have already said that some people are probably attracted to the idea that morality is simply a matter of opinion because they are tired of being told what to do all the time and resent being pushed around by authority. But if that is true, there is a big **logical error** in their thinking. You cannot say, 'I am going to believe that all morality is a matter of opinion because I have been bullied and bullying is wrong.' Why not? (You will find the answer in the Note below.)

Follow-up

Questions

1 What do we mean by 'moral language?' Give some examples in your answer.

2 Who were:
Jeremy Bentham
Epicurus
Karl Marx
and what are they famous for?

3 What is Hedonism?

4 What are the objections to Utilitarianism, and what do you think are its good points?

5 'Morality is just a matter of opinion.' How would you respond to somebody who said this?

6 'On the whole, atheist systems of morality have not been terribly successful.' Do you agree or disagree? Give reasons for your views.

For discussion

'Being good is about making people happy.' Do you agree?

Activity

Think of a time when you had to make a moral decision (when you had to choose between right and wrong). What did you do? Share these experiences in small groups (if you don't mind talking about them!).

NOTE: The answer to the question about bullying in this chapter is that it contradicts itself. 'Bullying is wrong' is being presented as an absolute fact which everybody will agree with. But if morality is just a matter of opinion there is no reason why anybody should agree with it if they don't want to.

The first five books of the Bible—Genesis, Exodus, Leviticus, Numbers, Deuteronomy—are called the Law of Moses or Torah. The Torah (which means 'law' or 'instruction') is at the heart of Judaism. Tradition says God gave it to Moses, the great Jewish leader who brought his people out of Egypt over a thousand years before the birth of Jesus. The Torah contains hundreds of rules or *commandments*, including the Ten Commandments (these are set out in Chapter 3).

By the time of Jesus, the Torah had been studied hard for centuries. Jewish teachers (*rabbis* or *scribes*) used to discuss which of the commandments summed up all the others. Jesus was himself a Jewish teacher, and in this story another teacher asks for his opinion.

 'Which commandment is the most important of all?'

Jesus replied, 'The most important one is this, "Listen, Israel! The Lord our God is the only Lord. Love the Lord your God with all your heart, with all your soul, with all your mind, and with all your strength." The second most important commandment is this: "Love your neighbour as you love yourself." There is no other commandment more important than these two.'

The teacher of the Law said to Jesus, 'Well done, teacher! It is true, as you say, that only the Lord is God, and there is no other God but he. And man must love God with all his heart and all his mind and with all his strength; and he must love his neighbour as himself. It is more important to obey these two commandments than to offer animals and other sacrifices to God.'

Jesus noticed how wise his answer was, and so he told him, 'You are not far from the Kingdom of God.'

Mark 12:28–34

Look at Jesus' reply. The first commandment Jesus quotes is about loving God. It was well known: it comes from Deuteronomy 6:4–5. It begins the prayer called the *shema*, with which synagogue services still start today. The second commandment Jesus quotes is from Leviticus 19:18. Most New Testament scholars say Jesus was the first rabbi to summarize the Torah in this way. The scribe agrees with Jesus: loving God and loving your neighbour is more important even than

worship in the Jewish Temple. Jesus is pleased with this response: the scribe is close to becoming a member of God's family or Kingdom.

So the two most important things, Jesus says, are:

- to love God

- to love your neighbour as yourself

Both are linked together. They are at the centre of Christian moral teaching (*ethics*).

What does 'love God' mean?

- Make sure that God is the most important thing to you in every aspect of your life

- honour God

- do what God wants

- love God as you would love a friend

What does 'love your neighbour' mean?

Clearly we shall have problems if we think 'love your neighbour' means 'go out with the person next door'! 'Love' here is not romantic love; and the word neighbour means *everybody*.

The New Testament was written in Greek. Unlike English, Greek has more than one word for love, including:

- *eros*: romantic or sexual love

- *philia*: friendship

- *storge* (pronounced 'storgay'): family affection

- *agape* (pronounced 'aggerpay'). This is the word used in Jesus' saying, where it means being concerned about other people, wanting their wellbeing, caring about them as much as you care about yourself. (The New Testament writers used this word, which was originally rather vague in meaning, because it was not as 'loaded' as the other words for love.)

To have *agape* for someone, you do not have to be *in love* with them.

Why should people love in this way? For Christians, the answer is more than just 'because it sounds like a good idea'. Christians believe that God *is* love. Everything God does is part of the outpouring of that love. If God created the universe, then love is part of

Jesus summed up God's rules for living in the two commands: love God and love others. Love is the principle at the heart of the Christian faith. The secret of good relationships is really to care about other people (our enemies as well as our friends).

the structure of the universe. People are designed to behave in a loving way.

This is explained by a passage from the First Letter of John (1 John) in the New Testament. Tradition says the author is Jesus' disciple John, who wrote John's Gospel. Modern scholars are less sure who wrote it, and whether the author also wrote the Gospel. The letter seems to have been sent to a number of early Christian communities or churches.

 Read 1 John 4:7–21

John is saying:

- God is love. Christians know this because God sent his Son, who died to bridge the gap between people and God.

- Because God loves people, they should love each other.

- When people do this, God lives in them and they live in God.

- God showed his love in sending Jesus.

- If we genuinely love God and one another there is no need to be frightened about being judged by God.

- Nobody can really love God and hate a fellow human being.

> **The heart of Christian ethics is NOT a set of rules or laws. The heart of Christian ethics is love, which has its source in God.**

The great early Christian scholar Saint Augustine of Hippo (AD 354–440) said:

'Love, and then do what you want.'

We have said that:

- Love is the basis of all Christian thinking about morals.

- The greatest commandment, Jesus said, was to love

God and to love your neighbour as yourself.

- Saint Augustine told his readers to love God and then do what they liked.

This sounds great. Christianity seems to be going along with the old Beatles song: 'All You Need Is Love'. But hang on a minute!

- You could love somebody very much and still give them bad advice because you did not know better. You would feel all right, but your friend might end up worse off than before.

- It can be very hard to know what is the most loving thing to do. For instance, the circumstances surrounding abortion or euthanasia raise very complex problems. If Christians are going to follow Jesus, they have to work these out.

- We can all lie to ourselves. We can convince ourselves that we are acting in a loving way when we are really being selfish.

So, although Christianity teaches that God is love, that does not mean Christians think that 'anything goes' as long as you love people or say you do. Real love is a big responsibility which requires some hard thinking. In the next chapter we shall be exploring how Christians go about deciding what is right and what is wrong.

Situation ethics

One writer who did think that love was all anybody needed was an American Protestant Christian called Joseph Fletcher. In the 1960s he published a book called *Situation Ethics*, which was also the name he gave to his system of moral thinking. It caused quite a stir at the time. Fletcher argued that it was pointless to try to look for moral laws which would cover every situation you could think of. Life was far too complicated for that. Instead he said that when they were faced with a hard moral decision Christians should simply ask themselves: 'What does love require of me?'

Fletcher thought that because every human situation is different, the answer to this question would be different in every case. So you could not say that something is always good or always bad: you had to take the *context* or situation into account, even when talking about breaking the law, killing people or adultery.

📖 Read St Paul's letter to Philemon in the New Testament

Philemon was an important member of one of the early Christian churches and, like all other well-off people of his time, he owned slaves. One of them was called Onesimus (pronounced 'Ohnessimuss'). Onesimus ran away from Philemon and somehow came into contact with St Paul, who converted him to Christianity. After a while St Paul sent him back to Philemon with this letter, urging Philemon to be kind to him.

In his other writings St Paul had said that Christians should always obey the law (see for instance Romans 13:1). Yet what Onesimus had done was certainly illegal. If Philemon had wanted to be difficult he could have punished Onesimus for running away and taken legal proceedings against Paul for keeping him.

The Letter to Philemon has sometimes been used by Christians wanting to argue in favour of a 'Situations ethics' approach to morality. This is because, although St Paul has a general rule that Christians should obey the law (Romans 13:1), he seems to be making an exception in the case of Onesimus—in his particular situation. However, the argument is flawed. Although it was illegal for a slave to run away, the law gave Philemon the right to decide whether or not to have Onesimus punished and take to court anybody who had helped him. So in this letter St Paul is simply persuading him to do something the law allowed.

There are other reasons why Fletcher's ideas are not as popular today as they once were. What do you think these might be? Look at what is said above.

Follow-up

Questions

1 In Mark's Gospel, which commandments did Jesus say were the most important? Quote them, and make a note of his conversation with the scribe.

2 Write down the different Greek words used for 'love', with their meanings.
What does the First Letter of John say about love? (Answer in detail.) Which sort of love is this?

3 Paul was the most famous early Christian missionary. He founded a large number of churches in the Roman world. He wrote letters or epistles to them: some have survived, and are included in the New Testament.

1 Corinthians is the name given to his first letter to the church in the Greek city of Corinth. The epistle (letter) dates from around AD 57. In it, Paul warns his Christian readers not to think that some are better than others: they are all members of the church, even if they do different jobs. He shows them what he calls the 'more excellent way'.

Read 1 Corinthians 13. What is Paul's view of love?

4 Essay: 'Using examples from the Bible, explain the Christian concept of love. How far is it relevant to today's world?'

5 (a) Explain what is meant by 'Situation ethics'.
(b) Why has St Paul's Letter to Philemon sometimes been used to uphold a 'Situation ethics' approach to morality?
(c) What do you think of 'Situation ethics'?
(d) What do you think Philemon shows us about early Christian attitudes towards slavery? Is there anything here which a modern Christian might find shocking or surprising?

For discussion

'Love, and then do what you want.' (St Augustine) Do you think this is enough, or do people need rules as well?

Activity

Make a wall display to show the different types of love: *eros, philia, storge,* and *agape.* You might like to use pictures from newspapers and magazines, or your own artwork.

The basics

All Christians believe four fundamental things about the world:

- it was made by God;

- it is essentially good, because God is good;

- the people who live in it really matter: they are valuable;

- but people have disobeyed God's commands; they have sinned against God and messed things up.

These four central ideas in Christianity are expressed in the Bible in the story of the Creation of the world. You should read this now.

 Read Genesis chapters 1–3

All Christians believe that the universe is a good place. It did not just happen by chance and without purpose.

In the early part of the Genesis story, notice how the writer says that every time God made something he 'saw that it was good'—he was pleased with it. The Bible seems to be saying that existence itself is a good thing: that life, the world, simply being alive, are gifts to be treasured.

? **The ideas that life is a gift and that the creation is good are central to Christian morality. Try to think of some things which threaten or deny this attitude to life and the world. What do you think a Christian response to them would be?**

Look at Genesis 1:26–27, the creation of men and women. It says that God made them to be like himself. They are made in **the image of God**. This is not saying that God has a body like ours! It means that people have a special kind of freedom and an ability to think, which the animals do not have. Like God, men and women can *choose* to do things. Christians call this **free will**.

Genesis and science

When people read the beginning of Genesis they sometimes ask 'But hasn't science disproved all of this? Surely Christians cannot still believe that the world was made in six days and that Eve had a conversation with a talking snake? What about the Big Bang, Evolution and all that?'

These are all good questions, and they are not new. When, putting forward the theory of evolution, Charles Darwin published his *Origin of Species* in 1860, it caused a tremendous row and some Christians lost their faith because of it. Others refused to believe that the new scientific discoveries were true and clung to a literal belief in the Bible story.

The vast majority of Christians today—including scientists—believe that science and the Bible both have their place in our understanding of the nature of the world. There is a difference, they believe, between moral or religious truth and scientific observation. Scientific and religious views of the world are like two different TV cameras covering an event from different angles. Both can give a 'true' picture. Each picture is 'complementary' to the other, so we need both views to get the full picture. Science on its own cannot answer all our questions. Why do we find it so hard to be good, for instance? It is questions like this that the story in Genesis can help us to answer.

The Roman Catholic Church teaches that there is no conflict between science and religion provided that scientific research is carried out within moral laws (Vatican II, *Gaudium et Spes* 36).

Charles Darwin's theory of evolution created a furore in the last century. This caricature appeared in *The London Sketch Book*, 1874.

NOTE: Free will and the image of God are ideas we shall explore in greater detail later on.

Very soon, things begin to go wrong. In Genesis chapter 3 we get a story about how people chose what was wrong and sin was introduced into the world. This story is called the **Fall** because it talks about how people 'fell' from the state of innocent goodness God wanted for them. Adam and Eve are banished for ever from the Garden and lose their innocence and happiness. Since this first sin—a kind of cosmic disaster people brought upon themselves—the world has never been the same. Once people chose the path of disobedience, turning away from God and learning to do evil, the whole of human society was affected and this was passed on from one generation to another.

NOTE: The idea that the whole of human society has been affected by sinfulness is called the doctrine of original sin. 'Doctrine' simply means 'teaching'. 'Original' means 'first'—from the very beginning.

What do you think Christians might point to as evidence for the truth of their belief in original sin—that something has gone badly wrong with the way people behave?

All Christians believe that God rescued the world from sin by becoming a man in Jesus Christ. He opened the way for people to be forgiven, to be reconciled to God, and finally to be reunited with him in heaven, despite their sins.

So how do Christians decide what is right, what are the most loving things to do?

Things begin to get more difficult here, because there are two main branches of Christianity which answer this question rather differently.

The Protestant approach

Protestant Christianity teaches that when sin was introduced into the world people became so tragically flawed that left to themselves they will always go wrong. But God has not left people helpless. He speaks to the world through the Bible, telling people about himself and how he wants them to live. For this reason

the Bible is often called 'the Word of God'. (The technical word for God telling people things is **revelation**.)

> *The Protestant churches broke away from the Catholic Church during the Reformation in the sixteenth century. The Protestant leaders (or Reformers) taught that New Testament Christianity had been corrupted by the Catholic Church. They rejected its claim that Jesus has given it authority over all Christians and insisted that the actual revelation of God was found only in the Bible.*

So when a group of Protestant Christians want to decide whether something is right or wrong, or when an individual Protestant is asking the same question, their first thoughts will be:

- What has the Bible got to say about this?

- How should what the Bible says be applied today?

For this reason (as well as for others) Bible study forms a very important part of Protestant religious life. By studying the Bible alone or together, Protestant Christians try to work out the way God wants them to live.

The most famous set of moral laws revealed in the Bible are the Ten Commandments:

God spoke and these were his words: I am the Lord your God who brought you out of Egypt, where you were slaves.

Worship no god but me.

Do not make for yourselves images of anything in heaven or on earth or in the water under the earth. Do not bow down to any idol or worship it, because I am the Lord your God and I tolerate no rivals. I bring punishment on those who hate me and on their descendants down to the third and fourth generation. But I show my love to thousands of generations of those who love me and obey my laws.

Do not use my name for evil purposes, for I the Lord your God, will punish anyone who misuses my name.

Observe the Sabbath day, and keep it holy. You have six days a week in which to do your work, but the seventh day is a day of rest

dedicated to me. On that day no one is to work—neither you, your children, your slaves, your animals, nor the foreigners who live in your country. In six days I, the Lord, made the earth, the sky, the sea, and everything in them, but on the seventh day I rested. That is why I, the Lord, blessed the Sabbath and made it holy.

Respect your father and your mother, so that you may live a long time in the land that I am giving you.

Do not commit murder.

Do not commit adultery.

Do not steal.

Do not accuse anyone falsely.

Do not desire another man's house; do not desire his wife, his slaves, his cattle, his donkeys, or anything that he owns.

Exodus chapter 20:1–17

How do Christians decide what is right and what is wrong? For the Church as a whole, and for individual Christians, the Bible provides basic principles.

Sometimes the modern world presents us with moral problems which would have been unheard of in Bible times: nuclear weapons and global warming are two good examples. These are not directly mentioned in the Bible. But by careful Bible study together, by helping one another, and by reference to those with special expertise, Protestant Christians try to work out what their position should be from the general principles laid down by the Bible writers.

 Look at the Ten Commandments again and try to work out which ones might be useful for Christian discussion on:
- **nuclear weapons**
- **pollution**
- **pornography**
- **advertising**
- **the care of the elderly**

The Roman Catholic approach

Roman Catholic Christianity teaches that God reveals his will (tells people what he wants) through the Bible too. But Catholic Christians also believe that God continues to speak to the world through the teaching of the Catholic Church. This too is part of God's revelation.

The Gospels say that Jesus gave his authority to teach to his twelve apostles and promised that the Holy Spirit would lead his disciples into truth after he himself had left them. (See Mark 6:6–12, Luke 10:16, John 14:16–17: 26.) Catholics believe that Jesus' promises have come true, and that this is the way it has happened:

Down the centuries the Holy Spirit has continued to guide the church. In particular, the authority Jesus gave to the apostles has been handed on to the people of God and especially the bishops who lead the Christian community. They have a special responsibility to help people understand what Christianity is about and to interpret the Bible. Very occasionally, all the bishops meet together with the Pope to sort something out. This meeting is called a **General** (or **Ecumenical**) **Council**. Catholics believe that what these Councils decide is especially guided by God the Holy Spirit and that God prevents them from making wrong decisions. The technical word for this is to say that General Councils are **infallible**.

Veritatis Splendor

In 1993, Pope John Paul II issued an encyclical called *Veritatis Splendor* ('The Splendour of Truth'). This was addressed to all the Catholic bishops. It was intended as a warning to them that some theologians were trying to set aside the usual Catholic understanding of right and wrong and were dangerously near saying that all that really mattered was what people decided for themselves. The encyclical was an attempt to put a stop to this sort of thinking, which the Pope saw as a great danger to the unity and life of the Church, by reminding Catholics that the authority of the Church to guide Christians in moral questions is supposed to come from God himself.

In Roman Catholic thinking the Pope has a special part to play in all of this. He is the chief bishop, just as St Peter was Jesus' chief apostle (see Matthew 16:18–19) and he is in charge of the day-to-day running of the church. As St Peter's successor he has special authority of his own. He can decide to make a declaration about Christian teaching without calling a General Council, and Catholics believe that if he does this he too is especially guided by God. But this special authority has been used very rarely. Usually the Pope teaches through special letters to the Church called **encyclicals**. Encyclicals try to sum up what the Church has to say about different things, so they are read by Catholics with great respect, although they are not regarded as infallible.

General Councils of the Church do not happen very often. There have only been twenty-one since the start of Christianity—roughly one every century. The last one was held between 1962 and 1965 and was called the **Second Vatican Council** *(Vatican II). We have already referred to it at the end of the box on Genesis and science, and it will come in again elsewhere. Vatican II set out the way the Catholic Church should respond to the modern world.*

So when a Catholic Christian wants to know whether something is right or wrong, his or her first question is likely to be:

- What is the teaching of the Church about this?

Roman Catholic theology says, thirdly, that people can work some things out for themselves. Catholic teaching emphasizes that original sin does not completely destroy the image of God in men and women. Despite the Fall, people still have the ability to recognize goodness and to come to important conclusions about the world around them. So God does not have to tell us everything: some things are obviously wrong because they contradict the way the world is made.

 NOTE: The technical word for purpose in the way the world is made is Natural Law. You do not have to believe in God to think of the world in this way.

 NOTE: The idea of Natural Law will be very important when we come to discuss Roman Catholic teaching about contraception (Chapter 10).

When a new moral problem comes up, the Church has to decide what position to take. Catholic theologians then argue about what the teaching of the Church ought to be. They will ask themselves three questions:

- What does the Bible say?
- Has the Church said anything in the past which might be useful?
- Can we work anything out from Natural Law?

The Pope and the bishops will have the final decision.

So let's sum up. Here is a diagram of how Christians decide right from wrong:

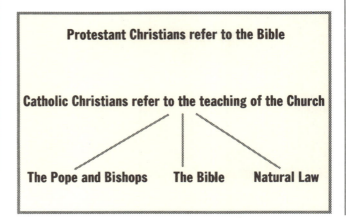

Problems within Christianity

1. Protestants and Catholics sometimes disagree about moral issues because of their different approaches to moral problems.
2. Protestant Christians may disagree among themselves. This is because of the way they interpret the Bible. Some say that the Bible must always be taken literally; others want to take account of the kind of writing (poem, story, history, letter) and the background; others again believe that the Bible writers were often influenced by the world around them, and want to take account of that in the way they interpret the writings.
3. Some Catholic Christians have difficulty accepting some parts of the teaching of the Church.

▓ Conscience

Somebody might ask, 'Is all this really necessary? Surely you should just trust your conscience and try to follow it as best you can?'

Christians agree that people should always do as their conscience tells them. But the trouble with saying 'Just follow you conscience' is that, like 'All you need is love', it only gets us so far. We can do wrong things with a clear conscience if we do not know that they are wrong. For this reason all Christians believe they have a duty to find out the right things to do—to have an 'informed conscience'.

Catholic Christians look to the saints to help them live out the teaching of the Church. These are Christians who, after their deaths, have been declared to have been especially holy. Catholic Christians believe that the saints help them in two ways: by providing examples of outstanding goodness, and by their prayers in heaven.

Follow-up

Questions

1 What do Protestant Christians mean by 'the Word of God?' Explain your answer.

2 Explain what each of these mean:
revelation
the 'Fall'
infallible
Natural Law
an informed conscience

3 What do Christians mean by the term 'original sin'?

4 Summarize what Roman Catholics believe about how God speaks to the world.

5 Re-read the beginning of the section on Hedonism in Chapter 2, then read Galatians 5:16–25 in the New Testament. Do you think a Christian could use the passage from the Bible in an argument on Hedonism? Explain your answer.

For discussion

'It does not matter what you do as long as you are sincere in what you are doing.' How do you think a Christian would respond to this statement?

4 The Sermon on the Mount

▨ The Sermon on the Mount

The **Sermon on the Mount** is the name given to the collection of Jesus' teaching in chapters 5–7 of Matthew's Gospel. For Christians, it is one of the best-known and best-loved passages in the Gospels, and indeed in the whole Bible. This is because it gives much of Jesus' teaching about how his followers should behave, and how they should live.

A whole library of books could be written on the Sermon on the Mount. Here we can only set the scene. Read the text of the Sermon carefully, and think hard about the issues raised.

▨ Background

Read Matthew 5:1–2

Matthew says Jesus taught on a mountain (or hill). In the Old Testament, Moses received God's Law or Torah on a mountain. So Matthew may well mean the reader to think of Jesus as the new Moses, who gives God's new law.

Many New Testament scholars say that the teaching in the Sermon on the Mount was given by Jesus on different occasions. Matthew had collected it together. At the time it was pretty revolutionary teaching, as it overthrew accepted values. It is *not* the rich, the successful or the powerful who are blessed by God, Jesus said. His kingdom was to overthrow accepted values.

? **After you have read through this chapter, see if you can work out why scholars say this teaching was given on different occasions. Do you agree with them?**

▨ The Beatitudes

The name given to the first section of the Sermon on the Mount—'Beatitudes'—comes from a Latin word meaning 'blessed'. People who are blessed by God are special to him. The people whom Jesus says are blessed are not the obvious ones—the rich, the powerful... (The Greek word used in Matthew's Gospel can also mean 'happy', which is how some English Bibles translate it.)

Read Matthew 5:3–12

Blessed are:

The poor in spirit or spiritually poor (those who realize their own helplessness, and trust utterly in God)	The Kingdom of heaven is theirs
Those who mourn	They shall be comforted
The meek or humble	They shall inherit the earth
Those who hunger and thirst to do what God wants	They shall be satisfied
The merciful	God will be merciful to them
The pure in heart (those whose motives are pure and good)	They shall see God
The peacemakers	God will call them his children
Those who are persecuted for doing what God wants	The Kingdom of heaven is theirs
Those who are insulted, persecuted and slandered for following Jesus	They have a great reward in heaven.

 To do: either write out the Beatitudes, or copy the summary given in this chapter.

 To do: the translation of the Beatitudes in the Authorized Version is especially beautiful. Try to get hold of a copy and read it.

A standard for others

 Read Matthew 5:13–16

Jesus is saying that Christians should set a good example for other people. But they should not be smug about it: they should not do it so that people will say how wonderful Christians are. All praise should go to God, not to them.

 Try to think of a Christian who put this teaching into practice.

Jesus and the Jewish Law

 Read Matthew 5:17–20

Jesus says that he completes and fulfils the Old Testament (the Law and the prophets of verse 17): he does not abolish it. The Torah, the Law of Moses, still applies.

 NOTE: This is a difficult passage. Scholars debate the question of what exactly Jesus thought of the Torah. Some think this section gives his teaching: all the Old Testament has been pointing forward to Jesus, who fulfils it. Others think that Jesus in fact thought the Torah no longer applied. Still others say he was not against the Torah, only against the rules of the Pharisees, or that his own attitude to the Torah was lax: he kept it, but was not very strict in applying it.

Anger (first antithesis)

Parts of the Sermon on the Mount are called the *antitheses* (which means contrasts). In the antitheses, Jesus takes a commandment from the Torah, and then gives his own teaching. Jesus' teaching either deepens or contradicts the old Law.

The Torah (first five books of the Bible—God's Law) is the focus of Jewish faith. Like this boy celebrating his Bar Mitzvah in Jerusalem today, Jesus would have learned the scriptures before he could become an adult member of the Jewish community.

Read Matthew 5:21–26

One of the Ten Commandments is 'Thou shalt not kill'. Jesus goes further: *he forbids people to be angry with each other.*

People do get angry, and Jesus taught that they can be forgiven. But they must not allow their anger to continue. People who are angry with, or quarrel with, their brother or their sister cannot worship God. And *everyone* is to be regarded as a brother or a sister. The quarrel must end; they must make up and put things right whether they are involved in a lawsuit or just an everyday dispute! Then God will accept their worship.

Burning rage, anger that is fed and nursed, is forbidden. It is not enough to hold back from killing someone: *wanting* to kill someone is forbidden. It is not enough to hold back from hitting someone: *wanting* to hit someone is forbidden. Despising people, or hating them and calling them names, is bad enough to be punished in hell.

 What does Jesus say about anger in the Sermon on the Mount?

 What might Matthew 5:21–26 have to teach about
– wanting to do people down (malice)?
– gossip?

 Is it ever true to say anger can be as bad as murder?

 'People who get angry will go to hell.' Is this what Jesus taught? Think carefully!

▌ **Adultery** (second antithesis)

 Read Matthew 5:27–28

'Thou shalt not commit adultery' is one of the Ten Commandments. Again, Jesus takes things further: his followers must not even want to commit adultery.

Jesus is not saying that people should not be human. He is not forbidding normal human desire which is part of human instinct and human nature. But he *is* saying that people should not deliberately decide to think about and dwell on the desire to have sex with someone to whom they are not married.

 Give Jesus' teaching about adultery.

 What do you think would be a Christian attitude towards pornography? Why?

 How might Jesus' teaching help to make for happy marriage?

 Read Matthew 5:29–30

Jesus is not telling his followers to tear out their eyes or cut off their hands if they do something wrong. What he means is that **life in the Kingdom of heaven**, which also means avoiding hell, **is the most important thing there is**. It is worth far more than an eye or a hand. (People in Jesus' time sometimes said the eyes led you into sin, including lust. There are some things it is best not to notice.)

▌ **Divorce** (third antithesis)

 Read Matthew 5:31–32

Here, Jesus refers back to Deuteronomy 24:1–4. The Law (Torah) allowed a man to divorce his wife if she were 'guilty of some shameful conduct'. Some rabbis or Jewish teachers said this meant adultery and nothing else. Other rabbis said it could mean almost anything, from a woman spoiling a meal to talking to a man she did not know. For a man, divorce in Jesus' day was easy, and the disgrace fell only on the woman.

In the Sermon on the Mount, Jesus allows divorce only on the grounds of 'unchastity' (which may mean having sex before marriage, but probably means adultery). However, in Mark 10:11–12 and Luke 16:18, Jesus appears to rule out divorce completely: he does not say it is allowed on the grounds of unchastity. It may be that Mark and Luke preserve Jesus' original teaching, which has been 'softened' by the time it reached Matthew, or by Matthew himself. (Matthew was written after Mark.)

Jesus' teaching on divorce raises a number of questions, which we shall discuss in more detail later, when we come to marriage and divorce. His teaching does, however, aim to protect women from unfair treatment, and emphasizes that marriage as God's original intention for people is a good thing.

 What does Jesus say about divorce in the Sermon on the Mount ?

Oaths (fourth antithesis)

 Read Matthew 5:33–37

Jesus says his followers are not to make oaths. There is no need to. They should be so trustworthy that people will accept what they say as true. (This is the thrust of the passage. Christians may say it is wrong to use bad language—even if they are not all very good at avoiding it !—and that may well be true, but this is not what Jesus is talking about here.)

Revenge (fifth antithesis)

 Read Matthew 5:38–42

Jesus quotes the Torah's rule on revenge (Exodus 21:24; Leviticus 24:20). This was designed to *limit* revenge: if someone knocked your tooth out, his tooth could be knocked out *and no more*. Jesus will not even allow that. Revenge is ruled out altogether.

 If anyone slaps you on the right cheek, let him slap your left cheek too.

Matthew 5:39

This is not inviting people to walk all over you. But Jesus' followers are not to retaliate, even if they are unfairly sued in court or forced to carry a pack for a Roman soldier.

Jesus also says people should give to those who ask, and should not refuse to lend their possessions to others.

 Learn verses 38–39

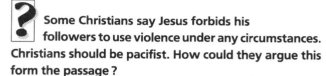 **Some Christians say Jesus forbids his followers to use violence under any circumstances. Christians should be pacifist. How could they argue this form the passage ?**

Other Christians say that Jesus is holding up an ideal: this is a standard to aim for, but violence may sometimes be necessary. Which idea do you think is better, and why ? Which idea do you think is closer to what Jesus actually taught ?

 If people refused to take revenge, how could that help to stop quarrels or fights ?

Love your enemies (sixth antithesis)

 Read Matthew 5:43–48

The book of Leviticus taught the Jews to love their neighbours (Leviticus 19:18). It seems that many in Jesus' time thought this meant they should only love fellow-Israelites, and hate their enemies. Jesus says they must go further: 'Love your enemies and pray for those who persecute you.' Anyone can love their friends: it is much harder to love people who hate you. (Jesus is talking here about Christian love or *agape*—see Chapter 2). Yet God loves everyone, and Christians must do so too. They must aim for the highest possible goal, even if they do not reach it: 'Be perfect—just as your Father in heaven is perfect !'

 Learn Matthew 5:44

 In what ways could Jesus' teaching, 'love your enemies', be applied during a war ?

Teaching about charity

 Read Matthew 6:1–4

When they help others, people have to think about why they are doing it. Do they really want to help, or do they just want to look good and enjoy it when people say how wonderful they are ? If they are just interested in the praise of others, that is their reward. God will reward

You cannot set your heart on money (and what it will buy) AND God, Jesus taught. People have to choose what is going to be most important in their lives, and what is not.

those who do not boast about it when they give.

 Would Jesus say that it is wrong to give money to charity ? Think carefully before your answer.

Teaching about prayer and fasting

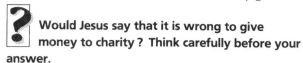

Read Matthew 6:5–18

When Christians pray or fast (go without food as a religious duty), they should not be interested in the praise of others: the object is to concentrate on God. Prayer is not about using lots of words and phrases that do not mean anything. The Lord's Prayer gives Christians the model or pattern they should use in prayer.

Notice the lines in the Lord's Prayer about forgiveness, which the Good News Bible translates:

> **Forgive us the wrongs we have done as we forgive the wrongs that others have done to us.**
>
> **Matthew 6:12**

People have a duty to forgive others, no matter how badly they have been wronged. This may be very hard to do. Yet unless they do it, God's forgiveness cannot work in them.

 Explain Jesus' teaching on forgiveness.

Look again at Jesus' teaching on revenge in Matthew 5:38–42. How might Jesus' teaching on anger and forgiveness affect Christians' views about punishing criminals ? (We shall look at punishment in more detail in Part Three.)

Treasure in heaven; the light of the body

Read Matthew 6:19–23

Anyone who places all his or her hopes in money and wealth will be disappointed. They can easily be spoilt or stolen. They do not last. Yet people who place all their hope in God will not be disappointed.

Jesus tells people to make sure their 'eyes are sound'. This is hard to understand at first, but it seems to mean something like this. People may have perfect sight physically, but they may be spiritually blind. They should make sure they are seeing things as they really are. Prejudice, jealousy or pride, for example, could stop them having a fair view of other people. And they should keep their 'sights' fixed firmly on God.

God and money

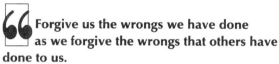

Read Matthew 6:24–34

- No one can serve two masters. 'You cannot serve both God and money.'

- Jesus' followers must not worry. There is more to life than food and clothes. God's fatherly care extends to the birds, the flowers and even to the grass, so he will certainly look after his people ! Instead, Jesus' followers should set their minds on God's Kingdom and on what God wants. Everything else will follow from that.

 Learn Matthew 6, verses 24 and 33

 What should Christians' attitude be towards money and what they own ? How do you think Jesus would expect them to use their money and wealth ? Give examples.

 Is it a good thing to worry ?

Judging other people

Read Matthew 7:1–6

'Do not judge others.' Why did Jesus say this ? We can suggest two reasons:

- Judgement can often be unkind, unfair or based on jealousy. So it may well be completely untrue !

- Nobody knows enough about another person to be able to write him or her off. We may judge someone for a particular thing he or she has done, without seeing the full picture.

Jesus pictured someone with a plank in the eye trying to get a speck of dust out of someone else's! Raising a laugh is a good way of driving a message home. No one is good enough to judge another person. People should concentrate on their own faults, and leave God to deal with the faults of others.

If people do judge others, they will only have themselves to blame if God judges them by the same rules.

 Why did Jesus say it is wrong to judge other people?

 Copy out Matthew 7, verses 3–5. You might want to illustrate this with a cartoon!

Ask and you will receive

 Read Matthew 7:7–11

Jesus teaches his followers to keep on praying. God will always listen, and he will always answer prayers. Those who truly seek God will find him. Those who truly want him to open the door will be admitted.

(Clearly, this passage does not mean that God will always give Christians what they want. He will answer prayers in his own way—and that may be unexpected.)

The Golden Rule

 Always treat others as you would like them to treat you.

Matthew 7:12 (Revised English Bible)

Jesus says this teaching sums up the whole of the Old Testament ('the Law and the prophets'). It is given the name of **the Golden Rule**: it is at the heart of Christian ethical teaching. It sums up the Christian law of love. **People should treat others in the way they would like others to treat them.**

The person who follows this rule, as William Barclay says, 'will try to forgive as he would wish to be forgiven, to help as he would wish to be helped, to praise as he would wish to be praised, to understand as he would wish to be understood'. This principle will rule life 'at home, in the factory, in the bus, in the office, in the street, in the train, at . . . games, everywhere'.

 Learn Matthew 7:12. As you work through this book, think about how far Christian teaching applies Jesus' Golden Rule, and where it falls short.

The way to follow Jesus

 Read Matthew 7:13–23

- The road to heaven is hard; the road to hell is easy and appears more attractive.

- Just as you can tell a tree by its fruit, so you can tell a good person and an evil person by their 'fruit'. Christians should beware of religious teachers who say one thing and do another.

- Only those who *genuinely* do God's will shall enter his Kingdom. So Christians cannot afford to be smug: the warnings apply to them too.

The two house builders

 Read Matthew 7:24–29

In his picture of the two men who build houses, Jesus teaches that it is obedience to his words which gives the sure foundation to life. Life founded on that obedience is safe, no matter what storms may come.

The value of the individual

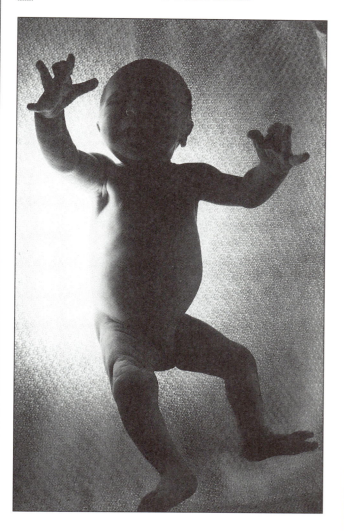

This does not mean that people are good all the time—far from it. But it does mean that people can recognize goodness for what it is. They can also choose their own futures by making plans, and they can choose the sort of people they want to be by making moral decisions. This is called having **free will**. It is the most important difference between humankind and the animals. As far as we know, animals' minds are not capable of recognizing goodness or making plans and decisions. Your dog can be trained to growl at a burglar but he could not work out why stealing is wrong, or choose to become a burglar's dog.

Free will means that people have very big responsibilities, and that things can go terribly wrong when they do not chose goodness. We have already explored this in Chapter 3.

Some atheist sytems of thought deny that people have free will. They say that although it <u>appears</u> to people that they are making choices, in fact they are doing nothing of the sort. According to this view, everything we do is a consequence of something else: upbringing, social background, our physical characteristics—even the way atoms and subatomic particles whizz around the universe. This kind of thinking is called **determinism** *because it says that our actions are determined by things outside our control.*

Communism (see Chapter 1) is an example of a kind of determinist system: Karl Marx thought that all human history and much human behaviour was determined by economic laws.

Christians believe that because God made people in his own image, every child born, everybody living in the world is immensely valuable. This is not just because their parents, family and friends love them. It is because each of them is the unique and unrepeatable image and likeness of God. The fact of Jesus' dying to rescue humanity doubly underlines the value God places on the individual.

What do Christians mean when they say that people are made 'in the image of God' (the phrase used in Genesis 1:27)? There is no simple answer. But there are two important points to make here.

1. Being made 'in the image of God' means that in some sense people's minds are like God's.

2. Secondly, Christians believe that being made 'in the image of God' means that people are called to share God's own eternal life. For human beings, life in this world is the beginning of a story which continues after death. Every individual has an eternal future—with God (in heaven) or for ever separated from God (in hell). Sometimes this is called having an 'immortal soul'. (Most atheist systems of thought deny that there is any future for the individual after death.)

So for Christians, each individual human life is sacred, not because it's a nice idea, but because each individual is made by God in his own image, and has an eternal destiny.

Christians and human rights

The twentieth century has seen two world wars and terrible crimes committed by the governments of some countries against enormous numbers of individuals.

Modern weapons have made such crimes particularly horrible, yet at the same time modern means of reporting news have made them harder to cover up for long. After the First World War, it became clear that something had to be done on an international scale to try to prevent large-scale atrocities. In 1948, after the Second World War was over, the General Assembly of the United Nations adopted and proclaimed its **Universal Declaration of Human Rights** in an attempt to meet this need.

The thirty articles of this Declaration articles set out the standards which UN countries agreed every nation should try to meet. The articles are summarized opposite.

The United Nations charter was unanimously adopted at the United Nations Conference in San Francisco, California, in 1945, at the end of World War II. Within three years the famous Universal Declaration of Human Rights was issued.

1. *Everyone is born free and equal.*

2. *Everyone has the rights set out in the Declaration.*

3. *Everyone has the right to life, liberty and security.*

4. *No one should be held in slavery.*

5. *No one should be tortured or subjected to cruel, inhumane or degrading punishment.*

6. *The laws of every country should recognize that everyone is a person.*

7. *Everyone should be treated equally by the law and should be protected.*

8. *A country's laws should protect everyone against violation of the rights set out in the Declaration.*

9. *No one should be arbitrarily arrested, detained or exiled.*

10. *Anyone charged with a criminal offence deserves a fair and public trial.*

11. *Everyone is innocent until proved guilty.*

12. *People should have their privacy, homes and families respected.*

13. *People have the right to move around their countries and to go abroad.*

14. *People can ask another country to protect them from genuine persecution in their homeland.*

15. *Everyone has the right to a nationality.*

16. *Adults have the right to get married and to have children. No one should be forced into marriage, and the family should be protected by the state as the fundamental unit of society.*

17. *Everyone has the right to own property and should not have it unjustly taken away.*

18. *People are free to think what they like and to practise their religions through worship and teaching, alone and in public.*

19. *Everyone has the right to freedom of speech.*

20. *People should be allowed to join associations and hold meetings, but no one should be forced to join any association.*

21. *Governments should be based on the will of the people. People have the right to take part in the government of their countries, either directly or by voting for their representatives.*

22. *People have a right to social security and to a share in their countries' material and cultural wealth.*

23. *Everyone has the right to work and to protection against unemployment. This includes the right to decent working conditions and pay, to equal pay for equal work, and the right to join a trade union. People should have a free choice of employment.*

24. *Everyone has the right to leisure time, including paid holidays.*

25. *People have the right to a decent standard of living for themselves and their families, which includes food, clothing, housing, medical services and social security. Mothers and children are entitled to special care and assistance. All children should be treated equally, whether or not their parents are married.*

26. *Everyone has the right to an education which should teach tolerance and understanding between all people. Primary education should be free. Parents have the right to chose the kind of education they want for their children.*

27. *People have the right to participate in the artistic and scientific life of their countries and to benefit from them.*

28. *Everyone has the right to live in a country where all of this is possible.*

29. *People have duties to the communities in which they live and must respect the legal rights of others as well as public order and morality.*

30. *No one should use any article of this Declaration in order to justify destroying someone else's rights.*

Amnesty International: two volunteers report

Amnesty works to seek the release of prisoners of conscience. That is, people who are imprisoned because of their beliefs, race, sex, language or religion. Amnesty also opposes torture, cruel treatment and executions.

As well as having campaigns on particular subjects or countries such as the murder of street children in Latin America or prisoners in Chile, Amnesty campaigns for individuals. One dramatic way this works is through the 'Urgent Action' network. In this scheme, Amnesty members are sent details very quickly of people who have disappeared or been arrested, and are asked to write to prison governors or heads of state, asking for their release.

For example, in June 1992 we received an 'Urgent Action' on behalf of Milot Batista, a member of a political party in Haiti, a poor country in the Caribbean. His party supported the president, Jean-Betrand Aristide, who had been overthrown by the army. Milot Batista was arrested by the new 'Anti-Gang' Investigation service, and most worryingly of all, had not been seen since. His family asked the Anti-Gang about him and visited all the local prisons without success—they were simply told that no one of that name was known there . . .

We were asked to write to the Prime Minister of Haiti and to the Anti-Gang chief or the Chief of National Defence, asking that Mr Batista be given security and safety in prison, access to his family and a lawyer, and be either charged with a crime or released at once. All these things are included in the Universal Declaration of Human Rights.

We do not always know the outcome of our appeals. But we know that about a third of all 'Urgent Actions'

bring some improvement. A prisoner may be released or no longer tortured, or may 'reappear' safe and sound, or receive medical or legal help.

As Christians we believe that an important part of our faith is to practise concern for other people. Amnesty, though not a Christian organization, gives us an opportunity to put our faith into action. St James' letter to the Christian church reminds us that 'Faith, if it does not lead to action is in itself a lifeless thing' (James 2:17). In other words, Christianity is not just for Sundays: Christians should show their faith by their good deeds.

Jesus tells us, 'Love your neighbour as you love yourself' (Matthew 22:39) and by 'neighbour' he meant everybody, not just people who live near you. There is another important passage in Matthew 25:31–46. There Jesus tells his followers that when they help people in need, such as those who are hungry or sick or in prison, they are doing that good deed for him. The Parable of the Good Samaritan (Luke 10:25–37) also reminds us of the need to help other people irrespective of their nationality or faith.

Some Christians are able to live out their faith by working among the homeless or helping in countries ravaged by famine or war. But, like most Christians, we live fairly ordinary lives and do not have the opportunity to work in these ways. Giving regularly to charity and participating in Amnesty International's Urgent Action letter campaigns provide us with practical ways of helping other people in need.

Michael and Norma Morrison

Christians welcomed the UN Declaration and support it whole-heartedly. Pope John XXIII saw it as a great step forward for the whole world, towards an international political authority which would advance genuine development. He discussed human rights in his encyclical *Pacem in Terris* in 1963. There he emphasized the Christian idea that people have rights because they are made in God's image:

> **Each individual man is truly a person... endowed with intelligence and free will. As such he has rights... which are universal and inviolable.**

The Second Vatican Council (Chapter 3) made the same point:

> **All men have a rational soul and are made in God's image... we should overcome and remove every kind of discrimination which affects fundamental rights... All such discrimination is opposed to God's purposes.**
>
> *(Gaudium et Spes* **29**)

The same kind of thinking can be seen in other Christian writings. A Church of England report on human rights issues said in 1977:

> **Rights can be established on the basis of the doctrine of the image of God.**

Of course you do not have to be a Christian to believe that the UN Declaration of Human Rights is a good thing. But for Christians today, supporting the UN principles is an important way of putting into practice what they see as the truth: that men and women are made in the image of God.

Sadly, human rights abuses still go on despite the UN Declaration. An important and influential organization which campaigns for the victims of human rights abuse is **Amnesty International**. Amnesty was started in 1961 in London by a lawyer called Peter Benenson. From very small beginnings it has grown into an international network of over half a million helpers of all races and religions. Two of its British volunteers are Michael and Norma Morrison. Like many others in Amnesty, Michael and Norma are practicing Christians. In the boxed feature opposite they describe Amnesty's work and how it relates to their faith.

Follow-up

Questions

1 Where does the phrase 'The image of God' come from? Be as precise as you can.

2 Why is the idea that people are made in the image of God important for Christians when they think about human rights?

3 Choose two of the articles from the United Nations' Universal Declaration of Human Rights and explain how you think these might be being broken today, either in your own country or abroad.

4 (a) What is determinism?
(b) Why do Christian thinkers disagree with determinism, and do you think determinism could affect the way people think about human rights?

For discussion

'The United Nations Declaration on Human Rights is not a religious document. It is pretty silly of the exam. boards to make us learn about it for an examination in Religious Studies.' What do you think of this statement? Give your reasons.

Activity

Here is an extract from a letter:

'I am becoming increasingly concerned by the frequent reports of human rights abuses we see in the news. I would like to do something about it all. Could this be God be asking me to do something? And if so, what can I do?'

Imagine that you are a Christian priest or minister who has received this, and write a suitable reply.

Further reading

Additional information is available from Amnesty International (see page 190).

6 The Problem of Pain

This book encourages you to think about a number of experiences which people find painful. There are sections dealing with abortion, racial prejudice and discrimination, physical and mental handicap, euthanasia, death, sickness, disease and poverty. Nobody could call these things a bundle of laughs. But they are worth studying because of the profound religious, moral and intellectual problems they raise and because they help us to look at and sympathize with the experiences of people who live in our community and share our lives.

In this chapter, however, we will be looking not at individual examples but at the problem of suffering itself—what Christian theologians call the **problem of pain**.

The problem of pain has to do with the meaning of our existence—it is a **philosophical** problem. It is a problem that has been struggled over and written about by many philosophers and theologians down the ages. This chapter is intended simply to help you to be aware of the things Christianity has to say about the problem of pain and to be able to write about it.

'Natural disasters' cause immense human suffering. The cyclone which hit southern Bangladesh, destroying buildings and creating the floods which isolated this farm, is just one of many examples.

What is the problem of pain?

The problem of pain lies in the existence of suffering. It has three main aspects which can be expressed as questions like this:

- Where does suffering come from?

- Is it possible to believe in a God who is good when the world is so full of suffering?

- Can suffering have any positive value or meaning?

We will look at each of these questions in turn.

Where does suffering come from?

Most Christian writers seem to think that the answer to this question depends on the sort of suffering you are talking about. Is it:

(a) suffering caused by human wickedness? (Some obvious examples are the horrors of war, murder, rape and exploitation. These are sometimes called **'moral evils'**.) Or is it:

(b) suffering which apparently 'just happens'?

(Examples include the suffering caused by natural disasters, disease, old age and the sufferings of the animal kingdom. These are sometimes called **'natural evils'**.)

Sometimes natural and moral evils can overlap—as when an earthquake (a natural disaster) causes the collapse of houses which have been built unsafely because of the greed of a contractor or property developer.

Traditional Christian theology says that a great deal of suffering is caused by sin. The idea goes like this (you may need to look at Chapter 3 again to help you):

God gives people free will. They are not God's puppets: they can genuinely choose how to live their lives. So people have a real choice to do or not to do things which alienate them from God—sins. Because God is wholly good—perfect—wrong choices lead further and further away from him and from perfection. The imperfection resulting from sin results in suffering, both for the sinner and for his or her victim.

What is worse, since the Fall the inheritance of original sin gives everyone a bias towards choosing the wrong things, and so much unnecessary suffering continues.

This teaching was developed first by St Paul, who wrote many of the letters of the New Testament, and was expanded by St Augustine of Hippo (354–430) and St Thomas Aquinas (1225–74). It seems to fit our experience of moral evils—our type (a) suffering.

Christians have sometimes tried to explain natural evils (our type (b) suffering) in this way as well. Here, the Fall is seen to have affected the whole of creation, corrupting what was once a perfect world. This idea, in its crude form at least, is not as popular as it once was. It seems difficult to believe that the sufferings of the dinosaurs as they became extinct were directly caused by the sin of a species which was not going to evolve for several millions of years!

Modern science has helped us to understand that some of the things which we call 'natural evils' seem to be necessary for the world to carry on at all. If volcanos did not occasionally erupt, enormous pressures would build up under the earth and blow it apart. If animals did not die off, there would be no room for new individuals and so no evolution. Even cancer cells and

diseases are risks that have to be taken for biological life to be sustained. But it still seems 'unfair' on people who live under volcanos or who get cancer.

This brings us to our second question.

Is it possible to believe in a God who is good when the world is so full of suffering ?

For a great many people the existence of suffering is the biggest reason for not believing in God and for disliking religion altogether. Perhaps you have yourself heard people say things like 'If there is a God, why doesn't he do something about all the suffering in the world?' or 'How come God allowed six million Jews to be murdered in SS camps?'

So for many people this is a very decisive issue. Let's explore it in more detail. The argument goes like this. According to Christianity, Judaism and Islam:

If God exists:

- God is absolutely **good**

- God is able to do anything: he is **omnipotent**

- God knows everything: he is **omniscient**

BUT suffering exists and God (if he exists) apparently does nothing about it.

So either:

- God knows about the suffering in the world and is able to help but does not want to. In that case he can't be good: he must enjoy people suffering.
  or

- God knows what is going on but is unable to help—in which case he is no longer omnipotent, and does not seem to be much use as a God any more.
  or

- God could and would help if he knew about suffering, but he does not. In this case it is God's omniscience which has gone out of the window. Once again, he does not seem much use like this.

Christianity, Judaism and Islam all teach that there is one God who is good, omnipotent and omniscient. But for many people (on the basis of the reasoning above) the very existence of suffering makes it impossible to believe that God can be all three at once. Since no

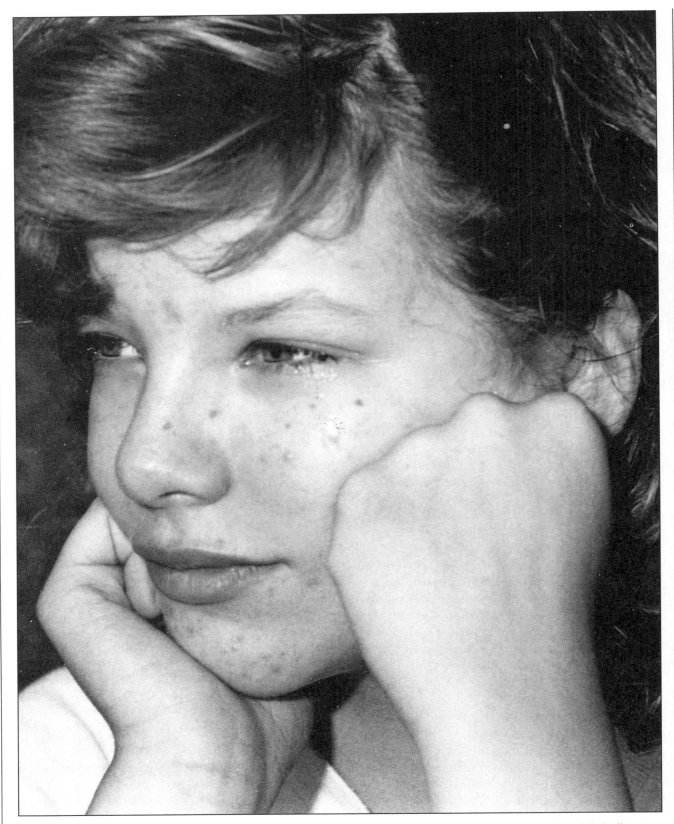

Who can measure the sum of human pain, or count the tears? Is it possible to believe in a God who is good when the world is so full of suffering?

other sort of God is worth having, they conclude that God does not exist.

Providing an answer to an argument like this is going to be a hard job for anyone who still wants to say that there is a God!

The most important thing about any argument is to look at its starting-points or premisses. Here the premiss is three-fold: God is good, omnipotent and omniscient. Given these basic ideas, the rest seems to follow automatically. So are Christians, Jews and Muslims wrong? Does the existence of suffering mean that there can be no God? Should everyone become atheists, as some people think?

But many Christian theologians point out that although God is omnipotent—can in theory do anything—there may be some types of action which God could do but which would change the nature of the world. It would stop being a real creation with its own independent existence.

Something like this may be happening with suffering. If God kept interfering with the universe in a direct way—if he kept intervening to take away all suffering and make it perfect—its whole nature would change. It would become part of God, people would lose their freedom, and there would have been no point creating it in the first place. So although God could in theory act to remove all the suffering in the world, in practice his hands are tied.

Even so, God is not powerless. He can work through people: doctors fight disease, and the Allies defeated Nazism in Germany, for instance. By using their freedom to choose the right things people can co-operate with God to remove suffering, and Christians would say that God can inspire and help them if their lives are open to him—even sometimes perform miracles through them. But that may be about the limit, if the world is not to become a puppet theatre with God pulling all the strings.

Think about this for a moment. Imagine you lived in a world where every time we were going to have pain or cause pain to anyone else, God prevented it from happening. Sometimes this would mean stopping you from doing things you had chosen to do. Would you have been able to grow up? Would you ever be really free?

This brings us to our final question.

Can suffering have any positive value or meaning?

Some suffering has a practical and very important positive value. Most of the physical pain people experience warns them that something is wrong. If you touch a flame and it burns, you instinctively pull your hand away. This limits the damage. So pain of this sort is a defence mechanism.

In the same way, mental pain can spur us on to do things that need doing. Being worried is unpleasant—it is a kind of suffering. But it can make us sit down and get on with a piece of coursework that is due in! Or the pain we feel on behalf of others can spur us to help.

So some suffering seems to be unavoidable—even important. But this is not always the case. Although physical pain is intended as a warning mechanism, a disease or injury can go on hurting long after the pain is useful. Mental suffering can turn into the nightmare of mental illness. Some suffering seems particularly terrible and pointless because of its victims: it is very hard to see what meaning there can be in the suffering of children.

Christianity does not say that all suffering is meaningful. Some things which happen in the world are against God's will. They are meaningless and cruel and nothing else. In John's Gospel there is a story of Jesus meeting a man who had been born blind. Jesus' disciples asked whether his blindness had been caused by his sins or those of his parents. In their way they were trying to find a reason for his suffering. Jesus' reply is very interesting:

> **His blindness has nothing to do with his sins or his parents' sins. He is blind so that God's power might be seen at work in him.**
>
> **John 9:3**

The story continues with Jesus curing him. God cares! Christians take comfort from that. And in the new life beyond death there will be no pain and suffering. In this extract from the New Testament, an early Christian writer describes what he has seen in a vision:

> **Then I saw a new heaven and a new earth…I heard a loud voice speaking from the throne: 'Now God's home is with mankind! He will live with them, and they shall be his people. God himself will be with them, and he**

will be their God. He will wipe away all tears from their eyes. There will be no more death, no more grief or crying or pain. The old things have disappeared.'

Revelation 21:1, 3–4

Finally, Christianity teaches that there can be spiritual value in suffering. Most important of all there is the suffering of Jesus on the cross. Christians believe that in Jesus' crucifixion God entered into the suffering of the world and reconciled humanity to himself: one of the most popular ways Christians have of thinking about this is to say that by his death Jesus paid the penalty due for the sins of the whole world.

When Christians themselves suffer they are encouraged to think of their sufferings in some way as sharing in Jesus' suffering (see Colossians 1:24) and of learning to sympathize with and feel love for others who suffer. In the Roman Catholic tradition especially, suffering—and particularly illness—is seen as an important sign that the world is imperfect and in need of God.

Follow-up

Questions

1 Write out the three questions which summarize the problem of pain.

2 Give five examples of suffering caused by
(a) moral evils
(b) natural evils
and explain the difference between them.

3 Suggest two occasions when moral and natural evils might combine to produce suffering.

4 How does Christianity account for the existence of moral evils?

5 Explain why the existence of suffering leads some people to reject religion.

6 What religious value do Christians see in some types of suffering?

For discussion

'When you look at the world, it's pretty clear that either God is evil or he doesn't exist at all.' What do you think? Discuss the statement in small groups and report back to the rest of the class.

Activity

God is on trial. The counsel for the defence and the counsel for the prosecution have to prepare their closing speeches to the jury. Divide the class up into an even number of small groups. Half the groups have to work out the defence speeches, and half the prosecution speeches. Each then elects a speaker, who presents the case to the rest of the class.

PART TWO

The Family

7 ▼ Family and Friends

How do you think people should behave towards one another?

To get you thinking, look at this passage from the New Testament. It is from one of the letters of St Paul, advising the early Christians about how they should behave towards one another:

> **No more lying, then! Everyone must tell the truth to his fellow believer, because we are all members together in the body of Christ. If you become angry, do not let your anger lead you into sin, and do not stay angry all day. Don't give the Devil a chance. The man who used to rob must stop robbing and start working, in order to earn an honest living for himself and to be able to help the poor. Do not use harmful words, but only helpful words, the kind that build up and provide what is needed, so that what you say will do good to those who hear you. And do not make God's Holy Spirit sad; for the Spirit is God's mark of ownership on you, a guarantee that the Day will come when God will set you free. Get rid of all bitterness, passion and anger. No more shouting insults, no more hateful feelings of any sort. Instead, be kind and tender-hearted to one another, and forgive one another, as God has forgiven you through Christ.**
>
> **Ephesians 4: 25–32**

The passage has some very religious language in it. But you do not have to be religious to agree with a lot of what it says. Most sensible people would say that we should not use harmful words, or harbour hateful feelings, and that we should always be kind. We are hurt when people insult us and we know that we should not insult people ourselves. We *know* this, no matter how many times we fail to behave as we should.

Read the passage again. List the qualities people need in order to live up to what the writer says. Now ask yourself, 'Am I anything like that? Never? Sometimes?'

Did you find your answers daunting? The virtues the passage requires may seem fine in theory, but very far away from everyday experiences. Sometimes we meet people it's easy to like. But often we meet people who are hard to get on with, and then it is much more difficult to be kind. This does not change as you get older. Adults also have to meet and work with people who get on their nerves. Most jobs are like most classrooms. You have to see people you dislike every day.

So it is extremely important for all of us to learn how to deal with people. The process of **socialization** begins very early.

▮ Family

It is in the family that most of us begin to learn how to live in a community. It starts soon after we are born. After a few weeks of life a baby wakes up to the fact that the warm thing which provides milk is actually another person. Another few weeks, and the baby has worked out (usually) that she has two parents—and that by smiling they can be made to smile back. So the process goes on.

Gradually we learn to understand language and use it for ourselves. Now the learning can begin in earnest. 'Say "bye-bye".' 'Say "thank you".' 'Wash your hands.' 'Don't hit your sister over the head with that iron.' 'Give Mummy a kiss . . .'

By talking to their children, by playing with them as well as by teaching and correction, parents are preparing them for interaction with others in the outside world. The process is a long one: it takes years.

Christianity teaches that our relationships with one another are important to God. In Matthew's Gospel, for instance, Jesus says that whatever his disciples do for others, is done for him (see Matthew 25: 31–46). Christians believe that love is the basis for all their relationships. It is in our families that most of us first learn to love: this is one reason why Christians place a very high value on family life.

Families come in all shapes and sizes but, whatever kind of family we belong to, this is where most of us take our first steps in relating to others. Young and old share in celebrations, too—in this case, it's grandfather's birthday.

WHAT IS A FAMILY?

For a great many people the word 'family' conjures up the simple picture of a husband and wife living in the family home with the children of their marriage. The technical word for this is a **nuclear family**. *This is a common pattern of family organization in Western countries.*

But even nuclear families are part of an **extended family**. *This wider group includes not just a couple and their children, but aunts, uncles, cousins and grandparents too. In some cultures it is common for all the members of an extended family to live close to one another—even in the same house.*

In the **single-parent family** *children are brought up by one parent. This may follow a separation, death or divorce, or may be the result of a decision not to marry.*

When parents marry again after a divorce or the death of a partner, the family may consist of a husband and wife who have children (or a child) by a first marriage. This is sometimes called a **reconstituted family**.

WHAT THE BIBLE SAYS ABOUT FAMILY

The Bible writers taught that children and parents have duties towards one another. One of the Ten Commandments says:

Honour your father and your mother.

Exodus 20:12

and this idea is taken up in the New Testament:

If anyone does not take care of his relatives, especially the members of his own family, he has denied the faith and is worse than an unbeliever.

1 Timothy 5:8

But this does not mean that Christian children are their parents' slaves. Parents must be reasonable. It's a question of give as well as take:

Children, it is your Christian duty to obey your parents always, for that is what pleases God. Parents, do not irritate your children, or they will become discouraged.

Colossians 3:20–21

Friends

From our first experience of living with others in our families when we are very young, we soon we begin to meet people of our own age and form **friendships**.

Childhood friendships play an important part in teaching us how to cope with other people. By playing together, young children begin to enjoy the company of others. In activities such as team games they learn how to co-operate and set their own wishes aside for the good of the group as a whole. The experience of losing out is painful, but it can be a very helpful lesson. By exchanging information and sharing experiences, children help one another to discover and to make sense of the world around them.

Parents have an important part to play. By welcoming their children's friends, they allow their own children to learn what it means to 'play host' to somebody else, and then encourage independence and fair play.

As we grow up we begin to form friendships which are less dependent on our families for support. At this stage it is almost as if we inhabit two worlds: one provided by our family, and another which we share with our friends. Each

Outside the family, it's friendships that matter most.

What the Catholic Church says about family

The Second Vatican Council (see Chapter 3) had quite a lot to say about family life. It talked about the duties of parents towards their children in two places in particular: the 'Declaration on Christian Education' (*Gravissimum Educationis*, 1965) and the 'Decree on the Apostolate of Lay People' (*Apostolicam Actuositatem*, 1965). Here is a summary of some of the important points:

From the 'Declaration on Christian Education':

1. Parents are primarily and principally responsible for their children's education: nobody else can be a really adequate substitute. Although society should help parents in their task of education by providing schools, parents' rights and duties must be safeguarded.

2. Parents must create a family atmosphere inspired by love and devotion to God and their fellow human beings so that Christian children can grow up to live out the faith they first received at baptism. They have a duty to send their children to Catholic schools wherever this is possible.

3. The family is the principal school of the social virtues which are necessary to every community and the place where children have their first experiences of a well-balanced human society.

From the 'Decree on the Apostolate of Lay People':

1. Marriage is at the heart of the family: parents have a duty to witness to the values of Christian marriage and to defend the idea of the family as a sacred institution. This may mean people's rights to housing, education, decent working conditions, taxation and social security.

2. Families as a whole should pray together and play an active part in the liturgical life of the Church. They should be places of hospitality, be active in the struggle for justice and peace, and perform acts of charity. Family life is particularly suited to showing the love of God by adopting abandoned children, showing a loving welcome to strangers, helping with education in schools and parishes, giving support to those preparing for marriage and caring for the elderly.

'world' has its own rules about how we behave and its own set of ideas. We experience a growing sense of independence from our parents.

During adolescence, we may use the 'rules' provided by our circle of friends to challenge our parents' authority. This can be a painful time for parents and children alike. It can be hazardous too, because we do not always have the skills to make wise decisions while we are growing up. Yet it is only by making our own decisions that we become truly adult. Parents simply have to hope that their children will eventually choose for themselves to adopt the good values they have learned at home.

In this chapter we have seen that both families and friendship are important. Christians believe that they are particularly important because they are ways in which we learn to love others—and that is what God wants. In the Gospels Jesus uses the language of family and friends when he talks about the relationship people have with God and with one another. Here are a few examples:

 This is how you should pray: 'Our Father in heaven . . .'

Matthew 6:9

Whoever does what God wants him to do is my brother, my sister, my mother.

Mark 3:35

 My commandment is this: love one another, just as I love you. The greatest love a person can have for his friends is to give his life for them. And you are my friends if you do as I command you.

John 15:12–13

Standing close to Jesus' cross were his mother . . . and the disciple he loved; so he said to his mother, 'He is your son.' Then he said to the disciple, 'She is your mother.'

John 19:25–27

A different calling

All Christians believe that marriage and parenthood is a way in which people can serve God. Many would say that God has given them a calling or vocation to married life: and most Christians do marry and have families. But a smaller number do not get married because they believe they have a different vocation—the vocation to the unmarried state or celibacy.

Monks, nuns and Roman Catholic priests share this vocation—though it is by no means limited to them. Monks and nuns live in communities which are rather like families. They call one another 'Brother' and 'Sister' and share the community belongings. By remaining unmarried they can give all their energy to the particular work they believe that God has given their community to do. Roman Catholic priests remain unmarried in order to serve their parishes and to be at the bishop's disposal without the distractions which family life might bring.

Follow-up

Questions

1 Do you think that people growing up always choose their friends wisely?

2 What dangers can there be in unwise friendships? How do you think worried parents can best cope with this?

3 Do you think there are any particular problems which might develop between parents and young people in a religious family?
    What do you think these might be? How should they best be dealt with by both the parents and their children?

4 What characteristics do you most look for in a friend?

5 What qualities do you think are most desirable in a parent of somebody between the ages of 13 and 19?

6 What do you think might be the advantages and disadvantages of
(a) the nuclear family and
(b) an extended family living near one another particularly for women?

7 What do you think might be the advantages and disadvantages associated with single parent and reconstituted families?

8 Summarize what you have learned about the teaching of the Second Vatican Council on the responsibilities of parents.

9 Sometimes young people experience conflict between their duty to their parents and their loyalty to their friends.
(a) Describe ONE situation in which such a conflict might arise.
(b) Describe the religious teaching or principles which you think might help young people in this sort of situation.

Activity

A teenager wants to go to a disco which goes on until midnight. The parents think this is too late. Role play the discussion the teenager has with the parents.

8 Marriage in the Bible

Can you see yourself getting married? What do you think marriage is? If you had to come up with ten key words to say 'marriage is...', what would you say?

In the four chapters which follow we will be exploring what Christianity has to say about marriage. We will begin by looking at the Bible.

Marriage in the Old Testament

There are several very important ideas about marriage in the Old Testament:

- The Old Testament writers believed that married love was part of God's purpose in creating people. Not accidental. Not a human invention. But God's good plan—part of the way the universe was made.

We can see this idea very clearly in the Creation stories in the Book of Genesis. The oldest of these contains a passage which we will keep coming back to in this unit. God has just made Eve:

 Then the man said, 'At last, here is one of my own kind—bone taken from my bone, and flesh from my flesh'...That is why a man leaves his father and mother and is united with his wife, and they become one.

Genesis 2:23, 24

The writer thought that marriage was so important, he put it right in the middle of the story of the Creation itself. To him and to the other ancient Jews, marriage was a fundamental part of being human and of God's purpose for mankind.

- The Old Testament writers also thought that married love should be creative and life-giving. Look again at the passage from Genesis. It says that the man and the woman 'become one'. Many scholars think that this is more than a romantic or poetic way of saying that men and women should be closely united in their marriages. Becoming 'one' (or 'one flesh') refers to sexual union with all its potential for creating new life.

So marriage is seen as something holy. It was part of God's plan in creating people and was itself meant to be creative. Because of this it was protected in the laws of the Old Testament, which the Jews believed had been given to them by God through Moses. In

particular, adultery—unfaithfulness in marriage—was condemned in the Ten Commandments:

 Thou shalt not commit adultery.

Exodus 20:14; Deuteronomy 5:18

Other Law books spelled out the details. The punishment for adultery in Old Testament times was death:

 If a man commits adultery with his neighbour's wife, both he and the woman shall be put to death.

Leviticus 20:10

According to the Bible, marriage has been part of God's good plan for human beings from the very beginning. It is the start of a new family unit, a relationship so close that the Bible says the two 'become one'. The hallmarks of marriage as the Bible describes it are absolute loyalty and faithfulness. The endless circle of the wedding ring symbolizes this lifelong commitment, worn from this moment on, for everyone to see.

This theme of the sacredness (sanctity) of marriage and the evil of adultery is taken up in the later books of the Old Testament, which were partly written in order to instruct people how to live their lives. In 2 Samuel 11–12 there is the famous story of King David's adultery with Bathsheba. Read it for yourselves in your Bibles. Stories like this were told to show how even the great heroes of Israel were expected to obey God's laws.

So, in the Old Testament:

- Marriage is part of God's purpose in the creation of men and women.

- Marriage is life-giving.

- Adultery is wrong.

But although the OT writers thought marriage was very important, they seem to have taken it for granted that a man could divorce his wife by giving her a written notice of divorce (Deuteronomy 24:1–4). (There is nothing about women divorcing their husbands.)

Marriage in the New Testament

There are two parts to the New Testament teaching about marriage:

- The teaching of Jesus about marriage and adultery.

- The teaching Saint Paul gives in his letters.

For both Jesus and Paul, the Old Testament was their 'Bible'. They knew the stories and the laws we have been looking at and built on them in their own teaching.

The teaching of Jesus

Although the Old Testament Law allowed divorce, Jesus did not. Look at the passage below from Mark's Gospel (see also Note below):

 Read Mark 10:2–12

At the time of Jesus there was a lot of argument among the rabbis about divorce. They all agreed it was allowed, but disagreed about the grounds for divorce. It depended what was meant by Deuteronomy 24:1, which talks about 'some impropriety' on the part of the wife as a reason for divorce.

The Pharisees in this incident were trying to get Jesus to give his opinion, and perhaps hoping he would make a mess of it. But Jesus is not interested in playing legal games. He dismisses the law that Moses gave, saying that it was allowed only because people were so sinful. The real truth is that there should be no divorce at all. Long before Moses, at the Creation itself, God had made men and women to become one in marriage, and that meant for life. To support what he has to say, Jesus quotes the passage from Genesis which we have already looked at.

So on one level, Jesus' teaching about divorce is much more strict than the Torah's. It goes behind the legal traditions of the Old Testament to an earlier tradition about Creation. It is as though Jesus is saying

that divorce was allowed for a while, but now that the Kingdom of God has arrived, people should live as God originally intended.

So Jesus said that anyone who got divorced and married somebody else was committing adultery. We have already seen that the Old Testament punishment for adultery was death. What did Jesus think about that? A story from John's Gospel helps us to answer this question:

 Read John 8:3–11

We have already said that on one level Jesus' teaching about marriage is very much more strict than the Torah's. In this story we can see that on another level it is considerably more lenient. What the woman has done is certainly wrong. Jesus tells her not to sin again, so it is not as though he thought what she had done did not matter. But in contrast with the law of Moses, this story shows us that the way of Jesus is one of forgiveness and reconciliation, not punishment.

NOTE: In matters of sexual morality and in his teaching about marriage, Jesus set extremely high standards. At the same time he offered the hope of forgiveness to those who had failed. Over the course of Christian history it has sometimes been difficult for the churches to do justice to both sides of his teaching: to uphold the rules which preserve the sanctity of marriage and at the same time to be loving and forgiving to people who find themselves in difficulties (see Chapter 10).

We can see this difficulty even in the very early church. In Chapter 4 we looked at the Sermon on the Mount, where Matthew has his version of the teaching of Jesus about marriage. It is almost identical to Mark's, but has an extra few words: '. . .any man who divorces his wife *for any cause other than unfaithfulness* commits adultery if he marries some other woman.'

New Testament scholars agree that Matthew's Gospel was written after Mark's Gospel, and that Matthew used Mark's words as a source for his own. Some deduce from this that Matthew thought Mark's version of Jesus' teaching about marriage was too uncompromising, and so he toned it down by adding the words we have put in italics. Matthew's local Christian community probably therefore allowed Christians to divorce and remarry in cases of unfaithfulness.

The teaching of St Paul

Paul wrote from about twenty to thirty years after Jesus' resurrection. He added a very important element to the Christian understanding of marriage by applying it to **the love Christ has for the church.** Paul wrote about this in his letter to the Christians at Ephesus.

 Read Ephesians 5:28–33

Paul is not the easiest writer in the world to understand. If you read the points below and then read the passage from Ephesians again, it may help:

- Paul (like Jesus) goes back to the Creation story in Genesis when he talks about marriage.

- Paul hints that Christ left his heavenly Father to become man and to find his 'bride', the church.

- He emphasizes the fact that in marriage the husband and wife become 'one flesh' and suggests that the two, in a sense, become a single entity.

- He says that each Christian is part of Christ's 'body' which is the church.

So Paul is saying that the unity and love between a Christian wife and husband is a symbol and a sign of the love between Christ and the church, and of the love which exists between Christ and each individual Christian.

To sum up the New Testament teaching about marriage:

1. Jesus, when he was questioned about divorce, referred back to God's intention in Creation. He said that people should not divide what God had joined together and that to remarry after divorce was to commit adultery (Mark 10).

2. Although the Old Testament punishment for adultery was death, Jesus' behaviour towards the woman taken in adultery showed a new way of dealing with people based on the love of God in forgiveness and reconciliation (John 8).

3. St Paul wrote about marriage as a sign of the love which exists between Christ and his church. The husband and wife are one body just as the church is the body and bride of Christ (Ephesians 5).

Follow-up

Questions

1 Which parts of the Bible would a Christian use to support the view that marriage is
(a) part of the way God has made the world and
(b) meant to be life-giving?

2 Summarize the Old Testament view of adultery. What was the punishment?

3 How would you say that the teaching of Jesus about marriage was
(a) similar to Old Testament teaching and
(b) different from Old Testament teaching?

4 In your own words, describe what St Paul taught Christians about marriage.

Activity

Prepare a short drama piece based on the story of the Woman caught in Adultery in John 8.

9

Christian Weddings

Christians believe that marriage has to do with people's relationship with God as well as with one another. In Chapter 8 we explored some important things the Bible has to say about it. Here we shall be concentrating on Christian wedding ceremonies and how these reflect Christian beliefs and practices to do with marriage.

What Christian marriage means

The Bible celebrates sex as the good gift of a good creator. It clearly affirms that our sexuality is God's creation, that marriage is God's institution, and sex is to be enjoyed within marriage.

There are five implications of the biblical definition of marriage in Genesis 2:24. Marriage is:

1. *Monogamous*—between one man and one woman.

2. *Heterosexual*—'a man and his wife'.

3. *Publicly acknowledged*—leaving parents meant a public, social occasion.

4. *Consummated in sexual union*—'one flesh'.

5. *Life-long*—'let no one separate'.

From *In Touch*, John Stott, 1993

In man and woman becoming 'one flesh', humanity has the possibility of exploring the depths of intimacy in its fullest glory—of giving and receiving, of knowing and being known, revealing and accepting. This, in essence, is the reward of living out the objectives of biblical marriage.

God designed marriage as a life-long commitment. For only then can the partners feel free, and confident, to grow and be grown. Only then can the partners be freed from the fear of rejection. Only then can they be confident that they can try again, and again. It is impossible otherwise to promise to love one another 'until death do us part'.

From *In Touch*, Jorge Atiencia, 1993

Christian weddings

Long before the wedding itself, most churches will expect the couple to attend marriage preparation classes. These will explore the meaning of Christian marriage and prepare the bride and groom for the wedding ceremony.

Christian wedding **ceremonies** nearly all have the same shape:

- An introduction explaining what Christian marriage is. Questions to ensure the lawfulness of the marriage.

- Special promises or vows which the bride and groom make committing themselves to one another.

- The giving and receiving of rings.

- An official statement that the bride and groom are now married.

- Prayers and blessings for the couple and then for the congregation as a whole.

- The signing of the Marriage Register and receiving of the marriage certificate. (This is a legal requirement which makes the marriage valid in British law.)

A Christian wedding can be elaborate or utterly simple. It is not the building, or the dress, or the size of the occasion (or bill!) that matters. The important thing is the promise, publicly made, to share the whole of life from this time on—no matter what the circumstances—with the chosen partner, and no other.

The **introduction** to a wedding service used in the Church of England says this:

> **Marriage is given, that husband and wife may comfort and help each other, living faithfully together in need and in plenty, in sorrow and in joy. It is given, that with delight and tenderness they may know each other in love, and, through the joy of their bodily union, may strengthen the union of their hearts and lives. It is given, that they may have children and be blessed in caring for them and bringing them up in accordance with God's will, to his praise and glory.**

From *The Alternative Service Book*, 1980

An Eastern Christian wedding

Wedding services among Eastern Orthodox Christians (and Eastern Rite Catholics) differ from the usual pattern familiar to most Christians living in the West, although both ceremonies share common elements. At an Eastern Christian wedding the service begins at the door of the church with the wedding vows and the exchange of rings.

The couple then process to a table at the centre of the church and the whole congregation listens to readings from the Scriptures. During this part of the service the couple hold lighted candles as a symbol of the presence of Christ.

Next, crowns are put on the heads of the bride and groom: the couple for a moment are king and queen and are to make their family an image of the Kingdom of God.

The Gospel story of Jesus changing the water into wine at the marriage feast in Cana is read. Prayers are said and a cup of wine is given to the couple to drink as a symbol of their new unity.

Finally the priest joins their hands and leads them around the centre table from which the Scriptures have been read. The circle they make is a symbol of the everlasting nature of the sacrament of marriage.

Although in Western Christianity the couple are said to marry one another by the vows they exchange, Eastern Orthodox theology takes a rather different view. There the emphasis is placed on the mystery and sanctity of marriage to such an extent that the priest is held to marry the couple.

'Are you ready freely and without reservation to give yourselves to each other in marriage?'

'Are you ready to love and honour each other as man and wife for the rest of your lives?'

'Are you ready to accept children lovingly from God, and bring them up according to the law of Christ and his church?'

The **marriage vows** themselves are usually considered to be the moment when the couple actually become married. Each of them says to the other in turn something like this (the words may change slightly depending on the sort of church):

> **I (name) do take thee (name)**
> **to be my lawful wedded wife/husband,**
> **to have and to hold**
> **from this day forward;**
> **for better, for worse,**
> **for richer, for poorer,**
> **in sickness and in health**
> **to love and to cherish,**
> **till death do us part.**

A wedding in the Eastern Orthodox Church has its own special rituals to express the commitment all Christian couples make in marriage.

Read the passage carefully again. You will notice that it emphasizes three things:

1. Marriage is about sharing your life completely with your partner (that involves being faithful).

2. It is about deepening your love for the person you have chosen by having sex together.

3. It is about having children and caring for them as God wants.

These three beliefs about marriage also stand behind the **questions** which the priest asks the bride and groom in a Catholic wedding:

The Sacraments

In Catholic theology, marriage is one of the seven **Sacraments**. This means that it is a visible sign of a special way God works to bring people close to him.

The Catholic Church teaches that there are seven Sacraments. Each of these is said to be 'an outward and visible sign of an inward and invisible gift, ordained by Jesus Christ, by which grace is given to our souls'. The Catholic Sacraments are:

- Baptism
- Holy Communion
- Confirmation
- Marriage
- The Sacrament of Reconciliation (Confession or Penance)
- The Sacrament of the Sick (Holy Unction)
- Ordination.

Most Protestant Christians only accept the first two of these as true sacraments.

When the couple give one another their **wedding rings** (sometimes only the bride has one) it is meant to be a symbol of two things:

- the promises they have just given to one another.

- the belief that marriage cannot be ended except by death, just as a ring has no ends.

In Britain most churches are licensed by the State as places where people can get married. Priests and ministers act as registrars for the State, giving out wedding certificates themselves and returning copies to Government records. But in some other countries the history of the relationship between the Christian church and the State has been more hostile than in Britain, and there Christians have to go through two marriage ceremonies—one to marry them in the eyes of the church, and another civil one to fulfil the legal requirements necessary for marriage.

In the Catholic wedding service and in the Church of England, the priest taking the wedding service acts as a representative of the whole Christian community. Strictly speaking he does not make them married: their vows to one another do that. But he acts as a kind of official witness, and now that the couple are married he leads the congregation in prayers for them and repeats the words of Jesus in Mark's Gospel:

 What God has joined together let no man put asunder.

Mark 10:9

*Catholic weddings frequently take place during a special Mass called a Wedding or **Nuptial** Mass. This is not compulsory, but is a popular choice particularly with couples who are both Catholics.*

During a Nuptial Mass the parts of the wedding service are interwoven with the usual order of the Mass. The questions for the bride and groom, the vows and the exchange of rings all happen directly after the priest's homily (sermon), during which he will have explained the meaning of Christian marriage.

Then the Mass progresses as usual until after the 'Our Father', when the priest gives a special blessing called the 'Marriage' or 'Nuptial' Blessing to the couple. Having the wedding within the Mass like this brings home to Catholics an important truth: that the couple's love as they give themselves to one another in marriage is a powerful symbol of the love of Christ who gives himself to Christians in the Eucharist.

Summary

- Christians believe that marriage is especially holy because **the love between a Christian husband and wife is a sign of the love of God.** The Christian ideal for marriage is rooted in the idea that Christian marriage is meant to be:

- **permanent**, just as God's love has no end;

- **life-giving**, like the love of God who creates the world;

- an **exclusive relationship** in which husband and wife remain faithful to one another just as God is faithful and keeps his promises.

Follow-up

Questions

1 Explain why Christians believe marriage to be especially holy.

2 Look back over the section 'Christian Weddings' and draw up a table which shows how each of these principles is reflected in what happens during the wedding ceremony. We have given you a start already:

Marriage is:		
a) permanent	b) life-giving	c) exclusive
Symbolised by rings	'Are you ready ..' Roman Catholic Service	The Marriage Vows

3 At what point in the wedding ceremony are the couple usually considered to be married? Describe the role of the priest or minister in this.

4 Explain why a Roman Catholic couple might be encouraged to celebrate their wedding during a Nuptial Mass.

For discussion

Many people who get married in church are not regular churchgoers. In groups, discuss why you think they still decide to have a religious wedding. Report back to the rest of the class.

Activity

Look again at the marriage vows in this chapter. Design a poster which could be used to help children to understand the meaning of the promises made in a Christian wedding.

NOTE: Not all marriages are permanent, life-giving or exclusive relationships. We shall explore some difficulties in marriage, and how Christians deal with them, in the next two chapters.

Most people love a wedding. There is something about seeing a young couple set out on married life full of trust and love for one another which moves us deeply. But the wedding day is only a beginning. We may hope that the road ahead will be full of joy, but it can sometimes be very hard indeed.

Most couples experience some kind of difficulty in their marriages at one time or another. You would hardly expect anything else in a lifelong relationship. Financial difficulties, overwork, illness and the threat of unemployment are common enough today. All of these can lead to other problems and can put real strain on a marriage. So can selfishness and lack of self-control.

Most married couples manage to work through their temporary difficulties. Sometimes a marriage may even be strengthened by the shared experience of trouble. But some couples' problems become so overwhelming that, despite their best intentions, their love for one another and the relationship itself is threatened. When that happens, people sometimes talk about 'marriage break-down'.

In this chapter and in Chapter 11 we examine some of these problems. They may not be anybody's 'fault'—they may just happen. And not all of them will lead to the marriage breaking down. But some do and we shall look at the options Christians have if that happens.

The fact that Christians have particularly high ideals for marriage (see Chapters 8 and 9) has two effects:

- some things raise particular problems for Christians which are not widely regarded as problems by society at large.

- Christians whose marriages have broken down feel specially embarrassed and guilty.

In Chapter 8 we saw that a Christian marriage is meant to be exclusive, life-giving and permanent. We are going to take each of these in turn.

Every marriage begins with high hopes and good intentions. But sooner or later problems arise. If these cannot be resolved, couples who care about their marriage will often turn to a skilled counsellor for help.

Marriage is meant to be exclusive— but people are sometimes unfaithful

If a married man has sex with a woman who is not his wife, or if a married woman has sex with somebody other than her husband, this is called **extra-marital sex** or **adultery.** The Christian churches are all agreed that adultery is a serious sin for the following reasons:

- It breaks the Commandments and goes against the teaching of Jesus (see Chapter 8).

- It breaks the promises or **vows** which the couple made to one another at their wedding (see Chapter 9).

- It nearly always involves deceiving one's wife or husband and so breaks the trust and threatens the honesty which is an essential part of marriage.

- It threatens the stable relationship between a husband and his wife which is necessary for the security of their children, if they have any.

- In Catholic theology, sex is the sign of the Sacrament of Marriage which shows Christ's love for the church. Extra-marital sex cannot be a sign of the Sacrament.

Sex before marriage (premarital sex) is widely accepted in secular Western society today. Many TV advertisements, books, magazines and films reflect the common belief that it is acceptable and usual for a couple to have sex if they are going out together. In part this is a consequence of the 'sexual revolution' of the 1960s, when many of the values held in society up till then were called into question. (In fact many people before the 1960s only paid lip-service to these values: they were having sex but keeping quiet about it.)

Despite the many pressures modern society brings to bear, traditional Christian teaching—for good reason—continues to say that sex should be kept for marriage and that outside marriage it is a sin. The reason for this is that as with adultery, sex outside marriage cannot really express the true nature of human sexuality as this is seen in Christian teaching:

One important point is that marriage offers security. But in the case of sexual relationships outside marriage, no public promises have been made, and neither the couple nor their family and friends can be sure about the future. This is particularly serious if a child is conceived. And for Catholics, there is no sacrament.

'Living together' or cohabitation describes a relationship in which a couple live as though they were married without going through a wedding ceremony. The Christian objections to premarital sex apply also to cohabitation. Many non-Christian couples argue that living together can be just as committed as marriage.

If marriage is meant to be life-giving, what about childless marriages?

Christian teaching stresses that the proper context for starting a new life—babies—is the loving sexual relationship of a wife and husband, which allows children to grow up in a stable and secure family.

That may seem like common sense. But sometimes things do not work out that way:

- one or other of the partners may be infertile—incapable of having children (or babies simply may not come);

- one or other of the partners may refuse sex.

Of course the couple may choose never to have children and use contraception to prevent them from being conceived.

Infertility causes great unhappiness to some couples: over two million people in Britain are estimated to be incapable of having children without special medical help.

Recent advances made in medical science have offered new techniques to help many couples facing infertility. In particular we now know how to fertilize a human egg (*ovum*) with sperm artificially outside the woman's body, and then replant the growing child in the womb. This is what people mean when they talk about 'test tube' babies. Its technical name is **in vitro fertilization** or 'IVF' for short (*in vitro* is Latin for 'in glass'). The world's first 'test-tube baby' was born in 1978, to the great joy of her parents.

Another technique sometimes used is **artificial insemination** (AI). Here sperm are introduced into the woman's body by means of an instrument instead of in sexual intercourse.

Christian teaching on modern infertility treatments

The Roman Catholic position: the Catholic Church attempted to deal with some of the problems raised by new techniques in the treatment of infertility in a document issued in 1987 and called 'Respect for Human Life in its Origin and the Dignity of Procreation'. This laid down guidelines for all who are involved in the treatment of infertility. Its basic principles are:

- that the proper place for the conception of children is within the loving sexual relationship of a husband and wife.

- that children are a gift and blessing from God.

- that because science makes something possible, it does not necessarily make it right. Scientists must continue to research into the causes of infertility while bearing in mind the requirements of the moral law.

- that all human beings have the right to life from the moment of conception: new techniques must respect that right.

Starting from these principles, the document goes on to outline the Catholic Church's position on IVF, AI and Surrogate Motherhood:

- According to the Catholic Church, IVF and AI are acceptable as long as:
  (1) 'spare embryos' are not created in IVF;
  (2) the sperm and the ovum belong to the married couple and are not donated by a third party;
  (3) IVF and AI are not used to replace the act of sexual intercourse in which husband and wife express their love.

- Surrogate motherhood strikes at the heart of the family and the dignity of motherhood and is not acceptable.

But despite the Church's reservations about these new methods, the document stresses that any child born using them is a gift of God's goodness and must be brought up with love.

Other Christian denominations do not take such a hard line on these issues as the Catholic Church. In 1984 **the Church of England** issued a report called 'Human Fertlilization and Embryology' which allowed for IVF in all its forms including the donation and use of sperm and *ova* by third parties. It also accepted experimentation on 'spare' human embryos up to the 14th day of their development. However, this report also said that surrogate motherhood was unacceptable.

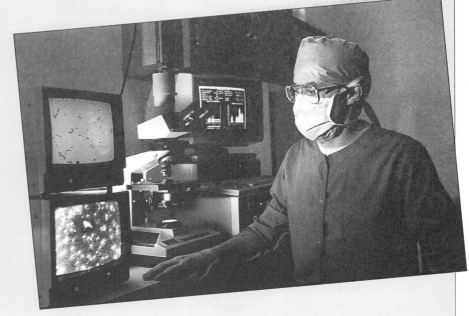

In vitro fertilization can sometimes be a way of solving infertility problems. Here a scientist uses a light microscope linked to TV monitors to check viability of sperm. Sperm may be provided by the husband (or be donated by a third party—which is a special problem for many Christians, and others too).

Despite the many good things which have come out of these new techniques, the Christian churches (and many non-Christians as well) have pointed out that they raise serious moral problems. A Christian couple faced with the problem of infertility would need to consider these very carefully. IVF allows for a number of possibilities which a Christian might consider wrong. Here are some of them:

- IVF and AI can both be done using either the husband's sperm or that of a donor. Many Christians think that the use of a donor goes against the idea of faithfulness in marriage.

- IVF sometimes results in the creation of 'spare' human embryos which are not wanted by the couple and which can be kept alive and used for medical experiments. This raises profound questions about the sanctity of human life. In particular, is it right to create life if we know that we are going to destroy it? To many people it seems we are in danger of 'playing God'. The creation of 'spare' embryos was a particular problem in the early days of IVF.

- Some women are unable (or find it inconvenient) to sustain a pregnancy. IVF could make it possible for a couple to ask another woman to carry a pregnancy through and give birth to the child. This is called **surrogate motherhood**. Many people are worried about this because of the practical and legal problems which might occur: what would happen, for instance, if the surrogate mother decided she did not want to give up the child? Many Christians would go further and say that surrogate motherhood strikes at the foundations of family life, particularly where money changes hands.

Infertility treatments and British law

In Britain infertility treatments are closely guarded by a licensing authority. Experimentation on human embryos (which may be frozen and kept until wanted) is allowed under licence for up to the 14th day of their development. IVF and AI, including the donation of sperm and *ova* (eggs) are allowed, but Surrogate Motherhood is illegal.

The laws controlling these things were put into force after the government set up the 'Committee of Enquiry into Human Fertilization and Development' in 1982. It made its report in 1984. Since the Committee's chairman was Lady Warnock, this is often referred to as the 'Warnock Report'.

The Committee took very serious notice of religious teaching when it was doing its work. On the whole Christians were happy that the Warnock Report set quite strict limits on what was allowed, although many (especially Catholics) think that it went too far in allowing embryo research.

Infertility can put great strain on a marriage where a couple long for children. A Christian couple may have the added burden of trying to choose a course of treatment which stays within the bounds of Christian teaching. In cases where one partner is Christian and the other is not, a great deal of understanding and help are likely to be required.

Sexual problems in marriage

Sex is creative not only in the sense of giving life to children. When things are going well, it cements the couple's relationship and affirms their love for one another, helping to keep the marriage fresh and alive. But sometimes underlying difficulties and tensions in a marriage affect the sexual relationship.

Tiredness, unresolved quarrels, the demands made by children, physical problems, or a host of other reasons, may lead one partner or both simply to 'go off' sex. The resulting guilt, resentment and embarrassment can lead to anger, jealousy or perhaps turning to someone else.

In extreme cases sexual problems can bring about the collapse of the marriage itself. St Paul seems to have been aware of this when he wrote about how necessary the sexual dimension and generous self-giving is for a Christian marriage.

 Read 1 Corinthians 7:3–5

The decision not to have children

Finally, a couple may choose not to have children and use contraception to ensure this. Over the past forty years discoveries in medical science have made contraceptives much more reliable than they used to be. In particular the development of 'the Pill', sterilization and vasectomy techniques make it possible for a couple to be more or less certain that no matter how often they make love, the wife will not conceive a child. (Sterilization and vasectomy are operations. Some people worry about the long-term medical affects of taking the Pill and use these as alternatives.)

All the Christian churches at one time taught that contraception was sinful. It was held that God intended sex for the creation of new life and people should not interfere with this. Three things have led most of the Protestant Christian churches to change their minds:

- Many people have become very worried by the increase in the world's population and see contraception as a way of controlling it.

- There has been a growing appreciation of the importance of sex as a way in which husband and wife share their love for one another and not just as the way children are created.

- The development of new contraceptive techniques means that using contraception does not actually interfere with the act of making love.

Many Christians feel that there is something selfish about a fertile married couple who go into marriage having already decided that they will never have children. A Christian wedding assumes that normally having children is part of what marriage is all about. But Protestant Christians today see no moral problem in using contraceptives to help them limit the size of their families or delay starting a family for financial or other practical reasons.

Roman Catholic teaching about contraception is rather different. In 1968 Pope Paul VI issued an encyclical called 'On Human Life' (*Humanae Vitae*) which re-stated the traditional teaching of Christianity. He thought that it was necessary to do this because of the increasing range of contraceptives which were being developed. Since then the Church's teaching has been re-emphasized by Pope John Paul II.

The Catholic Church's position on contraception is this:

- Sex has two functions: to express the love between husband and wife and to give life to children. In sexual intercourse the love between husband and wife becomes creative, like the love of God.

- The two functions of sex are naturally expressed in one action—making love—which is the sign of the Sacrament of Marriage.

- Contraceptives like the Pill, sterilization and vasectomy separate the creative function of sexual intercourse from the expression of love in an unnatural way.

- The use of contraceptives is contrary to Natural Law (see Chapter 3) and is therefore sinful.

- Contraception is also dangerous to society. As people accept its use, sexual immorality increases and women are increasingly seen as sexual playthings.

Because the Catholic Church disapproves of the use of contraceptives, many people think that Catholics believe that married couples should have as many children as they can. This is not true. In fact the Church teaches that married couples can and should limit the size of their families when necessary. This is meant to be achieved by 'natural' methods of birth control which take advantage of the fact that the wife is only able to become pregnant for a few days each month.

NOTE: Sometimes people have to have operations which, as a side-effect, make them incapable of conceiving or fathering children. Doctors may also occasionally have other reasons for prescribing pills usually used for contraception. The Catholic Church allows for cases like these because there is no deliberate intention to interfere with conception. Of course all the other moral laws apply: being unable to bear children because of an operation would not be a licence to commit adultery, for instance !

When Pope Paul issued *Humanae Vitae* in 1968 he was aware that it would disappoint many Catholics who had been hoping that the Church would find that using the Pill was acceptable. In *Humanae Vitae* he stressed that priests should handle the issue of contraception with great care and love, and he spoke of 'the difficulties, at times very great, which beset the lives of Christian married couples' and the 'deep distress' these can cause.

Many Catholic couples would agree that living up to the Church's teaching on contraception is a difficult and painful experience. But perhaps nobody should expect the Christian life to be easy.

Follow-up

Questions

1 Name two problems which can arise in marriage.

2 Give two reasons why Christianity teaches that extra-marital sex (adultery) is wrong.

3 Say whether the following statements are true or false:

- Christians have no objection to surrogate motherhood.

- The Catholic Church forbids all methods of birth control.

- IVF and AI are acceptable to all Christians, though with some restrictions.

- Experimentation on human embryos is legal in Britain.

- St Paul thought that married couples should be careful not to have too much sex.

4 (a) Explain one of the techniques which might be used to help infertile couples today.
(b) What moral problems, if any, are raised by this?

5 What were:

- *Humanae Vitae* (1968)

- the Warnock Report (1984)

- 'Human Fertilization and Embryology' (1984)

- 'Respect for Human Life in its Origin and the Dignity of Procreation' (1987)?

6 What does the Roman Catholic Church teach about contraception and birth control?

For discussion

'I think that living together is just as good as getting married. What difference does a wedding make?' A friend who claims to be religious says this. How would you respond? Discuss this in groups and report back to the rest of the class.

11 Christianity, Divorce and Remarriage

The Christian ideal is marriage for life. But if marriage is meant to be permanent, why do so many couples split up?

In 1989, 151,000 marriages in the UK ended in divorce—one of the highest rates in the developed world. Of course, not everybody in Britain is a practising Christian (only 50% of marriages even take place in church): but the figures do include a good many Christian marriages.

A divorce is a legal process involving the civil authorities (the State) which ends in a declaration saying that a marriage is at an end. Once this has been obtained, the couple are no longer married to one another under law. The State says they are free to marry again, although careful provision is made so that any children of the first marriage are looked after properly.

In the nineteenth century it used to be very difficult to get a divorce, but since then it has become increasingly easy. In the UK, divorce is governed by the Matrimonial Causes Act of 1973. This allows a divorce to be granted if it can be shown that a marriage has suffered what it calls 'irretrievable breakdown'. This can be demonstrated for instance, if the couple have been living apart for over two years, if adultery has occurred, or if there has been 'unreasonable behaviour' (violence, mental cruelty, or alcoholism, for example).

Many Christians think that the 1973 Act makes divorce too easy to obtain in Britain and does not do enough to encourage couples to overcome their difficulties. They would argue that the law has 'sold out' to a modern society which already tempts people to sexual unfaithfulness. As a result many young people have suffered the trauma of seeing their parents divorce and too many children experience what a 'broken home' means. As the idea of the family has been attacked, society has become increasingly violent and immoral.

Others would take an opposite view. They would say that a great deal of unhappiness was caused in the past by couples staying together 'for the sake of the children' and that making divorce laws hard only encouraged people—usually fathers—to desert their families. Easier divorces encourage a clean break and give a much greater degree of financial security to women who are often left to bring up children on their own.

Whatever the rights and wrongs of this argument, the Christian churches have to deal with divorced people, and this is a problem:

- On the one hand they feel that they have to uphold the sanctity of marriage as this is expressed in the Bible and especially Jesus' teaching.

- But on the other hand they know that they need love, support and care for people who have been divorced.

Different Christian denominations have come up with different ways of dealing with the problems. On the whole the **Protestant churches** take the view that Jesus' teaching is an ideal which married couples should try to live up to, but that sadly the problems faced by some couples mean that their marriages can and do end. In these cases the Protestant churches accept a civil divorce as an end to a marriage. A divorced man or woman may usually therefore remarry in a Protestant church, even if their original wife or husband is still alive.

The **Church of England** has changed its regulations about divorce and remarriage. Until recently it did not

Marriage breakdown and divorce are sad facts of life. Not all churches deal with the problem of broken marriages amongst Christians in the same way. The effect of family conflict on children is a major concern in the churches and in society as a whole.

Helping marriages in trouble

A number of organizations exist to help couples who are experiencing difficulties in their marriages. Two of them are Relate and the Catholic Marriage Advisory Council (CMAC).

Relate

Relate (The National Marriage Guidance Council) began in the early 1940s. It is a charity which depends on its clients for financial support, although it does receive some local government help with its work. Its marriage guidance counsellors are volunteers who undergo a two-year period of part-time training.

As an independent body which is not attached to any of the churches or other religious institutions, Relate believes that it is in a unique position to help people from all cultural and social backgrounds. It will help those who are living together as well as those who are not formally married, and it declares that its members are not expected to have any particular beliefs—except in the value and dignity of every human being.

Relate provides help for people in a number of ways:

- by providing counselling for people who are experiencing specific problems and conflicts in their marriages

- by providing counselling to help people deal constructively with what happens when a marriage ends in death, divorce or separation

- by helping married couples to enhance their relationship through therapy and counselling

- by offering education services and training in marriage and family life to professional groups such as doctors and social workers.

CMAC

CMAC—the Catholic Marriage Advisory Council—is the largest Christian counselling service in the UK. Like Relate, it opens its doors to anybody who seeks help and aims to accept them as they are. So you do not have to be a Christian or married for CMAC to help you. Unlike Relate, however, it bases its understanding of marriage on the Catholic principles we have looked at previously. CMAC offers:

- marriage guidance counselling with trained counsellors to help people develop the skills they need to deal with the problems they may be encountering

- an education service offering marriage preparation courses and help for parents and others involved in delivering sex education

- help for couples who want to know more about natural methods of family planning

- the opportunity for research into ways in which marriages can be sustained and enriched.

CMAC and Relate may look like rival organizations, but in fact they often work closely together. In 1991, for instance, the Home Office gave CMAC and Relate £100,000 for a joint project aimed at helping marriage and family life in inner city areas.

Both CMAC and Relate stress that their counsellors must put their clients first. They must be completely unshockable and unjudgemental. Their aim is not so much to offer advice, as to work through clients' problems with them, give the clients greater understanding of their own feelings and situations, and enable them to take control.

usually allow a divorced man or woman to remarry in church, although sometimes an informal blessing was given after a civil wedding in a registry office. Since 1981 however, the General Synod (the governing body of the Church of England) has given parish ministers the authority to remarry divorced people in church if they feel that this is appropriate, with the permission of their bishops.

The **Roman Catholic Church** again takes a rather different view from the other Christian denominations. It takes the words of the Bible literally: once a Christian marriage has taken place the two have become 'one flesh': the marriage is made by God and cannot be dissolved or ended by anything people do—only by death. It is indissoluble and irrevocable. So the Catholic Church says that a civil divorce is not enough. If a couple who have been married in church get a divorce from the State, the Church teaches that they are still married in the eyes of God. They are not free to marry again while their previous wife or husband is still alive. (Of course widows and widowers are free to marry again in all the Christian churches whatever the state of their previous marriages.)

However, the Catholic Church does allow for the possibility that there may never have been a real marriage in the first place, even though the couple went through a wedding service together. For instance:

- one of the partners might not have understood the marriage vows made at the wedding, or might have been forced into making them;

- one of the partners might have lied when making the marriage vows: for instance, he or she might never have had any intention of having children;

- the couple may never have consummated the marriage (had sexual intercourse together).

These are all examples of what are called impediments in the marriage.

In order to deal with cases like these the Catholic Church has a system of careful enquiries into marriages. If it can be proved that there was a serious impediment which prevented a real marriage from taking place then the Church will declare an **annulment**. This is a solemn declaration that from the very beginning no real marriage existed.

Catholics whose marriages have been annulled are free to marry in church even though the person to whom they were previously 'married' is still alive. (Of course, in this case the couple must have already obtained a civil divorce as well as the annulment—otherwise their marriage would break the civil law.)

Although getting an annulment is sometimes a difficult and lengthy process, Catholics whose marriages have broken down are encouraged to try. Catholics who ignore the process, get a civil divorce and then marry again in a registry office while they have a marriage partner still living are usually discouraged from receiving the Sacraments until their situation is sorted out. All of this can cause great pain to many who feel that they need the support of the Church at such a difficult time of their lives. In order to help them, the Church has set up a number of national and local associations for divorced and separated Catholics where friendship, help and advice can be found.

The Eastern Orthodox churches take the view that the church has the authority to end marriages, and the church itself will grant divorces. There even used to be a special service at which a marriage was ended. Remarriage is allowed in church, although the wedding service is not so jolly the second time around. You cannot keep on getting divorced, though. A third marriage is rarely allowed.

Follow-up

Questions

1 In Britain, divorce is governed by the Divorce Law Reform Act.

- In what year did this Act come into force?

- What is the significance of the term 'irretrievable breakdown' in the Act?

2 Can a divorced person remarry in any Christian church if he or she has a former wife or husband still living? Explain your answer fully.

3 In the Roman Catholic Church, what is meant by an annulment, and how does this differ from a divorce?

4 Describe the work of one agency which offers help to couples experiencing marriage difficulties.

5 What do you think are the most serious problems the church faces in dealing with divorce, and how do you think these can best be handled?

For discussion

'Divorce in Britain is too easy. We do not do enough to help couples to sort out the problems in their marriages' Do you agree?

Activity

Try to organize a speaker from CMAC or Relate to come to address your class.

'DID YOU KNOW? I'M PREGNANT AGAIN — WE'RE GOING TO HAVE ANOTHER BABY.'

'THATS BRILLIANT, CATHY! CONGRATULATIONS!'

When a couple announces that a new baby is on the way we usually think it is good news. The husband and wife in the picture are delighted: their friend shares in their happiness. Theirs will be a much wanted child, and over the course of the next few months they will look forward to his or her birth with increasing excitement. They will feel anxiety, too, as they hope that everything will be all right.

But scenes like this are not the whole story. For some people pregnancy can be very bad news indeed.

- It can be inconvenient and embarrassing.

- It always causes physical and emotional upheaval. It means that a woman has to take a break from her education or career.

- It can be difficult to pick up the pieces again afterwards, especially with a young child to look after.

- Sometimes women get pregnant without being married or in a stable relationship: and people are not always understanding or sympathetic to single mothers. Some of these mothers may be very young indeed.

- A number of babies are conceived every year after rapes and incest.

There are other things which may make a pregnancy unwelcome. Some people have incurable genetic disorders (conditions which start at the moment of conception) such as Down's syndrome, cystic fibrosis and haemophilia.

A number of factors can make the conception of a handicapped person more likely than it usually is: a history of haemophilia among men in a family, for instance, or the age of the mother in the case of Down's syndrome.

And things can go wrong during the pregnancy itself: German measles (rubella) caught by a pregnant mother can cause handicap in the growing baby (the foetus) in the womb. If parents know that there is a more than usually high risk of their child being born handicapped it will make them very worried about the future.

TESTS FOR HANDICAP

In recent years tests have been developed which can often show if a baby is going to be born handicapped. Among these tests the most commonly used are:

◆ **Ultrasound scanning**. *During a 'scan' a moving picture of the foetus is produced on a monitor screen by passing very high frequency sound-waves into the uterus and converting the 'echoes' into pictures. Ultrasound scanning has had the added advantage of allowing mothers and fathers to see their children for the first time before they are even born. Many find this an exciting and reassuring experience.*

◆ **Amniocentesis**. *In this test a small amount of the fluid surrounding the growing baby is drawn off and the foetal cells within it are examined for any genetic abnormality.*

If these tests show an abnormality in the pregnancy, the medical team may offer the mother an abortion.

So although pregnancy is usually a reason for celebration, there are some circumstances when it is very far from welcome. One option which most Western countries offer women who do not want take a pregnancy through to birth and child care is the chance of having an **abortion**.

What is an abortion ?

Doctors use the word 'abortion' to mean any death of a baby in the womb and its expulsion from the mother's body. This sometimes happens of its own accord: that is usually called a **miscarriage**. A miscarriage can be very upsetting to couples wanting a baby. But it may be so early in pregnancy that the woman is not even aware that she has conceived. It is thought that a great number of early pregnancies end in this way.

What most of us mean when we talk about 'an abortion' is a really a **procured abortion**. This is when the foetus or growing child is deliberately killed and removed from the womb. (That sounds so unpleasant that some people prefer to talk about 'terminations'.)

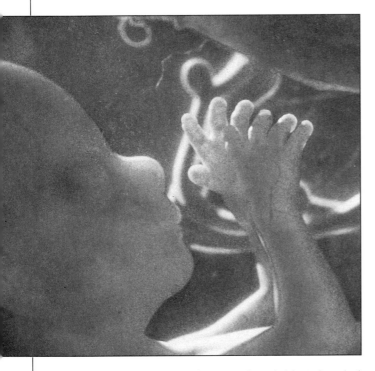

UK law allows abortion to be carried out up to the end of the 24th week of pregnancy. This photo shows the human foetus at about four months.

Abortion and the law

Abortion used to be a crime. In Ireland and some other places it still is. But in most Western countries the laws have changed and today it is possible to get a legal abortion. Since 1973 the law in the USA has said that a woman has the *right* to have her pregnancy ended in this way. She does not have to give any reason except that she wants it done. However, following a Supreme Court review of the law in 1989, some states have passed laws making abortions more difficult to obtain, in particular by restricting the number of abortions which can be performed on State property.

In Britain abortion used to be a crime under the Offences Against the Person Act of 1861. But in 1967 the Liberal MP David Steel introduced a bill into the House of Commons which became The Abortion Act of 1967. This Act was amended in 1990 and applies to the whole of the UK except Northern Ireland.

The Abortion Act

The law in the UK says that an abortion can be performed up to the end of the 24th week of pregnancy if two doctors agree that:

1. to continue the pregnancy would involve a risk of injury to the physical or mental health of the pregnant woman greater than the risks involved in having an abortion;
    or
2. that to continue the pregnancy would involve risk of injury to the physical or mental health of any existing children of the pregnant woman greater than the risks involved in her having an abortion.

However, the law allows an abortion at *any stage* of the pregnancy

1. if the doctors agree that continuing the pregnancy would involve risk to the life of the mother;

2. if they agree that an abortion is necessary to prevent grave permanent injury to the physical or mental health of the pregnant woman;

3. if there is a substantial risk that if the child were born it would suffer from 'such physical or mental abnormalities as to be seriously handicapped'.

The Abortion Act says that in most cases abortions in

Britain have to be performed before the end of the 24th week of pregnancy. That is because babies can be born alive and survive after then. (The technical expression for this is to say that they are *viable* after 24 weeks.) The 1967 Act originally took the limit of viability to be 28 weeks, but in recent years our skill at keeping very premature babies alive has increased. For this reason the limit was changed to 24 weeks in 1990. Abortions performed after 24 weeks are very rare at present.

The father of the foetus to be aborted has no right to be consulted or to object to the abortion, even if he is married to the mother. In 1987 a student at the University of Oxford lost his attempt in the courts to prevent his girlfriend aborting the child they had conceived.

The pressure for the liberalization of the abortion laws in Britain and the USA followed a number of 'hard cases' which showed up the apparent inhumanity of the laws which made abortion a crime. The most famous in Britain was **The Bourne Case** *in 1938.*

Dr Alex Bourne performed an abortion on a fourteen-year-old girl who conceived after being raped by several soldiers. He then gave himself up to the police. At his trial the judge ruled that Dr Bourne's action was done in good faith: the girl's condition, he said, was such that it could lead to a stage where there was a danger to her life. Dr Bourne was acquitted.

People who believe that today's abortion laws are too liberal often argue that 'hard cases' such as the Bourne Judgement have been used to open the way for abortion on demand.

Those countries which have legalized abortion have seen an enormous increase in its use. You can see from the graph that the number of abortions per thousand women living in England and Wales today is more than three times what it was when the Abortion Act came into effect in 1968.

Most abortions in Britain are performed under the part of the Abortion Act which allows abortion if the pregnancy involves a risk to the physical or mental health of the mother. Many doctors involved in abortion argue that if a woman is determined not to

have a child, to refuse her an abortion poses a possible threat to her mental health. For this reason the majority of abortions in the UK are performed for 'social reasons' on perfectly healthy pregnancies.

Other doctors believe abortions to be wrong and refuse to assist in them.

WHAT DOES AN ABORTION INVOLVE?

In most cases a general anaesthetic is given to the pregnant woman and the neck of the womb is opened (dilated). A special suction apparatus is then used to remove the contents of the uterus; larger pieces of foetal tissue (usually the head) are crushed and pulled out with forceps. Care is taken so that no tissue is left in the womb—this was a major cause of death among women in the days of 'backstreet' and 'do-it-yourself' abortions before the 1967 Act (see Chapter 13).

In very late abortions (very rare in Britain, although less so in the USA) the life of the foetus is first ended with an injection of drugs and then prostaglandin is administered to the mother. This is the hormone which begins labour: the dead foetus is delivered through the vagina.

Since the early 1990s a pill called RU486 has been available which will induce an abortion if it is taken within the first ten weeks of pregnancy. In Britain this is administered in hospital under specialist care and its use is controlled by the Abortion Law Reform Act.

DID YOU KNOW?

The United Nations Declaration of Rights of the Child (1959) says:

> *'The child, by reason of his physical and mental immaturity, needs special safeguards and care, including appropriate legal protection, before as well as after birth.'*

Do you think that British law provides such protection?

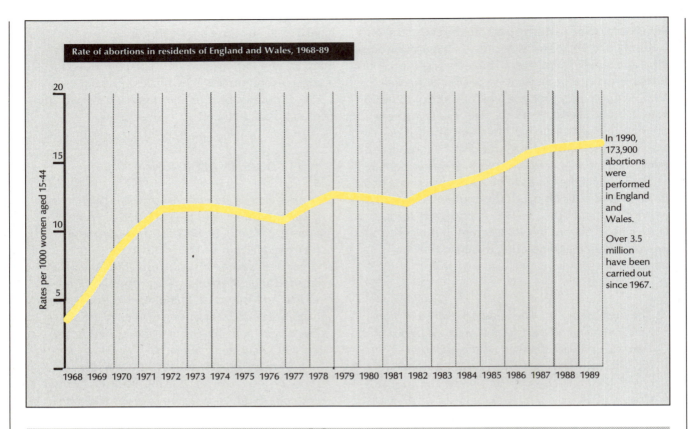

Rate of abortions in residents of England and Wales, 1968-89

Rates per 1000 women aged 15-44

20
15
10
5

1968 1969 1970 1971 1972 1973 1974 1975 1976 1977 1978 1979 1980 1981 1982 1983 1984 1985 1986 1987 1988 1989

In 1990, 173,900 abortions were performed in England and Wales.

Over 3.5 million have been carried out since 1967.

Follow-up

Questions

1 What is meant by the term 'abortion'?

2 (a) What law governs the availability of abortions in Britain today?
(b) In what year was it amended?

3 (a) What is meant when a foetus is said to be 'viable'?
(b) At what stage in the pregnancy does British law recognize the foetus as viable, and what effect does this have on the possibility of obtaining a legal abortion?

4 In some circumstances British law allows an abortion to take place at any stage of the pregnancy. What circumstances are these?

5 In 1992 the medical journals reported the case of a British woman planning to go on a skiing trip who found out that she was pregnant. She had an abortion rather than disturb her holiday plans. Explain how this was legal under the 1967 Act.

6 Describe another situation in which the news that a child has been conceived may be unwelcome.

In Chapter 12 we saw that abortion is legal and on the increase in most Western countries. Yet it remains extremely controversial. In the USA, where the photographs shown above were taken, it is a major issue in politics—one which can ruin a political career. Many people have very strong views, for or against.

Some common views

1. Many feminists think that people should have the right to ask for and get an abortion up to the moment of birth with no questions asked. This position is usually called support for 'abortion on demand'. Women have the right to control their own bodies, they say, and the foetus is part of a woman's body. Too often in the past men have made the rules in order to keep women in their control, and this is what has happened with abortion (see Chapter 37). Women have the *right to choose* what to do for themselves.

2. Others accept that the foetus is a human being, but argue that if a baby is unwanted it is like somebody who breaks into your house. In some countries (especially America, where this argument comes from) the law allows you to kill in defence of your property. Your body is your property, so you are justified in killing in defence of it. So although abortion is killing, it is justifiable homicide.

3. Some people think that abortion should be allowed, but only up to the point at which the baby is capable of being born alive and surviving outside the womb: before then they hold that it is really part of the woman's body and she should have control over it. (This seems to be the position of British law as far as normal pregnancies are concerned.)

4. Many people accept that the foetus is a human being or potential human being, and say that it should normally be protected. In some circumstances, however, they would argue that an abortion may be the most loving course of action. For example, in cases in which there is a high risk of very severe handicap, or when the pregnancy is the result of rape or incest. People might argue that unpleasant as it is, abortion may be the lesser of two evils. (This is a 'Situation Ethics'

argument: see Chapter 3. It is also the position of British law on the handicapped.)

5. Some people argue that human life begins at conception: the baby in the womb deserves the same protection as any other member of the human family. Abortion is therefore absolutely wrong: the liberalization of the abortion laws was a mistake, and abortion should be made illegal again in order to protect the unborn child.

6. Others agree that abortion is wrong, but say that it should nonetheless still be legal. They argue that in the days when abortion was illegal many abortions were carried out by backstreet abortionists, often in dangerous conditions. A number of women were killed by them. Others attempted 'do-it-yourself' abortions and died or became seriously ill as a result. Since people will always try to get abortions, society is better off providing safe conditions in which these can be performed. After all, there are a number of things which are absolutely wrong but which are not illegal like adultery, for instance. So the abortion laws should be relaxed sufficiently to allow women who are going to have abortions anyway to have them safely.

NOTE: What people have to say about abortion frequently depends on what they believe about 'the baby (or foetus) growing in the womb': is it or is it not a human being with human rights'? This is a very important point in Roman Catholic teaching on abortion.

In the debate about abortion even the language people use is important. Groups which campaign in favour of abortion on demand do not call themselves 'Pro-Abortion' groups but 'Pro-Choice' groups. The two most important of these in Britain are:

◆ *The National Abortion Campaign*

◆ *The Abortion Rights Action League.*

Both of these groups provide educational material designed to inform women about the options available to them under the law. They also attempt to influence politicians by lobbying MPs and by activity aimed at the political parties, trades unions and other groups.

Christians and abortion

Traditional Christian teaching places the highest value on human life, and therefore condemns abortion. One of the earliest Christian writings outside the New Testament—the *Didache*—says this:

> **You shall not kill by abortion the fruit of the womb and you shall not murder the infant already born.**

Nevertheless, if you were to ask all the practising Christians from all the denominations in a large town today what they thought about abortion, you would probably find all six of the arguments we have outlined above represented in their answers. Why? Here are three possible reasons:

● Christians are often influenced by the society around them as well as by their faith.

● There has been an increasing feminist influence in American and Western European Christianity since the 1960s.

● Some Christian denominations today do not give very clear teaching on abortion.

However, the biggest group in your survey would probably be those who had pretty strong reservations about it—in line with general Christian teaching.

Statements from the churches

The Church of England said in a report in 1984 that 'the foetus is to be specially respected and protected'. However, it went on to say that 'nonetheless the life of the foetus is not absolutely sacrosanct if it endangers the life of the mother.'

The Church of Scotland's Board of Social Responsibility in 1987 came to the conclusion that 'abortion has no moral justification and represents the unwarranted destruction of human life that is made in the image of God'. But it was careful to say that this was only in 'the great majority of cases'.

The view of the Protestant churches is that abortion is generally undesirable, but that it may be acceptable in some circumstances. It is not always clear what these circumstances might be, and perhaps for this reason a minority Protestant group ('Christians for Free

Did you know?

- Recent discoveries have shown that at the moment the ovum is fertilized by sperm, a genetically unique individual comes into being. The fertilized ovum takes half its genetic make-up from its father and half from its mother, and has some genes active while others remain 'turned off'. In this way it has its own genetic code which it reproduces at astonishing speed: the future baby's sex, colour of hair, fingerprints and all the other things which make people physically unique are decided at the moment of fertilization.

- By the third week of pregnancy the heart starts to beat regularly and the foundations of the nervous system have been laid down.

- The usual time for a pregnancy test is some time after the fourth week.

- By the sixth week the skeleton is complete and muscle reflexes are present.

- After seven weeks fingers, toes, and ears are all complete. Brain waves can be recorded, and milk teeth are present in the gums.

- After eight weeks all the major organs are functioning: liver, stomach, heart, kidneys and brain—even though the mother will not feel her child move for another two months.

- After eighteen weeks the baby moves its arms and legs, kicks and somersaults in the womb. It inhales and exhales amniotic fluid, grasps with its hands and sucks its thumb.

- After twenty weeks, hair is appearing on the head. The baby weighs about 500g/1lb, and responds to stimuli from outside. All it needs now is to grow.

- The limit for most abortions in the UK is twenty-four weeks.

Choice') campaigns for greater emphasis on what they see as a woman's right to make the decision to have an abortion. However, some Evangelical Christians, basing their views on the Bible, are firmly opposed to abortion.

Roman Catholic teaching

The Catholic Church teaches that deliberate procured abortion is a serious sin in all circumstances. In Catholic theology human life is said to begin at the moment of conception. From that moment it is sacred and everybody should try to protect it.

'Human life is sacred' Pope Paul VI said. 'All men must recognise that fact.' (*Humanae Vitae*, 1968.)

The Second Vatican Council (see Chapter 3) declared that 'Life must be protected with the utmost care from the moment of conception: abortion and infanticide are abominable crimes.' (Vatican II, *Gaudium et Spes* 51)

The Church's teaching was explained more fully in the **Declaration on Procured Abortion** (1974). This did three important things:

- It re-stated the traditional teaching of the Church, and pointed out as well that everybody (not just Christians) should have a proper respect for human life and human rights.

- It said that the movement for women's rights is a good thing when it frees women from injustice, but that this cannot be made an excuse for abortion, which denies to another person the fundamental right to life.

- It explained that although abortion was the killing of an unborn child, the reasons why people ask for abortions are sometimes very serious: they are the product of many 'sorrows and miseries'. The Declaration said that 'Every man and woman with feeling, and certainly every Christian, must be ready to do what he can to remedy them.'

This is the Declaration's teaching about when human life begins:

> **From the time that the a life is begun which is neither that of the father nor of the mother. It is rather the life of a new human being with its own growth. It would never be made human if it were not human already.**

NOTE: There are some occasions when an operation carried out for the purpose of curing a life-threatening disease might kill an unborn child. The Church teaches that these are permissible and necessary.

There are a number of groups which campaign for a change in the abortion laws to bring the number of abortions down or to stop them altogether. Their members include Christians (Catholic and Protestant), together with members of other religions, and of none. The most important of these groups in the UK are:

◆ *LIFE*

◆ *The Society for the Protection of Unborn Children (SPUC).*

LIFE concentrates its efforts on providing counselling and support for women who are pregnant or who think they might be. This is often done through parish groups. SPUC campaigns heavily for changes to the law by lobbying politicians, raising petitions and activity in political parties and trades unions. Both SPUC and LIFE provide educational material for use in schools and churches.

A BIBLE PERSPECTIVE

> **God created human beings in his own image,**
> **in the image of God he created them,**
> **male and female he created them.**
> **God blessed them and said to them,**
> **'Be fruitful and increase.'**
>
> **Genesis 1:27 (Revised English Bible)**

> **So the Lord answers, 'Can a woman forget her own baby and not love the child she bore? Even if a mother should forget her child, I will never forget you. Jerusalem, I can never forget you! I have written your name on the palms of my hand.**
>
> **Isaiah 49:15–16**

> **You created every part of me;**
> **you put me together in my mother's womb ...**
> **when I was growing there in secret,**
> **you knew that I was there**
> **you saw me before I was born.**
>
> **The Psalmist addresses God in Psalm 139:13 and 15**

> **Jesus said: 'Aren't five sparrows sold for two pennies? Yet not one sparrow is forgotten by God. Even the hairs of your head have all been counted.'**
>
> **Luke 12:6**

Follow-up

Questions

1 (a) Using the information given in this chapter, draw up a table. In one column put arguments in favour of legal abortions, and another column the arguments against.
(b) Use your table to write two speeches—one for and one against the legalization of abortion. Which one do you find the more convincing?

2 Name one 'pro-life' and one 'pro-choice' organization operating in Britain, and describe their activities in your own words.

3 Summarize the teaching of the Catholic Church about abortion.

Discussion

One of the most terrible aspects of abortion is what it does to our view of the handicapped. We are saying to them, 'It would have been better if you had never been born.' Discuss.

PART THREE

Citizenship

WOMAN BURGLED FOR THE FOURTH TIME THIS YEAR

Armed Robbery at Post Office

Maddock denies fraud charges

MURDERER OF PC COTTS GETS LIFE

Joyrider Kills Four in Accident

. . . community hall was destroyed by fire yesterday. Forensic evidence suggests arson was the cause . . .

. . . at a rally, a young man was assaulted by four youths on the grounds that he was coloured . . .

There is still no news of Sandra Peters, the seven year old who disappeared from her home on Thursday. Police continue to appeal for information, and Sandra's parents, fearing that she has been abducted, sent the following plea today . . .

Newspapers, television and radio bombard us with reports like these. Crime is widespread and affects many people. A crime is committed when a law made by the state is broken. Laws exist for the public good, to protect society. Since the state—the government—makes the laws, the state also decrees the punishment for law-breakers. Crime can be defined as

- an activity which is harmful to the public's good

- an activity which is forbidden by the criminal law, and which usually leads to prosecution.

Punishment

In the United Kingdom, if you break the law you may be

- **taken into custody** (People over 21 are sent to prison. Sometimes the sentence is suspended. This means the offender will not go to prison unless he or she offends again during a set period of time. People under 21 go to young offender institutions.)

- **fined**

- **given a set number of hours' community service**

- **conditionally discharged**: the offender makes and is made to keep a promise not to re-offend.

- **ordered to go to attendance centres**: these are run by the police. Young offenders go to them for a set number of hours. The programme includes the policy talking to offenders, and physical exercise.

Alternatives to punishment include:

- **probation orders**: offenders have to see a probation officer or attend a probation centre. A probation order can be combined with a community service order.

- **care**: some juvenile criminals—aged 18 and under—can be taken into care by the local authority.

- **cautions**: some offenders, especially juveniles, are given a formal caution by the police.

Britain does not carry out the death penalty, though other countries do. Torture, corporal punishment (birching, for example) and physical mutilation are also illegal in the UK, although not in all countries.

Most people agree that it is right to punish criminals. We have to ask why, and what punishment is for.

We can identify five possible aims of punishment:

- **Retribution** This means that:
  - offenders deserve to be punished—to suffer in some way for what they have done.
  - punishment is revenge
  - punishment aims to balance out the evil caused by the crime.

The Jewish Law or Torah, the first five books of the Bible, has this to say:

> **If anyone injures another person, whatever he has done shall be done to him. If he breaks a bone, one of his bones shall be broken; if he blinds him in one eye, one of his eyes shall be blinded; if he knocks out a tooth, one of his teeth shall be knocked out. Whatever injury he causes another person shall be done to him in return.**
>
> **Leviticus 24:19–20**

This commandment was originally designed to limit revenge. The victim could take an eye for an eye *but no more*. Jesus, however, ruled out revenge completely.

> **You have heard that it was said, 'An eye for an eye, and a tooth for a tooth.' But now I tell you: do not take revenge on someone who wrongs you. If anyone slaps you on the right cheek, let him slap you on your left cheek too.**
>
> **Matthew 5:38–39**

Jesus' words mean that Christians may not accept the idea of punishment as revenge. However, they may well accept that punishment is necessary to balance out the evil caused by the crime. A murderer owes something to his or her victim's family. He must pay in some way to satisfy their loss.

 Do you think criminals should be made to help or compensate their victims more?

- **Deterrence** Punishment puts people off committing crimes. People will not offend if they know they will go to prison for it. The philosopher Jeremy Bentham (1748–1832) said that punishments should be no harsher than they need to be to deter criminals.

Does deterrence work? Surely if it worked completely, there would be no crime! Do criminals expect to be caught—or think about being caught—when they commit a crime?

- **Containment** Dangerous criminals who could well re-offend should be kept away from other people. This is safer for them and for the public.

- **Reformation** Punishment should teach offenders to change their ways. If a criminal re-offends, his or her

An inside view

Probation officers are qualified social workers who specialize in working with the courts. They deal with both domestic and criminal matters.

Sally Miller has been a probation officer for the last seven years.

The probation service grew from Christian roots—a group called the Police Court missionaries, at the turn of the century. They took young offenders into their homes and communities, and tried to reform and rehabilitate them.

Our criminal justice system takes the responsibility for punishing the crime out of the hands of the victim. But more notice has been taken of victims recently, and some people say the courts are out of step.

People want offences against the person—violent offences, sex offences, murder—punished severely: to have that person locked up so that he or she can't do it again. The courts have tended to deal with offences against property—theft, fraud, shop-lifting, factory burglaries—very harshly. The law is now trying to make the punishment fit the crime.

I think punishment in this country is primarily for retribution. You can't reform a criminal by locking him up and taking away all his rights and responsibilities. That doesn't teach people how to cope when they go back into society. You might have had trouble coping anyway: perhaps you'd been homeless, you couldn't make ends meet, your benefit was very low and you turned to stealing, you'd been thrown out of home and you had to survive. In prison, food and shelter are provided for you in such a strict and regulated environment that you don't even have to make a decision about when you get up in the morning, let alone what to eat. So going to prison can't possibly help you learn to cope! People often re-offend afterwards.

Prisons are institutions, and people are institutionalized very quickly. They become dependent on the institution. If you take away all responsibility and provide a structured routine, the person very quickly loses the ability to make decisions.

Prisons vary. In the old Victorian prisons like Wormwood Scrubs and Wandsworth there is great overcrowding. There are no washing or toilet facilities: there are buckets which you have to slop out. You have to queue up for food. Some prisons offer work, like sewing mailbags, making shirts, clearing the prison. Inmates at Coldingley prison make all the road signs you see. Think about that when you're on the motorway! Prisoners might work up to a thirteen-hour week, and earn a total of about seven pounds. With that, they buy whatever they need apart from food: shampoo, soap, toothpaste, cigarettes, stamps, birthday cards. And they're not subsidized.

A typical day in prison might be something like this. You get woken up at 6 o'clock, slop out, get breakfast, go back into your cell, have lunch at 11.30 and go back to your cell. You might get a period of exercise or association. Then evening meal at 4.30, back into your cell, and you are locked up overnight. A lot of prisoners just go to sleep when they're locked up. It's a good way to pass the time. There's generally a prison library, so they might read. A lot of them write. They do things you do on your own, even if they're sharing.

Cells vary in size. A typical Victorian cell is built for one person, with only room for a bed and a chair. Overcrowding is a big issue, and they're working on it by cutting sentences and by building more prisons. The rioting in the 1980s proved the situation was at breaking-point: you simply can't do this to people and expect them to come out as law-abiding citizens. It's getting better: it's not often you get three in a cell now.

Problems when you share a cell might include tempers, high anxiety, infringement of personal space, homosexual assault . . . It's pretty much pot luck who you get put in with. Prisons develop their own hierarchies: there's status to be won and lost. You might gain status for being the toughest guy on the landing, or sometimes by your offence. 'He's a lifer!' And there are definitely unacceptable prisoners to the rest of the prison population, like sex offenders or child killers. They're called rule 43 prisoners, and are segregated for their own protection. The problem is that this can put all the sex offenders together, so in that way their views become the moral code. They encourage each other.

In theory, prisons should act as a deterrent. In practice, I don't know.

Crime is on the increase. Deterrence can work if the crime is pre-meditated (if it's thought about before it's committed). But some people just don't think it through.

Some prisons run groups or counselling led by a probation officer and a prison officer. There might be offending behaviour groups, sex offender groups, those sort of things, and movement towards rehabilitation by providing job search programmes, health education or facilities for doing GCSEs, 'A' Levels or Open University degrees. But there isn't too much of this, so prisons don't reform on the whole.

Prisoners can't compensate victims financially because they don't have any money. That's a real problem with custody. Compensation is a good idea: I think paying back for wrongdoing is very valuable. Probation officers have made some attempts to mediate between the offender and the victim, though it doesn't work for all offences. Having your house burgled is a horrendous offence for the victim, who may become very frightened and think, 'Was I chosen? Was I watched? Was I being spied on?' Often the offender can put their minds at rest: he did not see it like that: he just wanted to go in and grab the video. So he might say, 'No, I saw the milk bottles on the doorstep.' It's all about understanding and forgiveness.

I don't think criminals are a breed apart. We don't know what makes someone a criminal. If we knew that, the world would be a better place. We do know that some circumstances can make crime seem acceptable. Count up the number of

times you've broken the law! It might be by speeding, taking a pen from work, not telling someone you've been given too much change. Law-breaking is not a deviant act of the few.

Why am I still a probation officer? It's still rooted in Christianity for me. Being a probation officer is about forgiveness and acceptance and believing that people can change.

Do we put people behind bars to punish, to deter—or to make our society safer?

punishment has not worked.

- **Rehabilitation** Strictly speaking, this is not an aim of punishment, but something that should follow it. Offenders should be helped to take their place in society once their punishment is over. They should be helped to find work and to make a fresh start. The offender has paid back the debt to society.

Forgiveness

'Forgive us our sins,' Jesus taught his followers to pray, 'as we forgive those who have sinned against us.' Bitterness, being unable to forgive, destroys people from the inside.

Forgiveness does not mean letting people walk all over you! But it is important. Christianity follows Jesus' teaching in stressing that forgiveness is vital. It may be very hard, particularly for the victim of a crime. And it is not necessarily a once-for-all thing: it may have to be renewed.

Christians believe people can forgive because God forgives us. In some extraordinary way, Jesus' death has made that forgiveness possible. People can have a right relationship with God. They can stop worrying about whether they are 'good enough' for God. They can be set free: free to love, free to forgive, free to be truly human.

Jesus taught that people have to be ready and willing to forgive. But forgiveness has to be accepted too. (If you want to give me a present, I have to take it!) To accept forgiveness, I have to admit I've done wrong. I have to be sorry and want to change my attitude (even if it takes more than one attempt). I also need to repair the damage if I can. In the Roman Catholic Church the person who goes to confession has to be ready to make amends before he or she can ask the priest to pronounce God's forgiveness (absolution).

 NOTE: Roman Catholics and many other Christians confess their sins to a priest, whom they believe has the authority to absolve them, to tell them they are forgiven. This authority is given by Jesus Christ.

So there are two sides to forgiveness:

- giving (being ready to forgive)

- accepting (being sorry and ready to make amends).

Jesus' parable of the prodigal (or wasteful) son helps to make this clear.

 Read Luke 15:11–32

The son has behaved badly, but he is sorry. Ever since he left home his father has been waiting—and longing to forgive him. He brushes aside his son's prepared speeches: he is so delighted to see him that he throws a huge party! God's forgiveness is like that. And people's forgiveness should be like that too—swift and generous, not grudging like the older brother.

Jesus practised what he preached. Even on the cross, he forgave his executioners.

 Read Luke 23:32–43

BRITISH PRISONS

There are four categories for British prisons. Some prisons have one category, others have all four.

Category A: High security prisons for dangerous offenders such as terrorists or those serving the first months of a life sentence. Prisoners are usually escorted everywhere by two prison officers.

Category B: High security again. Lifers who have been moved from Category A.

Category C: For people serving up to about four years. The rules in these prisons are less strict. Prisoners are allowed to work and mix with other prisoners in the pool room or television room. This might be twice a week for two or three hours per day. Most prisons are Category C.

Category D: Open prisons. For first-time offenders and prisoners about to be released. There are no high surrounding walls, but a good deal of surveillance.

There are no categories for young offenders institutions.

Follow-up

Questions

1 In the United Kingdom, in what ways is crime punished? What other methods are used to deal with crime?

2 List five aims of punishment.

3 Article 5 of the United Nations' Universal Declaration of Human Rights says: 'No one shall be subjected to torture or to cruel, inhuman or degrading treatment or punishment.'

- What sort of punishment might Article 5 rule out?

- Do conditions in British prisons as discussed in this chapter break Article 5?

4 In the Lord's Prayer, Christians pray, 'Forgive us our trespasses (or 'sins'), as we forgive those who trespass (or 'sin') against us.' People have to forgive others if they want God to forgive them. This idea is also found in the parable of the unforgiving servant (Matthew 18:22–35).

- In full, explain what 'forgiveness' means.

- Summarize the parable of the unforgiving servant and explain what it is saying about forgiveness.

- Do the same for the parable of the prodigal son and for Luke's account of Jesus' crucifixion.

- How do you think Jesus' teaching might affect a Christian's view of punishment?

For discussion

Sally Miller says criminals are not a breed apart.

Is crime caused because some people are simply evil? Or does every human being have the potential to be a criminal? Discuss these in your groups and report back to the rest of the class.

Activity

How should criminals be punished?
Write to your school's police liaison officer and invite him or her to speak to your class about the reasons for punishment.

15 Capital Punishment

> **Some crimes are so terrible that they demand the death penalty. Almost all ancient societies practised capital punishment. Over half of the countries in the world still use it. It is a fitting way to deal with vicious criminals.**

Is it? A growing number of people believe that the death penalty is evil and should never be used. Here we look at the arguments on both sides. The issues raised are difficult. It is very important to think carefully and to weigh up the evidence before coming to a conclusion. Getting worked up or making up our minds before we start is not likely to help us find the truth!

Arguments for and against capital punishment

Retribution

FOR:

If you commit a terrible crime, you deserve a terrible punishment. Capital punishment shows society will not tolerate such crimes.

Religious people might point to God's words to Noah, after the story of the flood:

> **Man was made like God, so whoever murders a man will himself be killed by his fellow-man.**
>
> **Genesis 9:6**

In his letter to the Romans, Paul said that a ruler 'is God's servant and carries out God's punishment on those who do evil'. The Reformation leader Martin Luther agreed with Paul. Luther said God lends his authority to the state to punish those who do wrong.

AGAINST:

If murder is wrong, why is execution right? If you say the killers should be killed, should rapists be raped, torturers tortured and arsonists burned? It seems rather silly!

For the idea of retribution to work, the death penalty would always have to be carried out. But it is not. Some prisoners receive mercy, so the system is unfair and does not work. Even if the death sentence was always carried out, there would still be problems. It would be almost impossible to make such a law fair. In Singapore, for example, you can be executed for possessing more than 15 grams of heroin. So someone with 14.99 grams would live, but someone with 15.01 grams would die. Is that fair?

Not all Christians would take the words from the flood story as a command to execute murderers. Some take it to mean that *God's* justice will in the end catch up with those who do evil. Can it ever be right to kill a human being made in God's image? Others would say it is overruled by Jesus' words.

> **You have heard that it was said, 'An eye for an eye, and a tooth for a tooth.' But now I tell you: do not take revenge on someone who wrongs you. If anyone slaps you on the right cheek, let him slap your left cheek too...**
>
> **You have heard that it was said, 'Love your friends, hate your enemies.' But now I tell you: love your enemies and pray for those who persecute you.**
>
> **Matthew 5:38–39, 43–44**

Jesus never said anything directly about the death penalty, but words like these seem to rule it out. We know Jesus was friends with outcasts, who were thought to be scum or criminals. He wanted them to repent: to change their minds and their ways. It would be very odd if he also thought people like that should be killed!

When Paul was writing, he was trying to show that Christians were not politically dangerous. He did not deal with the problem of whether an evil ruler gets his authority from God. (Did Hitler?)

Desmond Tutu, Archbishop of Cape Town, South Africa, opposes capital punishment. So did Coretta Scott King, widow of Martin Luther King. Pope John Paul II survived an attempt on his life in 1981. He forgave the man who tried to kill him. He declared that the Papacy recommends mercy, even pardon, for those condemned to death. (However, the new 'Universal Catechism' of the Catholic Church supports the right of the state to execute people.)

Deterrence

FOR:

People will not commit serious crimes if they know they will die for them. The death penalty would deter would-be murderers or terrorists.

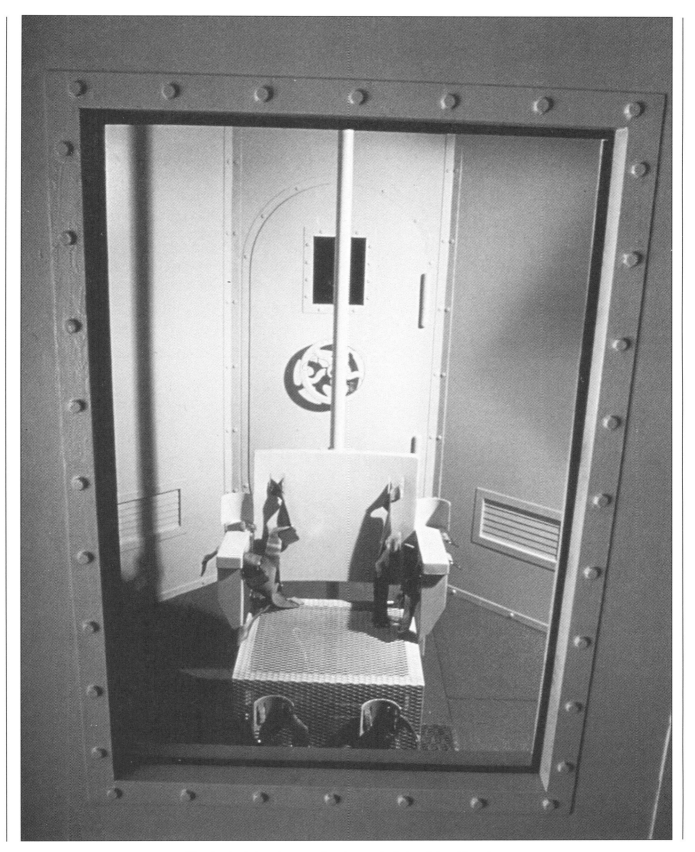

The electric chair: an impersonal modern method of capital punishment.

Capital punishment in the United Kingdom

1950 Timothy Evans was hanged for the murder of his daughter. He was innocent. The murderer was probably John Christie, who shared a house with Evans. Christie was hanged in 1952 for the murder of seven people. The Queen pardoned Timothy Evans in 1966, sixteen years after his death.

1964 13 August: the last two executions in the UK for murder.

1965 Parliament abolished the death penalty for murder. This was for an experimental period.

1969 Parliament finally abolished the death penalty for murder.

1979
1983 Debates in Parliament on
1987 whether Britain should bring
1988 back the death penalty. A large majority rejected the idea on each occasion.

No one has been executed in the United Kingdom since 1964.

Strictly speaking, however, criminals can still be executed

- in Jersey, for murder
- in the Isle of Man for murder, treason and genocide
- in England and Wales for piracy with violence
- throughout the United Kingdom, for high treason and for offences such as treason and espionage (spying) by members of the armed forces in a time of war.

AGAINST:

There is no evidence whatsoever that capital punishment is an effective deterrent. This is not an opinion. It is a fact. All the available evidence suggests the opposite. A report was produced in 1988 for the United Nations. This showed that execution was no more effective as a deterrent than life imprisonment. The report also said it was unlikely that capital punishment could *ever* be proved to be an effective deterrent. The United States Supreme Court, which allows the death penalty, accepts that it is not a deterrent.

Most murderers kill when they are very emotional, drunk or panicking. They are not capable of thinking properly. A deterrent can have no effect on people in that state. A study of 145 murderers was undertaken in Japan between 1955 and 1957. Not one of them thought about the death penalty at the time of the murder.

If deterrence worked, states which have the death penalty would have fewer serious crimes. They do not. If it worked, such crimes would rocket when the death penalty is abolished. They do not. Research demonstrates this. In Canada, the murder rate has actually gone down since capital punishment was abolished in 1976! Neither is there any evidence that drug traffickers are deterred by the death penalty.

Terrorists are generally prepared to die for their cause. Executing them turns them into martyrs. It often prompts more violence from the terrorist group in revenge.

Re-offending

FOR:

Capital punishment will stop any possibility of criminals re-offending. This will protect society.

AGAINST:

The same effect can be achieved by life imprisonment! One can never *prove* someone will re-offend, even if it is likely. The evidence shows that murderers rarely re-offend. Most murders are committed against a member of the same family. They are not likely to be repeated.

Leniency

FOR:

Capital punishment is kinder than a long prison sentence.

AGAINST:

This is not an argument for the death penalty. It is an argument for improving prison conditions.

Democracy

FOR:

Most people in most countries are in favour of the death penalty. If it is not used, governments are going against people's wishes.

AGAINST:

The fact that people believe something does not make it right. Christians believe morality comes from God. It is not just a matter of opinion. If something is right, it is right. If something is wrong, it is wrong. (See Chapter 3.)

If public opinion favoured torture, torture would still be wrong. It may be that most people who want the death penalty do not really know or understand the arguments. They may believe it works as a deterrent, which we now know to be wrong. Also, a democracy like the United Kingdom is a *representative* democracy. We elect people to represent us, not to vote for whatever we tell them.

Economics

FOR:

It is cheaper to execute someone than to keep him or her in prison for the rest of his or her life.

AGAINST:

It is also cheaper to let a hospital patient die than to carry on with the treatment! The death penalty is too important to decide on the basis of economics. In fact, capital trials in the USA are more expensive than life imprisonment! The legal costs are enormously high.

It is difficult to identify further arguments for the death penalty. (This is not necessarily important. One weighty reason may be better than six light ones!) There are, however, a number of other arguments against it. These are in the main provided by Amnesty International, a worldwide organization which campaigns against torture and capital punishment:

If the death penalty is available for one crime, it is a short step to argue that it should be used for other crimes. When does it stop being justified? Hanging murderers could be the 'thin end of the wedge'. History shows that the death penalty can be abused. It is often used by corrupt governments against their political opponents, particularly after a coup. It tends to be used against those who are disadvantaged or worst off

Abolishing the death penalty

35 countries have abolished it completely
18 countries have abolished it apart for exceptional crimes such as wartime offences
27 countries keep the death penalty, but never carry it out
So, over 40% of countries have abolished the death penalty in practice.

in society. The poor cannot afford good lawyers!

In South Africa, for example, blacks were more likely than whites to be hanged. Between June 1982 and June 1983, of 154 South Africans who were found guilty of murder

- 81 were blacks who had murdered whites—38 were hanged.

- 52 were whites who had murdered whites—one was hanged.

- 21 were whites who had murdered blacks—none was hanged.

The death penalty is too final. In many countries, trials are completely unfair. Even in countries with fair trials, mistakes can be made. Jesus himself was unjustly sentenced to death. A study carried out in 1987 in the USA found that 350 people found guilty of capital crimes this century were in fact innocent. (Twenty-three of these were executed).

Executions are brutal and cold-blooded. They appeal to sadism and viciousness. They brutalize those involved. *Even if* they acted as a deterrent—which they do not—they would still be wrong. Every human being has a right to life. Religious people believe this right is given by God. Governments cannot take this right away for bad behaviour, however appalling the offence.

The United Nations favours the abolition of the death penalty. In view of Amnesty International, capital punishment breaks Article 5 of the United Nations Declaration of Human Rights:

No one shall be subjected to torture or to cruel inhuman or degrading treatment or punishment.

Follow-up

Questions

1 What is capital punishment?

- Name five countries which have capital punishment.

- What crime is capital punishment most often used for?

- Give five methods of capital punishment.

- When was capital punishment abolished in the United Kingdom?

2 The Torah or the Law of Moses in the Old Testament lays down the death penalty for certain crimes. Murder is punished by death, but so are other offences. For example, if a witness accuses someone of a crime he did not commit, the witness is to be punished. He is to receive the penalty laid down for the crime he has lied about.

 Read Deuteronomy 19:15–21

No mercy is shown here: an eye repays an eye, a tooth repays a tooth. We have seen that Jesus did not agree with this.

Although Jesus said nothing directly about the death penalty, many Christians believe a story in John's Gospel shows he was against it.

 Read John 7:53–8:11

The Torah said adultery was to be punished by death. The Pharisees and the other experts in the Torah brought to Jesus a woman who had committed adultery. When you read it, think about

- why their question to Jesus is a trap

- what Jesus' reply means, and why it avoids the trap

- why some Christians would think this shows Jesus to be against capital punishment

- why other Christians would disagree with them.

Both the Torah and the Koran, the Muslims' Holy Book, lay down the death penalty for certain crimes.

Yet not all Jews nor all Muslims support the death penalty. The World Council of Churches favours its abolition, yet some Christians would disagree with this.

- Using examples, explain in full the *religious* reasons for or against the death penalty. Use the information in this question and in the rest of the chapter.

3 In detail, give three arguments for and three arguments against the death penalty.

For discussion

Do you think the death penalty is right? Explain your reasons.

'Britain should bring back hanging.' Discuss.

Further reading

We The Accused by Ernest Raymond (tells the story of a schoolmaster who is hanged for the murder of his wife).

When the State Kills: Amnesty International Publications.

Read Luke 20:19–26

This story appears in the Gospels of Matthew, Mark and Luke (the Synoptic Gospels). Jesus criticized the Jewish authorities (Luke calls them 'the teachers of the law and the chief priests' here), and they plotted against him. The question their agents asked was very clever. Jews hated paying Roman taxes. Not only were they very high: they were a constant reminder that the Jews were not their own masters. Yet God, not Caesar, should be the Jews' king! There were two traps in the spies' question:

- If he said, 'Pay the tax,' the people would stop following him.

- If he said, 'Don't pay the tax,' he could be handed over to the Roman governor, Pontius Pilate. His reply would make him a traitor against Rome.

Jesus' answer brilliantly avoids both traps. Caesar's head is on the coins. If people pay tax, they are simply giving Caesar what he owns.

Yet people owe more to God that they do to Caesar; so Jesus says

 Render to Caesar the things that are Caesar's; and to God the things that are God's.

Luke 20:25

Jesus' words show there is a difference between church and state. Religion and politics are not the same thing! (The 'state' means a community organized under a government).

Christians and non-Christians agree that the state has a duty to maintain law and order. The state exercises control over its citizens by making them obey the law. This should be for the good of all.

But should religion and politics *always* be kept apart? What is the Christian's attitude to the state? Here are some possible answers:

- **Paul** in his letter to the Romans says that the state is given authority from God. Christians must therefore obey it. (See 'Paul's view of the community' below).

- **Martin Luther**, the Reformation church leader, based his views on Paul. He said there were two kingdoms in existence: the Kingdom of God and the kingdom of this world. God rules people through both.

Everyone belongs to the 'kingdom of this world'. True Christians also belong to the Kingdom of God. The kingdom of this world brings about peace and prevents evil through its laws. The Kingdom of God brings about true faith. Both kingdoms are vital—like the two sides of one coin—but they should remain separate.

- Roman Catholic teaching, from the **Second Vatican Council** (Vatican II) does not mix up church and state, but gives directions for the ways states should behave. The aim of political authority, it says, is to achieve justice and the good of all (the 'common good'). This is why people should generally obey the state. Christians should not vote from selfish motives, but for the party that will best build up the common good. They should work with others, and set an example by the way they live.

Vatican II goes on to say that Christians who have political talents should be involved in politics. They should promote justice and oppose oppression and intolerance, dedicating themselves to everyone's well-being.

Other Christians generally would agree with this: religion must include caring for others in the community. The community exists on a local, national and international level. Christians can influence government only if they are involved at every level.

In the United Kingdom, as elsewhere, individual Christians engage in politics, although churches are not tied directly to political parties. An Anglican is not told by the Church of England what party to vote for, for instance. Christians from different churches are members of all the main political parties. Church members vote according to their consciences—Conservative, Liberal Democrat or Labour (although it would be very difficult to be a Christian and to vote for the British National Party). Many MPs are Christians. Most Prime Ministers have been Christians.

The senior bishops of the Church of England sit in the House of Lords. This is because the Church of England is established by law as the national church. The Queen is, nominally at least, the head of the Church of England, and many church matters are dealt with by parliament. Yet the state does not control the Church of England: the two are linked, but they are not identical.

If the government or ruler is evil, most people

(including most Christians) would say they do not have to obey it. Luther, however said that people should never rebel: under mob rule you would have a hundred tyrants instead of one. Others would say it is not as simple as that.

In the Acts of the Apostles, Peter and some of the other apostles are arrested by the Sanhedrin, the Jewish Council. The Council orders them to stop preaching about Jesus. Their reply is important:

 We must obey God, not men.

Acts 5:29

So Christians believe that if there is a conflict between what God wants and what a country wants, people should do what is right, even if that means breaking the law. However, they should continue to obey the government in all other respects where the government contributes to the common good (as Vatican II says).

Religious people have criticized governments for a number of reasons:

● The American civil rights leader Martin Luther King and the Archbishop of Cape Town, Desmond Tutu, both opposed racial discrimination. (See Chapters 19 and 20.) Both agreed that unjust laws should not be obeyed. In South Africa, apartheid—separate development for blacks and whites—was enshrined in law. Yet the World Council of Churches agreed with Desmond Tutu and the South African Council of Churches: it had to go. Tutu pointed out that God who led the Jews out of slavery in Egypt was not a God who wanted his people to keep out of politics! The Old Testament prophets frequently attacked the policies of their day when they oppressed the poor or ignored God's demands.

The state has a duty to maintain law and order. Here, police clash with rioters protesting against the poll tax, in Trafalgar Square, London.

Paul on church and state

Paul wrote his letter to the Christian community in Rome in about AD 58. Scholars often see the letter to the Romans as his greatest work. It gives his mature thoughts on the central ideas of Christianity. In chapters 12–14 Paul deals with the Christian community (the church), and the community of the world (the state).

 Read Romans 12–14

Romans 12: the Christian community

Christians should dedicate themselves completely to God's service. This is a living sacrifice: the best worship a Christian can give God. They should not be snobbish or proud, but modest.

The human body is made up of different parts which work together. The church is one body, too, and each Christian is a different part of that body. So they should work together. Each has gifts, such as speaking God's message, serving others, teaching, encouraging others. These gifts should be used for the good of everyone.

Love is the key to it all. Christians should

- hate what is evil
- hold on to what is good
- show respect for each other
- work hard and serve God
- be joyful
- be patient in their troubles
- pray
- share their possessions

- welcome strangers into their homes
- pray for those who hate them
- be sensitive to other's needs.

Revenge is ruled out: they should live in peace with one another and leave revenge to God. Evil should be conquered by good.

Romans 13:1–7: the community of the state

In AD 49 the Emperor Claudius ordered all the Jews to leave Rome. Paul knew of this, as did his readers. Would the Christians be in trouble too ? It was important not to offend the authorities. (Trouble, of course, did come later. The first persecution of Christians, under the Emperor Nero, began in AD 64.)

Paul believed that the state's authority came from God. Therefore, if someone disobeys the state, he or she is disobeying God. People who do what is right do not need to be afraid of rulers. People who do evil should be afraid: the ruler is God's servant who will execute God's punishment. Christians should also obey the state because their consciences tell them to. And they should pay taxes.

Paul does not deal with the problem of obeying an evil government. The government he is writing of seems to be carrying out its duties fairly and justly. He is also looking at the duties of a citizen rather than at the duties of a government. It is unlikely he would say that people should always obey the government, no matter what.

Not all Christians agree with Paul that the state gets its authority from God.

Romans 13:8–14 and chapter 14: The Christian community

Paul tells the Christians to live by the one rule, 'Love your neighbour as yourself.'

He reminds them that Jesus will return soon. Christians need to live in the light of that.

They should respect each other's views over matters that are not vital. Some Christians are vegetarians, others are not. Some believe certain days to be special, others do not. They may show their faith in different ways, but they are one family.

Paul tells them not to do anything that might make a fellow Christian stumble. They should not eat a certain food if it offends someone. Paul says the Jewish food laws no longer apply, but we still should respect others' views.

Christians should aim for peace, and the things that strengthen each other.

- Since 1979, influential members of the Church of England have frequently criticized some policies of the Conservative Governments. The Church of England report *Faith in the City* (1983) argued that the government did not do enough to help the poor. This view has also been voiced by the Archbishop of Canterbury, George Carey. (See Chapter 28.)

There are many other examples. Vatican II says the Church has a right to pass moral judgements, even in political matters. Whenever human rights or the salvation of souls demands it, the Church must speak out.

Freedom of speech

Everyone has the right to freedom of thought, conscience and religion; this right includes freedom to change religion or belief, and freedom, either alone or in community with others and in public or private, to manifest his religion or belief in teaching, practice, worship and observance.

Article 18, Declaration of Human Rights

Everyone has the right to freedom of opinions and expression; this right includes freedom to hold opinions without interference and to seek, receive and impart information and ideas through any media and regardless of frontiers.

Article 19, Declaration of Human Rights

Christians and non-Christians alike accept these two Articles from the United Nations Universal Declaration of Human Rights.

THE ROMAN CATHOLIC POSITION

Vatican II says the basis for the right to religious freedom is human nature. We are designed to seek the truth. Therefore we should not be hindered in our search, and no one should be forced to act against his or her conscience. This is because our conscience tells us God's law. Religious people should be allowed to speak publicly and bear witness to their faith. However, they should also respect others' rights. They should not force people to agree with them, or use dishonest methods to win their agreement.

People in the UK are free to think and speak as they please. However, we do not have absolute freedom of speech. The law limits freedom of speech in three main ways:

- **Abusive or threatening words or behaviour** are illegal—they could lead to a breach of the peace. This means that they
  – could give someone good reason to suspect danger, or
  – they are intended to cause violence, or harassment (constant or repeated annoyance), or to distress or alarm someone.

- **Libel or slander**   It is illegal to make a false statement about someone which damages his or her reputation.
     When a statement like this is written or broadcast, it is called libel. When it is spoken, it is called slander.

- **Racial hatred**   It is a criminal offence to use threatening, abusive or insulting words when these are likely to produce racial hatred. They might be written, or spoken in a public place. Incitement to racial hatred can be punished by a heavy fine and/or up to two years' imprisonment.

Follow-up

Questions

1 What is
(a) the state?
(b) freedom of speech?

2 (a) Explain what happened when Jesus was asked whether the Jews should pay taxes.
(b) 'Render to Caesar the things that are Caesar's, and to God the things that are God's.' What does this mean?

3 Explain the views of:
(a) Paul
(b) Martin Luther
(c) The Second Vatican Council
about the authority of the state. What are the differences between them?

4 How and why might Christians be involved in politics?

5 'We must obey God, not men.'
(a) Who said this, and why?
(b) Give two examples of religious people or groups who have spoken out against a government.

For discussion

Some religious people refuse to pay part of their taxes. This may be because they do not agree with what their taxes are spent on. For example, a pacifist Christian might note that, say 5% of his or her country's taxes are spent on arms. He or she might then refuse to pay 5% of the tax demand.
        This is illegal. Should it be? Why?

What reasons lead people to support freedom of speech?

Explain how and why freedom of speech is limited by law in the United Kingdom.

Should people have a right to express their views, however unpleasant those views are?

Activity

Do some research in a library on either Dietrich Bonhoeffer or Thomas More, two Christians who opposed the power of the state and died for it. Prepare a three-minute talk on one of them. It might be interesting to use a tape recorder for this.

17 Racism 1

> **Are you blonde? Then you are a creator and preserver of civilization. Are you blonde? Then you are threatened by perils.**

This is a quotation from a German magazine called *Ostara* at the beginning of this century. *Ostara* said there was a struggle in history between two groups: the heroic men, the Heldings, and their enemies, the small ape-like animals called the Shrattlings.

The blonde-haired, blue-eyed master race of the Aryans would fight and destroy the inferior mixed races in a coming battle. A new, pure people would be born. The animal men would be sterilized, removed by force to the 'ape jungle' and wiped out by hard labour and extermination. The Aryans, the 'sons of the gods', would utterly destroy the children of the Shrattlings and would rule the new, beautiful world.

What do you think of *Ostara*'s ideas? You might think that whoever wrote this was off his head and very nasty. Yet the words struck a chord with a young German who read them when they were published. His name was Adolf Hitler.

Hitler went on to concoct his own theories about race. This led to the murder of six million people. According to Hitler and the Nazis, they were the cause of everything that was wrong in Germany. These men, women and children started the war, they caused the economic problems, they were the cancer at the heart of the state. The extermination of the Jews, only fifty years ago—in your parents' or your grandparents' time—was the end-result of racism. It was racism that led to the gas chambers of Auschwitz and Dachau.

Racism (or racialism) is prejudice against people of another race or ethnic group. *Prejudice means pre-judging: making up your mind about someone or something when you have not considered the facts or the evidence.*

Racists believe that human beings can be divided up into racial groups. Most of these will be inferior. The racist's own group will of course be the superior race: probably the only superior race.

One form of racism is **colour prejudice.** *This is prejudice against people who have a different colour skin from your own.*

Racial discrimination *puts racism into practice—treating people badly or unfairly because they are from a different race or ethnic group.*

It was racism that led to the Holocaust, yet racist attitudes and racial discrimination still persist. Protest and laws can go so far—but the problem lies deep in the human spirit.

The 1991 census in Britain showed that 5½% of its population belonged to ethnic minorities. It defined people as white, black Caribbean, black African, black (other), Indian, Pakistani, Bangladeshi, Chinese, other Asian and 'other' (not included in other groups). Most coloured immigration into the UK took place this century, particularly in the 1950s and 1960s, when the British government asked people to come and work here. Some others came as refugees from countries where they were persecuted, such as Uganda or Vietnam. Many were born here. The vast majority have British citizenship.

A glance at the history books shows that immigration is nothing new. There is no such thing as a 'British race': immigrants have been coming in for centuries! Romans, Vikings and Normans settled here; the Irish, French, Poles and Jews came, and so on. If we want to hate people for being immigrants, we will have to hate everybody in the country! Yet British white racism continues.

Why are people racist ?

Here are some possible answers:

- Racists believe that you can divide humanity up into biologically different races. These 'biological differences' mean you can predict how someone will behave, or what he or she will be like.

This way of thinking has its roots in the fifteenth and sixteenth centuries, when European nations went on their voyages of discovery to what they called the New World. It allowed people to claim that colonizing other countries and enslaving their people was morally acceptable: they belonged to 'inferior races', not to the 'superior race' to which the white colonists belonged.

Biologists and social scientists have investigated the idea that people can be divided into races and that you can predict what they will be like. They say it is scientific nonsense. It is very hard to talk about different 'races' of *homo sapiens* (human beings): it has little scientific meaning, and the supposed 'races' are hard to define. Many scientists say that the only race as such is the species: *homo sapiens*. (For this reason, some think we should take about 'ethnic groups' rather than 'races'. It puts more weight on the groups to which people may feel they belong, without implying that humans can be classified in terms of race.)

- People inherit many of their attitudes from their parents and from their peer groups. So they may be brought up to be racist. Children below three or four years old are not prejudiced: people clearly have to learn to be racists, it is not something rooted in their nature.

- We tend to be afraid of things or people we think are different from us in some way. Fear can lead to hatred.

- People who are hard up or out of work want someone to blame. It is easy to say, 'It's their fault, coming over here and taking our jobs. They should go back to their own country. (Between the wars, there was massive unemployment and poverty in Germany. The Jews were an easy target to blame for the country's problems.)

- The concept of the 'out group', which is quite easy to understand. Some people find it hard to come to terms with the fact that there is an unpleasant side to themselves—what St Paul calls 'the unspiritual nature', or the 'old nature'—which fights against God and goodness (Romans 7:14–25). It is hard to admit that we can be bad, selfish, vicious, cruel. One way to cope with it all is to project it onto others. Even if we are not aware we are doing this, we can still do it. 'It's not me, it's them.' 'They're all lazy, stupid, dangerous, violent, corrupt: I'm not.' 'I'm a nice person: it's other people who are bad.' Thinking about others like this makes us feel better.

A group that stands out in some way becomes a good target, hence the term 'out group'. It does not really matter what the group is: any will do. But common targets are: ethnic minorities, Jews, or, for many in Northern Ireland, Protestants or Catholics.

Looking down on other people makes us feel superior. Much of sexism, for example, can be explained by this.

- Prejudice can melt away when people are confronted with the facts. Yet they may not want to know. Stupidity and ignorance are dangerous, yet many prefer them to reality.

Controlling racism

Racist attitudes and behaviour in Britain are strictly controlled by the law:

- It is illegal to use threatening, abusive or insulting words in public, when racial hatred is likely to be stirred up. The penalty may be a heavy fine or even imprisonment.

- It is illegal to practice racial discrimination in such areas as:
    Employment. It is illegal to offer someone a job, or to refuse them a job, on the grounds of their colour or race. Employers must not discriminate against ethnic groups when they train, test, transfer, promote, discipline or dismiss employees.
    Education. Schools cannot refuse to admit pupils on the grounds of their race, and must ensure that all have access to the same benefits, facilities and services.
    Housing. Councils must not discriminate against people on racial grounds when they allocate council houses. It is also illegal to refuse to sell or rent a home to someone because he or she is from a

Eugenics

The word 'eugenics' comes from a Greek word meaning 'well-born'. It was coined in 1883 by Sir Francis Dalton, a British doctor. Dalton wanted to 'improve' the human race by carefully matching parents. He believed that people's characteristics were inherited from their parents. It had nothing to do with their education or how they were brought up. It was all to do with biology. So, criminals, prostitutes, poor people and alcoholics all inherited their problems from their parents. To get rid of such problems, all you had to do was to stop 'undesirable' people from having children. Then their negative characteristics would not be passed on.

Dalton was influenced by Charles Darwin's theories on evolution. In nature, Darwin said, only the fittest animals survived, which meant the ones who could cope with their environment. Dalton was therefore proposing that careful and selective breeding would ensure that only the 'best' humans would be born.

But who is to say who the 'best' human beings are ? And what right does anyone have to say that one group is 'better' than another ?

The Nazis said the best humans were the Aryans. In Nazi Germany, it was illegal for an Aryan to have sex with a Jew. While the Jews were being exterminated, the Nazis set up selective breeding programmes to ensure a supply of pure Aryan blood. The SS ran baby farms for children born to parents of 'pure' blood. The fathers were often SS officers. Lists were drawn up of desirable racial characteristics: hair colour, eye colour, the shape of the nose. In occupied countries like Poland, many children who conformed to these characteristics were taken away from their families and given to Nazi foster parents in Germany. Many other children, who did not conform, were killed.

Earlier this century in the United States, laws were passed forbidding marriage between blacks and whites. (This was, until quite recently, also the law in South Africa.)

In practice, then, eugenics has often been racist. It has also been used against the disabled. Again, earlier this century in the United States, epileptics and the mentally ill were forced to be sterilized.

The idea that criminals, prostitutes and the poor inherit their problems biologically from their parents is scientific nonsense. Although intelligent people often have intelligent parents, this is not always the case. It is certainly not just to do with biology. Upbringing, education and society play a major role.

Still today, some people want to limit the number of children born to poor parents. Some couples want only a boy or only a girl, and say it is acceptable to abort a child of the 'wrong' sex. (This is illegal in Britain.) Recent scientific research suggests it may be possible to detect whether a foetus will be homosexual in later life. The conclusions of this research are by no means certain, but it raises grave questions if it turns out to be true. Will people want to abort such foetuses ? Should they be allowed to ?

It is hard to see how any Christian could agree with parents being allowed to choose the sex of their babies. Will there come a time when science enables parents to choose their children's eye colour, hair colour, height or anything they like ? Children are human beings, made in the image of God. They are not consumer commodities to be packaged, selected and chosen like a brand of washing powder in a supermarket.

particular ethnic group, or to demand a higher rent from them.

Community life. Everyone, regardless of ethnic origin, has the freedom to

— use any place open to the general public
— stay in a hotel or guest house (if there are vacancies)
— use banks, insurance and financial services, transport and travel facilities, places of entertainment, refreshment or leisure facilities
— use the services offered by any profession, such as solicitors, doctors and so on.

The **Commission for Racial Equality** (CRE) was set up by the government to act as a watchdog and to promote good relations in the community. Its fifteen members have backgrounds in business, politics, race relations or the trade unions. It works towards eliminating all discrimination, and to ensure that everyone has equal opportunities in all areas of life, regardless of his or her colour. If someone claims that discrimination is taking place, the CRE investigates the incident and can order the offender to stop. Its order can if necessary be enforced by the courts.

Follow-up

Questions

1 What is
(a) racism
(b) colour prejudice
(c) racial discrimination?
Now look up the word 'xenophobia' in a dictionary and explain how this is different from racism.

2 (a) Give examples of groups against whom some people might be racially prejudiced.
(b) Give three reasons why some people are racist.

3 'Racism often goes hand in hand with recession, inflation and unemployment.' Work out what this statement means.

4 (a) What does 'eugenics' mean?
(b) In detail, give an example of when a programme of eugenics was carried out.
(c) 'Eugenics can never be right.' Do you agree? If so, why? If not, why not?

For discussion

'Freedom of speech is a human right, but British law will not allow that freedom to racists.'

'My right to swing my arms ends where your nose begins.'

(a) Is there a connection between these two statements?
(b) Is it ever right to limit freedom of speech? If so, why? If not, why not?

Activity

Have you ever been judged unfairly? How did you feel? Reflect on your experience and write a short poem or descriptive piece about your feelings. You might want to share this with the rest of the class.

Further reading

Read Aldous Huxley's novel, *Brave New World*, about a world in which eugenics has gone mad.

18 Racism 2: The Bible and Race

The Bible condemns racism. We can see this by examining passages from

- the **Old Testament**
- the life and teaching of **Jesus**
- the experience of the **early church** and the letters of **Paul**.

The Old Testament

The Law of Moses (the Torah) is at the heart of the Jewish faith. The Jews believed that God gave it to Moses on Mount Sinai.

God's people had a special responsibility to treat people of other races in the right way.

 Do not ill-treat foreigners who are living in your land. Treat them as you would a fellow-Israelite, and love them as you love yourselves. Remember that you were once foreigners in the land of Egypt. I am the Lord your God.

Leviticus 19:33–34

This passage from the Torah comes very soon after the commandment, 'Love your neighbour as you love yourself.'

Jesus said that this was one of the two greatest commandments. Here, the Jews are told they must apply it to foreigners, including those of a different race, who live in Israel. They are to be treated just as well as fellow Israelites. The Jews, once a minority group of slaves in Egypt, must treat their own minorities well.

? Britain today is a multi-racial country. What does this passage say to people now?

The teaching of Jesus

Jesus taught that God's kingdom was open to everybody. It did not matter whether or not you were Jewish. What mattered was how you responded to Jesus' invitation to God's kingdom.

The case of the centurion's servant

 Read Luke 7:1–10

The Jewish elders in this story spoke very highly of the Roman officer or centurion. (A centurion commanded a hundred men.) He was not a Jew, but was sympathetic to Judaism: he had built the local synagogue and probably worshipped the Jews' God. And he had great faith in Jesus. Jesus responded to the centurion's faith by healing his servant (or slave). It did not matter that the centurion was a Gentile, and a Roman at that! Jesus' highest praise is reserved for a foreigner, for someone of a different race:

 I tell you, I have never found faith like this, not even in Israel!

The case of the good Samaritan

Jesus taught that God's kingdom was not only open to the Gentiles; it was also open to the Samaritans.

The Samaritans lived in the region of Samaria (see map). In 721 BC, this area had been conquered by a great world power called Assyria. The Assyrians deported many of the Jews who lived there, and replaced them with Assyrian settlers who intermarried with the Jews who remained.

By the time of Jesus, Assyria had long since ceased to exist. But the Samaritans were still there. Most Jews would have nothing to do with them: they despised the Samaritan religion. And they despised the Samaritans for being of mixed race. Racial prejudice was a feature of first century life, as it is today.

 Read Luke 10:25–37

The expert in the Torah asked Jesus how he could gain eternal life. When Jesus asked him what the Torah said, he picked the two commandments which Jesus himself taught were the greatest: to love God, and to love your neighbour as yourself. We have already seen that the second of these comes from Leviticus. In Leviticus, the command to love your neighbour applied to foreigners as well. Yet by Jesus' time, many wanted to restrict it to Jews alone. So, the expert in the

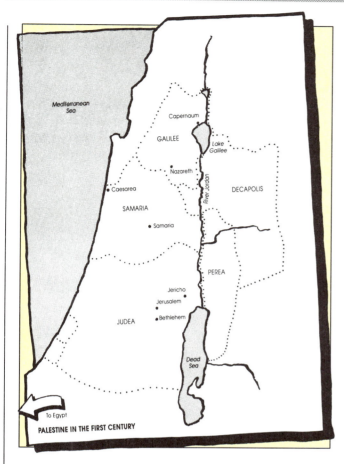

PALESTINE IN THE FIRST CENTURY

Torah asked Jesus, 'Who is my neighbour?' The parable answered the question. Who was it who helped the injured man? Not the people of his own race, but the Samaritan.

When Jesus got to the point when a Samaritan came along, people would have thought that the 'baddie' had arrived! Yet there is a sting in the tail. It is the Samaritan who cares for the wounded man, not the Jewish characters. Racial origins were irrelevant: the test was which one loved his neighbour as himself!

Jesus ends by saying, 'You go, then, and do the same.'

The Samaritan's compassion is a model for everybody. Jesus teaches that everyone is your neighbour. Love knows no boundaries or distinctions.

The early Christians

The Acts of the Apostles was written by Luke and is the second volume to his Gospel. It tells the story of the early church from Jesus' ascension into heaven until Paul's imprisonment in Rome in AD 61–63.

The early church faced a number of problems. Many Jews who became Christians said Gentiles should be circumcised and should keep the Torah. In other words, Gentiles had to become Jews before they became Christians. (Jewish Christians who thought like this were called Judaisers.) Peter and Paul both got into trouble with these 'Judaisers' because they did not insist on this point.

Peter's lesson

 Read Acts 11:1–18

Gentiles did not keep the food laws from the Torah: their food was not kosher. Jews could not therefore share meals with them. This is why the Judaisers attacked Peter.

In Peter's vision, the sheet was full of all kinds of animals: not all of them were kosher. As a Jew, he refused to eat the non-kosher food, even when the Lord told him to! He was then told to go and visit Cornelius, a Gentile centurion. Cornelius and the other Gentiles in his house heard Peter preach and received the gift of the Holy Spirit: God had shown that they were Christians and they were baptized.

The vision showed Peter that there was no longer a distinction between clean (kosher) food and unclean (non-kosher) food. He was told, 'Do not consider anything unclean that God has declared clean.'

The same principle clearly applied to people. The vision, and what happened at Cornelius' house, showed that there was no distinction between 'clean' people (Jews) and 'unclean' people (Gentiles). Racial differences were not important. Both Jews and Gentiles were included in God's kingdom.

Paul's teaching

Paul, the great early Christian missionary, also believed that there should be no distinction between Jew and Gentile. Christ had sent him to the Gentiles.

One of Paul's group of new Christians—the church in Galatia—was troubled by Judaisers. They said that the Christians there had to be circumcised and keep the Torah if they wanted to be saved. Paul vigorously protested against this.

 Read Galatians 3:26–29

Paul tells the Galatians that what matters is faith. It is not the Jews who are Abraham's true descendants, but those who have faith in Christ.

> **So there is no difference between Jews and Gentiles, between slaves and free men, between men and women, you are all one in union with Christ Jesus.**
>
> **Galatians 3:28**

> **There is no longer any distinction between Gentiles and Jews, circumcized and uncircumcized, barbarians, savages, slaves, and free men.**
>
> **Colossians 3:11**

Christians today would say that, if there is no distinction between Jews and Gentiles, slaves and free men, men and women, there is no distinction either between black and white ! Paul's letters rule out racism altogether.

Follow-up

Activity

Use seven index cards and label them up as in the example below. (You might want to draw them out in your file or notebook if this is easier.) Fill in one for each Biblical passage we have examined in this chapter.

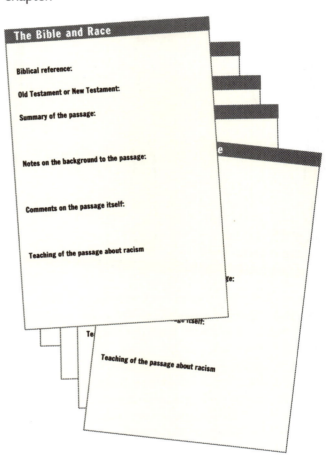

The Bible and Race

Biblical reference:

Old Testament or New Testament:

Summary of the passage:

Notes on the background to the passage:

Comments on the passage itself:

Teaching of the passage about racism

Study 1: The teaching of the Roman Catholic Church

The Roman Catholic Church, with the other denominations, strongly opposes racism. Roman Catholics accept the Bible's teaching on the subject, and agree with measures in society to combat racial hatred.

The Second Vatican Council, in 1965, produced a *Declaration on the Relation of the Church to non-Church Religions (Nostra Aetate)*. This is what it said about racism:

> ❝ **The Church reproves, as foreign to the mind of Christ, any discrimination against people or any harassment of them on the basis of their race, colour, condition in life or religion.**

Following *Nostra Aetate*'s publication, Pope John Paul II asked the Church's 'think tank' on Justice and Peace to produce a fuller report on the subject. This report (published in 1988) was called *The Church and Racism*. Its teaching many be summarized as follows:

- Every human being is created in the image of God (see Chapter 5). God offers salvation to everyone, to all nations.

- The Roman Catholic Church has condemned racism in the past:
  - When the European explorers of the fifteenth and sixteenth centuries went out to the 'New World', many of the inhabitants were killed and enslaved. The Popes at the time condemned this absolutely, and Catholics who kept 'Indians' as slaves were excommunicated (expelled from the Church).
  - Later, the slave trade in African black people was outlawed by Pope Leo XIII in his encyclical (letter) *In Plurimis* (1888).
  - The Catholic Church joined others in teaching that the Nazis' practices were morally outrageous. Pope Pius XI taught that those who put race, the people or the state at the centre of things, were overturning the order established by God.
  - The present Pope, John Paul II, condemned the fact that Christians had contributed to the slave trade.

- Apartheid in South Africa must be abolished. (See Chapter 20) The future in South Africa should be based on the principle that every person is of equal dignity. [Note: the South African government under Nelson Mandela has now abolished apartheid.]

- Prejudice against immigrants is based on fear: fear of the presence of others or of people who are 'different'. Yet differences between people brings enrichment. They should be welcomed. Respect for others is essential, and it is completely wrong to discriminate against immigrants or refugees.

- Scientific developments in the future may bring new dangers. It would be quite wrong to use genetic engineering to produce 'perfect racial specimens'. (See the box on eugenics in Chapter 17.)

- 'We must hold strongly to convictions about the dignity of the human person and the unity of the human family.' Everyone has the same nature and origin: we are created by God in his image. Christ's work of saving us means we all have the same calling from God and share the same destiny. It is true that individuals have physical and mental differences, but discrimination based on sex, race, colour, social conditions, language or religion is utterly wrong. Discrimination like this must be stopped because it is alien to God's design.

- The Church therefore supports everything in the world which works against racial discrimination and which supports human rights.

- The Church
  - wants to change racist attitudes, including those found among her own members
  - asks God to open people's hearts and appeals to people's moral and religious sense
  - offers a place in which people can be reconciled (brought together)
  - wants to see more initiatives between different ethnic groups to welcome each other, share ideas with each other and to help each other
  - tries to live by the message which she proposes to all human beings: **'Every person is my brother or sister.'**

Study 2: The work of Martin Luther King Jnr

One particular Christian who is famous for his work in opposing racism is the American Baptist minister, Dr Martin Luther King.

In the Southern States of the USA, in the 1950s and 1960s, discrimination against black people was common. It had been going on for a long time, and the situation was in danger of becoming like that in South Africa (see Chapter 20). Blacks' earnings were only about half those of whites. Many did not have the vote, and certain public places were said to be for 'whites only'.

On 1 December 1965, a tired black woman refused to give her bus seat up to a white. For this 'offence', she was arrested. This led to a bus boycott: black people refused to use the buses in the area as a protest against the way they were treated by society. The boycott was led by Martin Luther King, who at the time was a Baptist preacher in Alabama. It brought him recognition as the head of the Civil Rights Movement, which campaigned

for equal treatment of blacks and whites.

Martin Luther King refused to support the idea that white people were all evil. Some black radicals believed this. Instead, he taught that Christian love was the way forward. Love was the supreme moral norm. 'Love,' he said, 'is the only force capable of transforming an enemy into a friend.'

His convictions about love came, of course, from Jesus. He supported non-violent protest as the way forward. It had worked for Gandhi, the great Indian leader, in getting the British to leave India, and King used Gandhi's tactics (see Chapter 37). Even when he received death threats and his own home was bombed, he insisted that the black community should not fight back.

In 1962, King met President Kennedy and asked for greater understanding towards American blacks. The following year, he led a march of a quarter of a million people, black and white together, on the capital city of Washington. The march campaigned in favour of the new Civil Rights Bill, which aimed to ease the situation of black people. The bill became law. In 1965, King met President Johnson and asked for further reforms to remove the remaining obstacles to racial equality. The right to vote was universally granted to black adults that year.

Martin Luther King was awarded the Nobel Peace Prize in 1964. He was assassinated in Tennessee in April 1968. His ideals live on in American life through the work of many, including his widow, Coretta Scott King, and his friend the American Baptist politician, the Reverend Jesse Jackson, who ran for President in 1984.

His message may be summed up in a quotation from a speech he made in Washington at the end of the march in 1963:

> **I have a dream that one day all God's children, blacks, whites, Jews, Gentiles, Protestants and Catholics will be able to join hands and sing in the words of the black people's old song, 'Free at last, free at last, thank God Almighty, we are free at last.'**

Follow-up

Questions

1 Write your own notes, in as much detail as you can, on:
(a) the work of Dr Martin Luther King, and
(b) the teaching of the Roman Catholic Church on racism and racial discrimination. Don't forget to identify which document this teaching comes from.

2 'Love is the only force capable of transforming an enemy into a friend' (Martin Luther King). Do you agree with this idea? Is it important?

Activity

Copy out and learn a quotation from *Nostra Aetate*, *The Church and Racism*, and Martin Luther King.

NOTE: Don't confuse Martin Luther King (the twentieth-century black American civil rights leader) and Martin Luther (the sixteenth-century German monk who was a leader in the Protestant Reformation). Many people mix them up !

20 Racism 4: South Africa

South Africa is a multi-racial country. The chart below shows the colour mix in South African society:

In a just society, you might expect the blacks to have the largest say in running the country ! Yet only whites had the vote until 1987, and even then it was extended only to 'coloureds' and Asians, not to blacks.

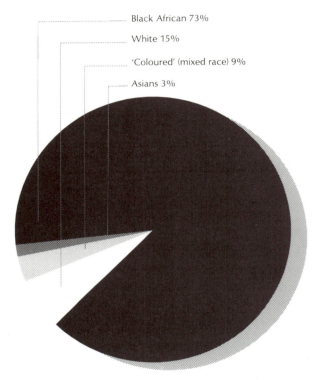

Black African 73%

White 15%

'Coloured' (mixed race) 9%

Asians 3%

The whites ran the country to their own advantage. The black population was forced to live in 'homelands'. This meant that 73% of the population lived in 13% of the land of South Africa. The other 87% of the land went to the whites and the other groups.

Black Africans could not choose where they wanted to live. Three-and-a-half million blacks were evicted to the black areas, the 'homelands'. Their old homes were bulldozed, frequently to make way for new housing for the whites.

The 'homelands' were nothing of the kind. They were not the ancient homes of the black tribes. They were poor, overcrowded, and had few resources. It was hard to grow food in them. Slums developed. Those blacks who managed to get jobs had little choice but to become short-term workers on low pay in white-run farms, factories and mines. The men would bus out of their townships to work. Many had to stay in hostels in the white areas, seeing their families only once a year, at Christmas. Poverty gave them little choice but to separate from their wives.

Blacks working in white areas had to carry a passbook if they wished to remain there for more than seventy-two hours. Harsh penalties were used against those who had no passbook. Blacks could be detained without trial for ninety days at a time, and those periods were renewable.

Some of the 'homelands' received limited independence from the South African government. Nine million blacks lost their South African citizenship as a result. They then had no nationality, since no one outside South Africa recognized the independence of these homelands.

The white population jealously guarded its privileges. Blacks who spoke out were imprisoned. Amnesty International's files demonstrate that many were tortured and died in police custody. Not surprisingly, there was and still is a great deal of unrest in the black areas. Disturbances were savagely put down by the heavily armed police force: scenes of policemen using tear gas, whips and bullets on crowds became common on foreign news broadcasts. Many blacks, frustrated by the government's refusal to improve their lot, fought amongst themselves. Inter-tribal killings became common. Violence bred violence.

The whole system of legalized racism was given the polite name **Apartheid.** The Afrikaans word means 'separateness' or 'apartness'. (Afrikaans is the language of the descendants of the Dutch settlers in South Africa, the Afrikaaners.) The Dutch Reformed Church in South Africa compared the Dutch settlers to the Israelites in the Bible. When the Israelites came to the promised land, they subdued the Canaanites who were already there. If the Dutch were like the Israelites, the blacks were like the Caananites. Apartheid was God's will.

This view was condemned by all other Christian churches, and is rejected today by most of the Dutch Reformed Church itself. Apartheid was condemned by the United Nations and by the international community. The South African government of Nelson Mandela has now abolished apartheid.

The history of apartheid

1948 The National Party white government of South Africa sets up apartheid. Previous racist actions and practices now become law.

1960 The **Sharpeville Massacre**. Police kill 69 blacks and wound 186 others who were peacefully demonstrating against pass laws requiring people to carry passbooks.

Government bans two black freedom organizations: the **African National Congress (ANC)** and the **Pan-African Congress (PAC)**.

The ANC becomes an underground organisation. One of its leaders, **Nelson Mandela**, co-ordinates its campaign of sabotage, attacking property to try to de-stabilize the government.

1964 Nelson Mandela and others sentenced to life imprisonment for sabotage.

1976 The **Soweto uprising**. 400 people killed in rioting in Soweto and other black townships. **Steve Biko**, a black opponent of the government who spoke out against the massacre, dies in police custody.

1978 **P.W. Botha** becomes prime minister.

1979 Black trade unions are legalized. Anti-apartheid leaders denounce this as little more than a gesture.

1984 –86 Following violence in the black areas, the government imposes a **state of emergency**. Thousands of those opposed to the government, including children, are imprisoned without trial. The police are legally immune from prosecution. Many people are tortured and killed.

1985 Government lifts the ban on multi-race political parties and on mixed race marriages.

1986 The **pass laws** are abolished.

1987 The government proposes to alter the Group Areas Act, which set up the homelands.

New constitution: P.W. Botha now State President.

Limited power in parliament is given to 'coloureds' and Asians, though not to blacks.

The United Democratic Front (UDF: a body comprised of community, labour, student, church and women's groups) urges boycotting of the first 'coloured' and Asian elections. Only 20% of 'coloureds' and Asians vote as a result.

1989 **F.W. De Klerk** becomes state president.

1990 11 March: **Nelson Mandela released from prison. The ban on the ANC, the PAC and other groups is lifted**.

August: the **ANC abandons its policy of armed struggle** against the government.

1,500 political prisoners are released.

Exiles who had fled South Africa because of their opposition to the government, return.

1991 **Government repeals** (undoes) the **Groups Areas Act**, which set up the homelands.

1993 Whites-only referendum on De Klerk's programme to abolish apartheid. The result supports the reforms.

De Klerk and Mandela awarded Nobel Peace Prize.

17 November: **signing of a new constitution** to end 300 years of white minority rule and 45 years of apartheid; agreement on an electoral Bill paving the way for general elections in April 1994—the door opens for democracy for all.

1994 April: the General Election results in a victory for Nelson Mandela and the ANC. President Mandela's government abolishes apartheid.

NELSON MANDELA

Nelson Mandela was born in Transkei, South Africa, in 1918, the heir to a tribal chief. He became the organizational leader of the African National Congress.

Mandela was sentenced to life imprisonment in 1964 for sabotage, treason and conspiring to overthrow the government. After twenty-six years, on 11 February 1990, he was released.

Even before his imprisonment, Mandela was seen as the figurehead for the black people's struggle in South Africa. He is still the figurehead today. Mandela is a moderate who wants a political system that will treat all in South Africa fairly, whatever their ethnic origin.

He has proposed that those who committed crimes against the blacks under apartheid should be pardoned: people should look forward, not backwards. He warns against promising grand schemes that cannot be carried out. Yet he stresses that blacks are in urgent need of more housing, with electricity and proper sanitation, better education and better employment prospects.

Mandela led the ANC to victory in the 1994 general election in South Africa. His government has abolished apartheid, but immense problems remain for the black population. Wealth needs to be redistributed to help the poor; violence continues; the education system is in need of reform. 46 years of black suffering caused by apartheid cannot be solved overnight. The process of bringing justice to all South Africans is a long one.

When he was released from prison in 1990, he quoted from the speech he made at his trial in 1964:

'I have fought against white domination, and I have fought against black domination. I have carried the idea of a democratic and free society in which all persons live together in harmony and with equal opportunity . . . If needs be, it is an ideal for which I am prepared to die.'

BISHOP TREVOR HUDDLESTON

Trevor Huddleston went to South Africa in 1943 to take charge of a church in Sophiatown, an area with a large and poor black population. He raised the money to build the children schools and nurseries, and successfully campaigned for black children to have free school meals (in 1945 only white children were allowed them).

Bishop Huddleston constantly attacked apartheid. He denounced the government when, in 1955, Sophiatown was demolished and its inhabitants evicted and re-settled. He attacked the pass laws. The government called him an extremist, and had him spied upon.

His lifelong friendship with Archbishop Tutu started when Tutu was a child. The young Desmond Tutu was tremendously impressed by the simple courtesy of Huddleston in raising his hat to Tutu's mother. It was practically unheard of for a white to show this kind of respect to a black.

Like Desmond Tutu, Trevor Huddleston stated that Christianity was totally opposed to the system in South Africa.

'Christians are not only commanded to love. We are commanded to hate what is evil, and nothing is more evil than apartheid.'

DESMOND TUTU

'I am puzzled about which Bible people are reading when they suggest religion and politics don't mix.'

The World Council of Churches condemned apartheid, and the South African Council of Churches declared it a heresy: a false teaching which perverts Christian truth. Desmond Tutu, the Anglican Archbishop of Cape Town and Head of the Anglican Church in Southern Africa, is one of the best-known church leaders who proclaimed this message. He denounced apartheid as 'one of the most vicious systems since Nazism,' saying that the day he was proved wrong on this would be the day when he would burn his Bible.

In both the Old and New Testaments, God is shown to be on the side of the slaves, the oppressed, and the victims. God rescued the Jewish slaves in Egypt, and led them to freedom in the Promised Land. 'What a political God!' Archbishop Tutu commented.

When the politics of their own day led to the rich getting richer and the poor getting poorer, the prophets of the Old Testament spoke out. Christians today, Desmond Tutu says, must test government policies against Christian teaching. God, who was on the side of the Israelite slaves in Egypt, is on the side of the black victims of apartheid in South Africa.

When the National Party government condemned Tutu, saying churchmen should not meddle in politics, he replied, 'I will not be told by any secular authorities what gospel I must preach.'

Desmond Tutu's opposition to apartheid stemmed from his Christian faith. Prayer, Bible reading and the church's worship are all essential for him. He has a magnetic personality, and is an electrifying speaker with a tremendous sense of humour. It is hard to be hostile towards someone who can make you laugh, and it gets the message across. He points out that it is ridiculous to discriminate against people on the grounds of a 'biological irrelevance' like skin colour. You might as well discriminate against people because their noses are too big!

Desmond Tutu supported economic sanctions

against South Africa, even though it was treason to do so. If international companies stopped investing and other nations stopped trading it would put great pressure on the National Party to end apartheid. Black people would be hurt by sanctions, but their hurt would help to gain their freedom. He told the government that time was running out. 'What are blacks expected to do in such a situation,' he asked. 'Fold our hands?'

Yet he opposes violence. In 1985, a young woman called Maki Skosana was mutilated and then murdered by an angry crowd, who thought she was a police informer. In a sports stadium, Tutu addressed 30,000 people telling them:

'If you do that kind of thing again, I will find it difficult to speak for the cause of liberation . . . Our cause is just and noble . . . You cannot use methods to attain the goal of liberation that our enemy will use against us.'

Desmond Tutu is against violence, but if all else fails he could justify Christians using violence to overthrow an evil government.

The National Party government had confiscated Tutu's passport several times. He continued with his message despite being rubbished by the pro-National Party South African press, receiving frequent obscene telephone calls and death threats. The National Party government funded a body calling itself 'The Christian League' to campaign against the South African Council of Churches and especially against Desmond Tutu. What chance had the National Party government got, he asked, against the prayers of millions of Christians for the ending of apartheid?

Desmond Tutu was awarded the Nobel Peace Prize in 1984. He received it on behalf of all those who sought to end apartheid. When he was enthroned as Archbishop in 1986, he praised God, for whom, he said, no one is a nonentity:

'I pray that Our Lord would open our eyes so that we would see the real, the true identity of each one of us; that this is not a so-called "coloured" or white or black or Indian, but a brother, a sister—and treat each other as such.'

Follow-up

Questions

1 (a) What does 'apartheid' mean?
(b) How did apartheid affect black people in South Africa?
Answer in as much detail as you can.

2 Explain in detail why Archbishop Desmond Tutu and Bishop Trevor Huddleston opposed apartheid. To support your answer, give examples of some of the things they have done and said.

3 Why are
(a) Nelson Mandela, and
(b) F. W. De Klerk
important people to know about when you discuss apartheid?

4 Look back again at the four chapters on racism. Plan thoroughly and then write an essay to answer the question:
'How and why does Christianity oppose racial prejudice?'

For discussion

'One of the things to blame for the origin of prejudice is religion. Religion causes prejudice.'

'Nelson Mandela's idea of a multi-racial society where everyone lives together in harmony sounds good, but it's an impossible dream.'

'Christianity hasn't helped the blacks in South Africa. Only politics can do that.'

'Religion and politics don't mix. Christians should stay out of politics.'

In small groups, discuss at least two of these statements. Then share your findings with the rest of the class.

Activity

Nelson Mandela was elected President of South Africa in April 1994. Find out about some of the changes his government has made in South Africa since his election.

If your school has a CD ROM in the library, it may well have back issues of a good newspaper on disk. You can use the key words 'South Africa', 'apartheid' and 'Nelson Mandela' to identify the relevant articles.

21

Class Prejudice

Look at each of these pictures in turn. Do you think people have set ideas about . . .

—how he or she might talk? (Think about the accent!)

—what he or she might do for a living?

—their names—Henry, Jemima, Beryl, Bill—or what?

—the sort of school he or she might have gone to?

College or university?

—the sort of home they live in? What sort of town it would be in?

—what he or she might be interested in?

—favourite television programme? Daily paper?

—what political party might he or she support?

Now some more questions:

- Which person do you think is
    working class?
    middle class?
    upper class?

- Do you agree or disagree with the following statements?
    'They're a bunch of snobs.'
    'They've got more money than sense.'
    'They're too smug and cosy, that lot.'
    'They're all stupid and ignorant.'

And some more:

- Would these three people ever mix or get to know each other? Why?

- Are these questions fair? Are the pictures themselves fair, or unkind?

- This sort of exercise can be quite funny! Even so, can your answers be taken seriously? Are they fair?

Most people in Britain understand terms like 'upper class', 'middle class' and 'working class'. Yet it is hard to say exactly what makes you one or the other. We could look at factors like

—income and wealth

—education

—occupation

—family background

—status: the way people in the community think about you

—lifestyle

But the whole thing is slippery. What class is a man whose father is a retired army major, who has a double-barrelled name, but who works as a farm labourer? What class is a woman whose parents worked in the factory down the road, but who has 'A' levels and is at university?

Some would also say the term 'middle class' is too broad, and should be divided into 'upper' and 'lower' middle class. Others would say the 'upper class' does not really exist: they are simply middle class.

Some would say the whole business is silly. But the British seem to be very conscious of class. It often strikes people whom come to this country from

overseas! People tend not to mix too much with others who they perceive to be of a different class. Is this true of you?

Suppose I dislike you or am suspicious of you simply because you are from a different class. There is no other reason: I just know what you will be like, because your class are all like that. This attitude is one of **prejudice.**

Prejudice means pre-judging: making up your mind about something or someone when you have not considered the facts or the evidence.

If you change your mind when you have considered the situation, or when you have got to know the person and have realized that you were wrong, you are no longer prejudiced. But if you bury your head in the sand, or say, 'I've made up my mind: don't confuse me with the facts,' or continue to think badly about someone because they are a member of a group you dislike, that is prejudice.

If you treat people badly or unfairly simply because you are prejudiced against them, that is called discrimination.

Some are prejudiced against others or discriminate against them on the grounds that they are

—from a different social class (sometimes called 'classism')

—of another race (racism or racial discrimination: see Chapters 17–20)

—from a different religion

—of the other sex or gender (sexism)

—old (sometimes called 'ageism')

—disabled.

(What other groups could be added?)

It is certainly true to say that prejudice between the social classes in the United Kingdom is common. (Did this come out when you discussed the pictures above?) What about discrimination on the grounds of class?

- Karl Marx (see Chapter 1) said the working classes were kept down by the capitalists, who had the money and controlled industry and business. The system worked against working-class people: they were definitely discriminated against. It was up to them to rise up against the capitalists by revolution. The communist society that followed would be a perfect society.

- In British politics, the Labour Party has aimed to improve the lot of working-class people. The Conservative Party under John Major spoke of a 'classless society': social class would no longer be a barrier for people. The Liberal Democrats agree with the other two parties that class should not divide people: discrimination on class grounds is wrong.

Why are people prejudiced? Why do they want to discriminate? Ignorance, upbringing and refusing to think all play their part. It is worth looking back at the idea of the **out group** (see Chapter 17).

Christianity teaches that every human being is created in God's image. Christ died for every human being alike. Everyone is equally precious to God. Jesus taught that people should love their neighbours as they love themselves, and everybody, without distinction, is a 'neighbour'. So Christians believe that prejudice and discrimination are wrong, whether they are directed against people of a different class, race, religion, or whatever. People should certainly not project their own sins and shortcomings onto others, onto an 'out group'. They should recognize their own faults, turning away from them: in a word, they must repent. It is no good thinking, 'Other people are the ones who need to get sorted out, not me.' As Jesus said in the Sermon on the Mount in Matthew's Gospel:

> **Why, then, do you look at the speck in your brother's eye, and pay no attention to the log in your own eye? How dare you say to your brother, 'Please, let me take that speck out of your eye,' when you have a log in your own eye? You hypocrite! First take the log out of your own eye, and then you will be able to see clearly to take the speck out of your brother's eye.**
>
> Matthew 7:3–5

THE PARABLE OF THE GREAT BANQUET

 Read Luke 14:15–24

Jesus did not give any direct teachings on the subject of class, but this parable teaches on the subject.

Most Jews in Jesus' time were looking forward to the arrival of the Kingdom of God. They sometimes pictured it as a big celebration meal, with God's chosen people as the guests. The Messiah, God's anointed king, would be the host.

In Jesus' time, people were invited twice to meals. So the guests have already been invited, and have accepted. Everything is ready, and the host is looking forward to welcoming them all. Yet when the servant goes to invite them for the second time, they are all too busy. God's Kingdom—and his invitation to enter it—is the most important thing there is, yet there are always people who are 'too busy' to hear God's call.

So the people who were sure of their places end up by losing them. And their places are taken by others: by beggars, cripples, the blind and the lame, who represent those to whom society closes its doors, but for whom Christ's door is always open. When there is still room, the invitations fly out to those on the country roads: the Gentiles, the non-Jews, who fill God's community of the church. The smug, outwardly religious people turn down God's invitation. It is the others who accept it, and whom God accepts.

The parable shows, once again, that God invites everybody to his table. Social distinctions—of class, of race, of sex, of age, even of religion—are not relevant. Christianity teaches that what matters is not what other people in society think of you. What matters is whether or not you accept the invitation God sends in Jesus Christ.

Follow-up

Questions

1 (a) What is prejudice?
(b) Name four groups against which some people are prejudiced.
(c) What is discrimination?

2 Explain the meaning of the term 'out group'. (See Chapter 17.) How does it help us understand why people are prejudiced?

3 'If you want to be prejudiced, that's up to you. No one else has the right to tell you what to think.' Think about what you have learnt from this chapter and from the course so far. Is this statement correct? Explain your answer.

4 The following sentences tell Jesus' parable of the great banquet, but they are in the wrong order. Put them right:

- The master told the servant to go to the town's streets and alleys and bring in the poor, the crippled, the blind and the lame.

- Another wanted to try out his new oxen!

- The master said to the servant, 'None of those men who were invited will taste my dinner!'

- When everything was ready, he told his servant to tell the guests.

- They all made excuses: one had to look at a field he had just bought.

- So the master told the servant to bring in the people from the country roads and lanes.

- The servant found the guests and told them it was time for the feast.

- When that was done, there was still room.

- Another did not want to accept the invitation because he had just got married.

- A man was giving a feast.

- The servant told his master, who was furious.

5 'It is wrong to be prejudiced against people from a different social class.'
Why would a Christian agree with this statement?
Your answer should include a look at Jesus' parable of the great banquet.

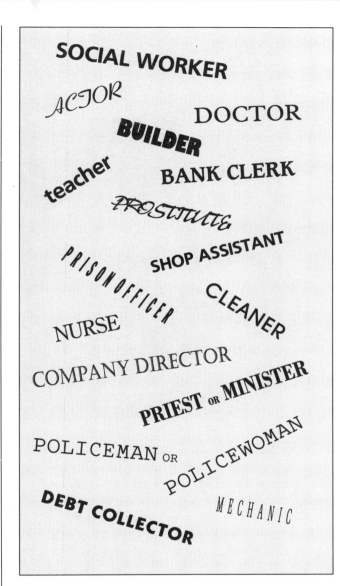

SOCIAL WORKER
ACTOR
DOCTOR
BUILDER
teacher
BANK CLERK
PROSTITUTE
SHOP ASSISTANT
PRISON OFFICER
CLEANER
NURSE
COMPANY DIRECTOR
PRIEST OR MINISTER
POLICEMAN OR POLICEWOMAN
DEBT COLLECTOR
MECHANIC

Look at the jobs above. A bizarre collection! Could you put them in order—from the 'best' job to the 'worst' job?

or:

—from the job 'best for a Christian' to 'worst for a Christian'?

If you managed to order them, what criteria did you use?

What makes a job good or bad? The size of the pay packet? Job satisfaction? How 'useful' it is? Or something else?

Christians often talk about 'vocation' when they are discussing work. 'Vocation' is sometimes applied to jobs. 'Vocation' comes from a Latin word meaning 'to be called.' A 'vocation' therefore is

—a call from God to be a Christian and to carry out a Christian job

or more simply

—the idea that people are called by God to do a certain job or work. (A call from God need not mean a flash of lightning and a booming voice! It might take the form of a strong feeling that something is right, or a more vague idea that what you are doing fits in with what God wants.)

- Sometimes 'vocation' is applied to a very specialized calling, such as the call to be a priest or minister or to the religious life (as a monk, friar or nun). An old-fashioned Roman Catholic view was that the religious vocation (to life as a monk, friar or nun) was better than the call to life in the world. The Second Vatican Council in the 1960s rejected this idea, although the call to the religious life is still seen as a vocation.

- The Protestant Reformer Martin Luther (1483–1546) said the Christian's vocation was no more and no less than to do the 'work of the world' to the best of his or her ability.

Jesus said that Christians should serve God and serve others. ('Serving others' means helping them, caring for them, giving them what they need. 'Serving God' means following him, obeying him and loving him.) This is, after all, what Jesus himself did, as he said to his disciples:

> **If one of you wants to be great, he must be the servant of the rest; and if one of you wants to be first, he must be the slave of all. For even the Son of Man did not come to be served; he came to serve and to give his life to redeem many people.**
>
> **Mark 10:43b–45 (the 'Son of Man' is Jesus)**

One of the most obvious ways of living out the Christian life at work is to be involved in a 'caring profession'. The caring professions are those in which people can most obviously care for and serve others. Doctors, nurses, teachers, ministers and priests and social workers could be classed as caring professions. (What others could be added to this list?) Perhaps personal satisfaction and doing good are more important to people in caring professions than the size

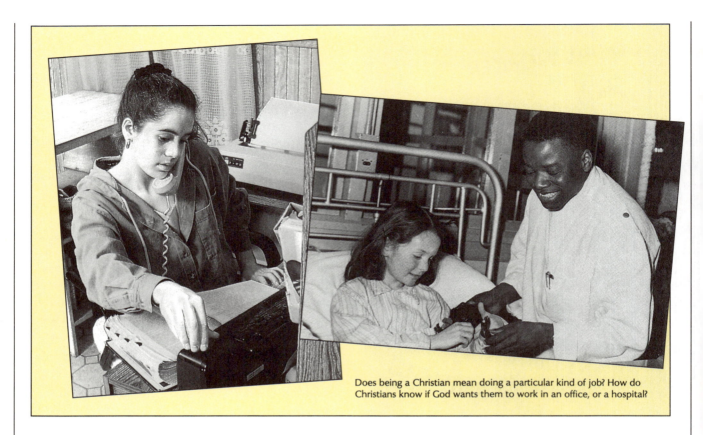

Does being a Christian mean doing a particular kind of job? How do Christians know if God wants them to work in an office, or a hospital?

of the pay packet. (Do you think this is true?)

Look back to what Luther said: Christians have a vocation to serve God and to serve others in any job they do. Faith is a way of life, and is not limited to a handful of professions. If a person can have a vocation only to a caring profession, it seems more that a little unfair. It limits vocations largely to middle-class occupations. What about working-class ones?

Suppose we define work as *a means of loving God by serving human need*. Then any job in which we can do this is acceptable. People need to buy such things as food and clothes, so shop work can be a vocation. If they need banks, then working in one can be a vocation. Places of work need cleaning, so being a cleaner can be a vocation. If people need cars, then being a mechanic can be a vocation, and so on. (Jesus was a carpenter, after all!)

The letter to the Colossians says:

> **Whatever you do, work at it with all your heart, as though you were working for the Lord and not for men.**
>
> **Colossians 3:23**

Clearly, there are some jobs in which it is hard to see

how this could be done. It is difficult to see how a Christian could justify being prostitute—although it is important to remember that Jesus' love and care included prostitutes and other 'bad characters' or 'sinners', he did not approve of what they did!

Christianity also teaches that it is wrong to exploit others. (This means using them for your own advantage and to their disadvantage.) This applies as much at work as anywhere else. In the Old Testament, the prophet Amos condemned the people of his own time for using others for their own gain. This was in the eighth century BC, but it is still relevant today.

 Read Amos 8:4–6

Amos condemns his fellow-Israelites who do not care about those in need:

— They cannot wait for the sabbath, the Jewish holy day, to be over. (Work was forbidden on the sabbath.) Then they can rip people off by overcharging them.

— They sell bad wheat at prices hungry people cannot afford.

—They are prepared to sell people into slavery if they cannot repay their debts.

Amos said that God would punish the nation for such crimes. Making money out of others' misfortune can never be right.

Is work a curse?

In the creation story in the book of Genesis, Adam and Eve are punished for disobeying God. After the fall, Adam is told that his cultivation of the land will become painful and hard. Yet it would be wrong to think that all work is a curse. It can be mindless, desperately boring, crushingly hard and de-humanizing—in a word, *drudgery*. Yet it can also be very enjoyable and fulfilling, like Adam's cultivation of the Garden of Eden before the Fall. It depends, perhaps, on how creative it is and on how much of yourself you can put into a job. Knowledge of a vocation can mean that your work is not automatically a curse.

What should all this mean for *employers and employees*? Both have rights (the things they are entitled to) and responsibilities (duties to each other). These are often controlled by a contract. The contract is a written agreement. It sets out what the employee can reasonably be expected to do, and what the employer will do in his or her turn.

Jesus taught people, 'you shall love your neighbour as yourself'. Christians believe that this applies to employers and employees, too. They should behave with this kind of love (care and concern) for each other. They should not think of each other as enemies! Instead, they should co-operate (work together) for the good of all concerned.

Article 23, sections 2, 3 and 4 of the United Nations' Universal Declaration of Human Rights sets out the responsibilities of employers and the rights of employees:

2. Everyone, without any discrimination, has the right to equal pay for equal work.

3. Everyone who works has the right to just and favourable remuneration (pay) ensuring for himself and his family an existence worthy of human dignity, and supplemented, if necessary, by other means of social protection.

4. Everyone has the right to form and to join trade unions for the protection of his interests.

('Just' means 'fair' or 'fitting in with justice'.)

The United Nations' Declaration is not a Christian document, although it has been influenced by Christian theology. Christian teaching agrees with the documents. For example, Pope Leo XIII (1810–1903) said workers have a right

—to be treated as persons

—to receive a living wage so that they can look after themselves and their families

—to join a trade union.

Someone might say this is all very well, but what happens if co-operation breaks down? What happens if employers or employees do not behave fairly? There are clearly things that can be done in such situations, such as going to court or going on strike. But this should be done fairly, and probably as a last resort. The harm that a strike or a prosecution does should be no more than is absolutely necessary. And steps should be taken afterwards on both sides to restore good relations.

The Old Testament book of Deuteronomy is the last of the five books of God's Law or Torah.

 Read Deuteronomy 24:14–22

A good deal of this section is relevant here. Deuteronomy says:

● Workers should be paid a fair wage. It does not matter whether they are Israelites or foreigners. It is a sin to refuse to pay them.

● Foreigners, orphans and widows all have rights! It is wrong to take the last thing a widow has as security for a loan. They are entitled to the crops of fruit that are left after the harvest. (How could this sort of idea be applied to agriculture today?)

Many Christians believe that workers should be paid a fair wage, even though work should be more than just a money-making exercise. But this raises a further question:

How should our money be used?

 **Read 1 Timothy 6:6–10;**
Mark 10:17–31; Luke 12:13–21

Jesus said, 'A person's true life is not made up of the things he owns, no matter how rich he may be.' Jesus' parable of the rich fool in Luke, his words to the rich man in Mark, and the advice given in the first letter to Timothy all show this. There is more to life than money.

Jesus said to the rich man, 'Go and sell all you have and give the money to the poor, and you will have riches in heaven; then come and follow me.' Some Christians take this to apply to everybody. Others think it applies only to some but not to others. Monks and nuns actually take a *vow* of poverty. (See Chapter 28 on Mother Teresa for an example of someone who puts this into practice). Most Christians, however, agree that there is nothing evil in having money; the important thing is to use it in the right way. The tenth Commandment is:

> ❝ **Do not desire another man's wife; do not desire his house, his land, his slaves, his cattle, his donkeys, or anything else that he owns.**
>
> **Deuteronomy 5:21**

So greed is totally unacceptable. Wanting more and more is not the Christian way. Loving money for its own sake can lead people to ignore the needs of others and to ignore God. As 1 Timothy says, 'the love of money is a source of all kinds of evil'.

Follow-up

Questions

1 (a) What does the word 'vocation' mean?
(b) Explain as fully as you can the Christian teaching about vocations.

2 Why did Amos condemn the other Israelites in the eighth century BC, and what does Deuteronomy say about the way workers and foreigners, widows and orphans should be treated?

Do these passages from Amos and Deuteronomy have any relevance to life today? If so, how?

3 What does the United Nations' Universal Declaration of Human Rights say about employers and employees?

What does Christianity say about employers and employees' rights and responsibilities?

4 Look again at the passages from 1 Timothy 6:6–10, Mark 10:17–31 and Luke 12:13–21.

What do they suggest the Christian attitude towards money should be?

For discussion

In groups, discuss these ideas:

'The caring professions are better than other jobs.'

'The love of money is a source of all kinds of evil.'

'Taking a day off when you are fit to work is no better than stealing.'

'God expects people to work.'

British Coal announces massive job losses

Receivers called in to local firm . . .

Jobless figures rise to highest for five years

Government blames unemployment rise on world recession

Headlines like these are all too common. Most of us have some experience of unemployment, with members of our family, or our friends, out of work. It is very likely that many of you reading this book will be unemployed at some stage in your lives, perhaps sooner rather than later. That is a very uncomfortable thought.

It is easy to say, 'It's their own fault if people don't have jobs: they're just lazy.' Yet it is much more complicated than that.

Economists identify several types of unemployment. Looking at some of these helps us to see what causes the problem.

Structural unemployment

This is caused by an employer losing business because people no longer want what he or she can sell (demand for these goods or services has gone down). Much of the massive rise in unemployment in the 1970s, 1980s and 1990s was caused by the decline in manufacturing industry. Industries closed, and there were not enough jobs available for the people who were put out of work.

Frictional unemployment

This is caused by the delay in moving from one job to another. The delay can be made longer by factors like

- the cost of moving house
- the fact that new skills have to be learnt, and
- the fact that the person seeking work may not know that there is another job available.

Casual unemployment

This is a type of frictional unemployment. People are casually unemployed when they are pausing between short-term jobs in such industries as building or agriculture. When the pause between jobs like these happens regularly and is caused by the weather or by seasonal demand, it is know as seasonal unemployment.

Technological unemployment
(a type of structural unemployment)

This is people being replaced by machines. In an automated factory, working people are replaced by computers and robots.

Residual unemployment

This is a general term used to cover everything else. A tiny minority of people actually refuse to work.

Others become, or are seen as being, unemployable. Some employers are less than keen to employ a person who has been out of work for a long time. This is because

they are afraid he or she has forgotten skills and has got out of the rhythm of working. They may therefore prefer to employ people who have not been without a job for such a long period.

What should the government do about unemployment? Politicians and economists disagree as to how much they can—or should—interfere. Conservatives tend to prefer to leave it to market forces. Let the employment level sort itself out: too much meddling only makes matters worse. The Labour Party believes that the government should do more to help the unemployed and to create jobs. The Liberal Democrats tend to take a position somewhere between the two. All three parties agree that training is essential if people are to find new jobs.

Certainly, being unemployed is tough. It can cause all kinds of personal and family problems and tensions. Here are some:

- **Boredom.** It becomes very difficult to fill the day when you are no longer working, and lack of money aggravates the problem.

- **Loss of self-esteem.** In the Western world, 'What do

Being out of work is tough, and not just because money is tight. Our society values people for what they do, not what they are. Time for change?

you do for a living?' is often the first question people ask. Your position in the scheme of things is defined by your job. If you have no job, you can feel as if you have no value. (Politicians and the media often don't help. They talk about jobs being shed, and unemployment figures—statistics, not people.)

- **Loss of companionship at work.** Some find this one of the hardest things about life on the dole. Missing the company of your workmates can make you very lonely.

- **Poverty.** Unemployment benefit is not usually very much compared with lost wages. How do you feed the family? Pay the electricity bill? Replace worn-out clothes? Buy children Christmas presents? If they cannot keep up their mortgage repayments, whole families can be made homeless. Banks and building societies repossess homes. The recession of the early 1990s saw the largest ever number of repossessions in Britain.

● **Anger and depression.** Most unemployed people have lost their jobs through no fault of their own. In addition to all their other problems they may be angry and depressed. Unemployment can be a real factor in marriage break-up. Riots too—where anger explodes—are a feature of times of recession. A minority, finding they cannot cope, resort to violence.

Despite all this, there is a danger that people stop thinking of unemployment as a problem. It has grown rapidly over the last thirty years and many have simply become used to the idea. This can lead to thinking of the unemployed as no more than numbers; pawns in the games played by economists and politicians as they talk about 'acceptable levels of unemployment'.

Yet Christianity teaches that human beings are priceless: they are of infinite value. It is wrong to think of a person's worth in terms of the job he or she does. What matters is their value in God's sight. Anything that leads to people being treated as less than fully human is wrong. So business problems should not be solved by making people unemployed if there is another way. And the unemployed should not be treated as worthless hangers-on who sponge off the rest of society.

Christianity supports measures

— to stop people from feeling that they are of no value now they are jobless

— to ease people's situation if they are poor

— to offer counselling and help if people are in distress

— to help people find ways of using their time constructively, especially if jobs are hard to come by.

Many churches run schemes for the jobless in their areas. These might include social clubs, support groups, counselling and practical help in job clubs, which help people to find and to apply for jobs. These would, of course, be run in co-operation, not competition, with schemes organized by the wider community.

Paul's second letter to the church at Thessalonica (2 Thessalonians) is sometimes referred to in connection with unemployment.

 Read 2 Thessalonians 3:6–13

Paul wrote the letter in AD 51. He tells his readers in the community to keep away from lazy people who refuse to work. After all, Paul and his companions kept up their jobs when they were in Thessalonica, and did not laze around! Paul says people who refuse to work should not be allowed to eat.

Is this relevant to today? It is important not to be hasty. Times and situations change. Paul was writing for a particular situation, not attempting to lay down rules for all time. It seems that the people who were refusing to work thought that Jesus would return very soon. The second coming was just around the corner, the Day of Judgement was at hand, so why bother working? Paul, however, believed that they should wait for Jesus and also get on with their everyday lives. And they were making a nuisance of themselves: Paul says they 'do nothing except meddle in other people's business' (verse 11). He instructs the church to put them out of the community until they are so ashamed that they change their minds.

Follow-up

Questions

1 What is unemployment?
What causes it?

2 Find out how much unemployment benefit is at present. What can it pay for? It is enough? Next lesson, compare your findings with those of the others in your class.

3 Karl Marx, the founder of communism, called religion 'the opium of the people': a drug to make them forget their misery. How could someone's religious faith help him or her if she or he became unemployed?

4 What does Paul say in 2 Thessalonians about people who refuse to work? Is what he says relevant to today? If so, why? If not, why not?

For discussion

'People are unemployed because they're lazy.' Do you agree?

The United Nations' Universal Declaration of Human Rights says, 'Everyone has the right to work' (from Article 23, (1)). Yet many would say this is unrealistic: there are no longer enough jobs.
    Can we talk about people having a right to work?

Activity

Follow the news carefully for a week on the radio and television and in the newspapers. Find out as much as you can about unemployment in Britain today. You could concentrate on the following areas:

- If unemployment is rising, which areas of the country are most badly affected? Which industries or employers? What are the present unemployment figures, and how does this compare with figures in the recent and not so recent past?

- If unemployment is going down, in which areas is this occurring, and how many people are still without jobs?

- What steps are being taken to reduce unemployment and to help the unemployed?

Present your findings to the rest of the class.

Most of us know someone who is or who has been unemployed. From what you know from them and from your reading of this chapter and from studying the news, write a report to answer the question, 'What is it like to be unemployed?'

Find out how the churches in your area are helping, or would help, people who are unemployed.

If you were to write a list of the ways you spend your time, it would probably include

—sleep

—school and homework

—travelling to and from school

—shopping

—bathing, showering and washing

—getting up

—going to bed

and so on. Someone a little older, perhaps with a family, would add such things as looking after children, housework and cooking, and would change 'school' for 'work' if they were employed.

The time left after these things is free time or leisure time. Leisure time is concerned with things we want to do, instead of the things we have to do. We tend to think that people should enjoy their leisure time (as well as work and school!).

All Christians accept the principle that human beings need one day out of the seven for rest and worship. Sunday, the day of Jesus' resurrection, is the day when Christians meet together.

Article 24 of the United Nations Universal Declaration of Human Rights says:

> **Everyone has the right to rest and leisure, including reasonable limitation of working hours and periodic holidays with pay.**

Christians are very much in favour of this. The Second Vatican Council, for instance, set out the benefits of leisure: leisure time allows people to develop their talents, to give time to their families and to social, cultural and religious activities.

All Christians would agree that fun, happiness and enjoying life are gifts of God. When God made the world, the account in the book of Genesis says, he saw that it was 'very good'. It was meant to be enjoyed. Christianity is not a killjoy religion. Jesus said he had come to give life in all its fullness. He was criticized by people who thought he was not glum and gloomy

In our free time, we can choose what we do—lie in bed or do aerobics; spend time with friends or on the computer. The Bible says people need time to rest and worship as well as work.

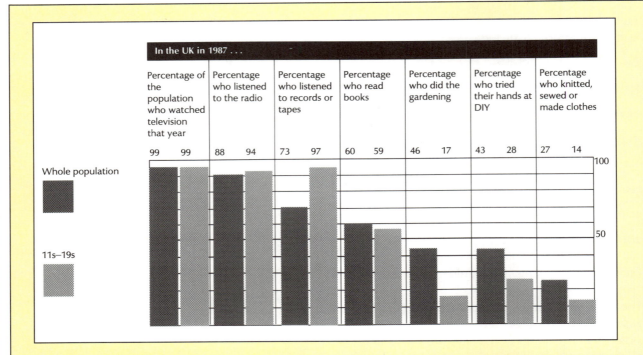

	Percentage of the population who watched television that year		Percentage who listened to the radio		Percentage who listened to records or tapes		Percentage who read books		Percentage who did the gardening		Percentage who tried their hands at DIY		Percentage who knitted, sewed or made clothes	
	99	99	88	94	73	97	60	59	46	17	43	28	27	14

In the UK in 1987 ...

Whole population

11s–19s

In 1988–89...

98% of all homes had a television

53% of all homes had a video

18% of all homes had a home-computer

How much television did people watch each week in 1989?

Age 4–15: 18 hours 27 minutes

16–34: 20 hours 34 minutes

35–64: 26 hours 7 minutes

Over 65: 36 hours 29 minutes

(Average figures which exclude hours spent watching video tapes!)

In 1989–1990 ...

19,466,000 went to watch football league games

5,400,000 went to watch greyhound racing

4,924,000 went to watch horse racing

3,575,000 went to watch Scottish football league games

2,250,000 went to watch Rugby Union in England

1,689,000 went to watch Rugby Football league

1,650,000 went to watch motor sports

751,000 went to watch Test or County cricket

25,000 went to watch motorcycle sports

In 1989 ...

11 million people attended a West End theatre performance

6.5 million people went to Blackpool pleasure beach

4.7 million people went to the British museum

2.4 million people went to Alton Towers

2.2 million people went to the Tower of London

Source: Central Statistical Office
Social Trends 23

Millions choose to watch sport in their leisure time. Others opt for activity.

enough. Because he enjoyed sharing meals—and drinks, too—with his friends, they labelled him 'a glutton and a drinker' (Matthew 11:19). Jesus even compared the Kingdom of God to a huge celebration meal (Luke 14:16–24). When he and his disciples went to a wedding reception, he supplied the wine when the host's ran out (John 2:1–11). He wanted his disciples to relax when they had been working hard (Mark 6:31). Christians are meant to be of the same mind as Jesus in all these things.

But Christianity does not dictate *how* people should spend their free time—whether to read science fiction or Dickens; whether to listen to rock or Beethoven.

The great Christian principles are that people should love God and love others. Everything is tested against these standards. Playing the bass guitar when I promised to help wash up is therefore wrong. Riding a motorbike without a silencer at 4 a.m. in a residential area is also wrong. Filling our thoughts with pornography is wrong.

Many people—Christians especially—will choose to spend some of their leisure time helping to meet specific needs. Of course, religion is a way of life, and helping others is not just something for one's free time! However, human need is great, and time has to be found. A house-bound old lady might need someone to dig her garden. A youth club might need volunteers to help run it. The local branch of the Samaritans might need new volunteers.

Some will choose to devote free time to working for a charity or other organization. They might drop envelopes through local doors during Christian Aid Week, distribute collection boxes for The Children's Society, or write letters for prisoners of conscience sponsored by Amnesty International. If these things are not done during people's leisure time, it is hard to see how some of them would ever get done.

A day for rest

In the Ten Commandments in the book of Exodus, God says:

> **Observe the Sabbath and keep it holy. You have six days in which to do your work, but the seventh day is a day of rest dedicated to me. On that day no one is to work— neither you, your children, your slaves, your animals, nor the foreigners who live in your country. In six days I, the Lord, made the earth, the sky, the sea, and everything in them, but on the seventh day I rested. That is why I, the Lord, blessed the Sabbath and made it holy.**
>
> **Exodus 20:8–11**

These verses have always been important in Judaism. Work is forbidden on the Sabbath, the Jewish holy day. This runs from sundown on Friday to sundown on Saturday. Orthodox Jews have a number of rules to help ensure they do no work whatsoever on the Sabbath. Many Christians regard Sunday, the Christian holy day or 'the Lord's Day'—as a new Sabbath. They argue that this commandment forbids all but essential work (such as that of doctors, the police and so on) on the Lord's Day. People should not work, but should be free to rest and worship.

However, Jesus said:

> **The Sabbath was made for the good of man; man was not made for the Sabbath. So the Son of Man is Lord even of the Sabbath.**
>
> **Mark 2:27–28**

This means that human needs are more important than rules and regulations. So maybe Christians should not be too strict about Sunday. It can be argued that people who need to work, or who simply want to work, should be allowed to do so. The commandment was designed to ensure that people had at least one day off to rest and worship, rather than simply to ban work. It is a principle the Creator has given to people for their good.

It is of course possible to be too lazy!

People knew this well before the time of Jesus, too. The Book of Proverbs is a collection of sayings from the Old Testament, the Jewish Bible.

 Read Proverbs 6:6–11

Proverbs tells lazy people to go and have a look at ants! Ants are busy and industrious: they do not laze around in bed all day!

(In ancient Israel and in other countries nearby, 'wise men' frequently drew lessons from looking at animals' behaviour.)

Follow-up

Questions

1 What does the United Nations Universal Declaration on Human Rights say about leisure?

2 What is the Christian view of leisure? Answer in full.

For discussion

Is it morally acceptable to spend £50 on a restaurant meal when people are starving elsewhere in the world?

Activity

Work out your timetable for a 'normal week'. Write it up on a table like the one here.

How much time did you spend:

- in bed?

- in school?

- travelling?

- in the bathroom?

- How much time did you spend on leisure activities? What did you do, and how long did you do each activity for?

- Now compare your findings with the rest of the class. What were the most popular activities?

- Could any of these activities be objected to on moral and/or religious grounds?

'Just say no,' the government anti-drug slogans run. But many people say yes.

Why do people take drugs?

Here are some of the reasons:

- **as an escape.** Drugs can help people to forget—that they are lonely, depressed, unhappy, unemployed or poor. Some people claim that they offer an alternative when reality becomes too threatening. Perhaps this helps to explain why solvent abuse has increased so much in recent years.

- **because of peer pressure.** If your friends take drugs, it can be very difficult for you to resist. People are afraid to be different.

- **for kicks.** People also *want* to be different. Some are attracted to drug taking simply because it is illegal, just as children sometimes like being naughty for the sake of it. Some think taking drugs makes them different from— perhaps superior to—everyone else. It can be a way of asserting independence for our parents, perhaps of hitting back at them.

- **because they want to** (despite the dangers). They may be attracted by the 'alternative culture', such as the 'rave scene' connected with ecstasy.

- **because they are addicted.** They are unable to stop taking the drug. There are two types of addiction:
  - physical: the body becomes dependent on the drug, as with heroin or nicotine.
  - psychological: taking the drug becomes such a habit that although the body can go without, the mind cannot—as with cannabis. Psychological addiction can be just as powerful as physical addiction and many who take drugs regularly want to stop, but cannot.

A woman with pupils contracted after snorting heroin smokes a hand-rolled cigarette. A major problem in the prevention of drug abuse is that society condones the social use of some drugs, such as tobacco and alcohol.

Should people be allowed to take drugs?

YES

- The law should not interfere with people's private lives. It should be up to the individual whether to use drugs or not, even if they are harmful.

- Making drugs illegal does not stop people taking them. Legalizing them would allow the police and the courts to concentrate on other things.

- Legalizing drugs would break the power of organized crime. It would also stop drugs being adulterated by suppliers. (This means adding other substances to the drug so that it is impure, thus adding to the dangers.) If drugs were available from legal sources, the quality could be carefully monitored.

- If there is a demand for drugs, it is good business sense to supply them.

- Cannabis is said to be less harmful than tobacco. Other drugs should remain illegal, but cannabis should be legalized.

NO

- The law should protect people from themselves. People who are depressed, unhappy or on a high at a 'rave' are not in a fit state to make a rational decision about taking drugs. Anyone who really knew the risks would not take them.

- Drug use does not only affect the individual. We have obligations to our family and friends who worry themselves sick about us. You have no right to risk becoming very ill, even dying, when it will make others desperately unhappy or grief-stricken. Nor do you have a right to cost the health service thousands of pounds for your treatment. Individuals do not belong to themselves. We all belong to each other. Christians would say we also belong to God.

- Taking drugs is selfish and self-obsessed.

- Life is the greatest gift anyone can have. If you take a drug which could kill you, you are throwing one of God's most precious gifts back in his face.

- Drugs often become the most important thing in an addict's life but there are better things to live for than getting a regular supply of a dangerous chemical.

- Cannabis should remain illegal. We do not know about its long-term effects. They may be severe.

- Taking drugs helps organized gangs of particularly nasty criminals.

- Taking drugs is illegal. We may not like the law, but if we choose to disobey it, we must be prepared to suffer the consequences.

- Coming off addictive drugs is a terrible experience. The 'cold turkey' or withdrawal symptoms are extremely unpleasant: they include chills, aches, spasms or depression. The craving continues: far worse than the craving for food when you are on a diet.

- We already have two 'socially acceptable' drugs: alcohol and tobacco. These already do enough damage, and we don't need any more !

The dangers of drugs

The effects of most drugs vary from person to person. Some may not be affected much; others may have a severe reaction. It is dangerous to believe that because X took drug Y and it didn't do him any harm, that will be true for everyone else !

Taking a lot of drugs adds to the dangers. It could even be fatal. Taking one drug while another is in your system is also extremely dangerous. Pregnant women users risk harming their babies. Users who share needles are in the high-risk groups for hepatitis and AIDS. Drugs obtained on the illegal market are frequently impure. They may have other substances added, such as glucose, talcum powder or even scouring powder. This increases the risks.

Many drugs exaggerate the user's mood. If he or she is depressed, the possible consequences are clear.

Drugs are expensive. It is very sad that some decide to steal or become shoplifters or prostitutes to finance the habit. Others find their general standard of living declines as more of their income is spent on drugs.

Types of drugs

- **Heroin** (class A) is derived from the opium poppy. It is often adulterated by suppliers.

  It is physically and psychological addictive, and people can become 'tolerant' of it. This means they require it to remain 'normal'. If they stop taking it, withdrawal symptoms are extreme. The dangers of long-term use include the damage caused by injecting, decreased appetite and apathy. Overdosing causes coma or death.

- **Cocaine** (class A) comes from the Andean coca plant. Refined cocaine is called crack. Cocaine can produce attacks of panic or extreme anxiety. It can be psychologically addictive, and after-effects include depression and tiredness. Those who use the drug regularly can become nervous, even paranoid. It can cause death from heart failure.

- **Solvents** include glue, paint, aerosols and so on. Solvent abuse is most common between the ages of twelve and sixteen.

  Children have died—some the first time they sniffed glue—from suffocation or heart failure. Risks for very long-term users include brain damage or damage to the liver and kidneys.

- **Cannabis** (class B) comes from the plant *cannabis sativa*. There are various forms: resin, herbal cannabis or marijuana, and oil prepared from the resin. It is illegal to grow it, supply it or possess it, or to allow others to smoke it in your house.

  It can produce attacks of panic or amplify depression. We do not know what the effects of long-term use are. Users can become psychologically addicted, although it is probably not physically addictive.

- **LSD** (Lysergic acid diethylamide) (class A) is a manufactured drug. It is hallucinogenic (causes hallucinations) and 'trips' can last up to about twelve hours.

  'Bad trips' can produce depression or panic, and the user may feel very disorientated. Long-term use can produce serious anxiety or 'flash backs' to previous 'trips', well after the drug was taken. These can be very upsetting. It is psychologically addictive.

- **Ecstasy** (E) (class A) can be extremely dangerous: people have died after taking only one tablet. It can also produce anxiety attacks. We do not know what its long-term effects are. It is quite possible they are severe.

(This list is not complete: these are simply some of the more common drugs.)

Drugs and the law

British law reflects society's attitude as a whole towards drug abuse. The three main relevant laws are the Misuse of Drugs Act 1971, the Drug Trafficking Offences Act 1986, and the Intoxicating Substances (Supply) Act 1985.

- **The Misuse of Drugs Act 1971**
  Drugs are classified as class A (the most dangerous), class B and class C. All classified drugs are dangerous and illegal.
  - It is an offence to possess these drugs.
  - It is also an offence to supply them (to sell them or even to give them away) unless you have legal authority.
  - It is illegal to allow anyone to supply drugs in your house, or even offer to supply them.
  - It is illegal for parents to allow their children in their house to share drugs with one of their friends.
  - It is illegal to allow someone to smoke cannabis in your house.
  - Users who are first offenders may be fined, and acquire a criminal record. Regular offenders or suppliers can go to gaol.
  - The maximum penalty for drug trafficking is life imprisonment.

- **The Drug Trafficking Offences Act 1986**
  Under this Act drug traffickers can be gaoled for life and may also have their property confiscated.

This is a heroin-user's kit. Heroin is a dangerously addictive drug.

- **The Intoxicating Substances (Supply) Act 1985**
  Under this act it is illegal to supply any such substance to a person under eighteen if you know he or she is intending to inhale the fumes. The penalty is six months' imprisonment or a £2,000 fine.

Schools or Sixth-Form or Tertiary Colleges consider drug taking to be a serious offence. Pupils who use drugs, even if they have done so only once, are usually expelled. The pupils also have to face the police and the courts. At universities and colleges, student drug users also risk being 'sent down' or expelled.

Despite the dangers a small minority of people think the drug laws are too strict. Some of them want to legalize cannabis, while others want to legalize all drugs. The box on page118 gives some of the main arguments.

Follow-up

Questions

1 Why do people take drugs?

2 Outline the British law covering the use of drugs.

For discussion

Despite information, teaching and campaigns, people still take drugs. Why do you think the message fails to get across? How could it be made more effective?

Does the Christian doctrine of original sin (look back at Chapter 3) have any bearing on the issue?

Activity

Appoint two speakers for each side to debate the motion:

'This house believes that the decision on whether or not to use drugs should rest with the individual, not with the state.'

(The debate will be more effective if the speakers write their speeches before it is held.)

NOTE: Two organizations which help drug users and their families are: The Standing Conference on Drug Abuse and Adfam National (addresses on page 190).

PART FOUR

Responsibility for Others

26 Poverty 1: The Bible and the Poor

In this chapter we look at why care for the poor has always been important for Christians.

Of course, it's not only Christians who care about those in need. Many people of goodwill give money to charities, raise funds and campaign to help the less fortunate people of the world. But Christians do it for very specific **religious reasons** and we will explore these first.

Where it begins

Christianity gets its tradition of caring for the poor from its beginnings in Old Testament Judaism. The writers of the Old Testament books lived at different times and in different situations, but they hammer home the idea that God cares about the poor and wants them treated well.

- This is based on the Jewish belief that all men and women are created in the image of God and are equal in his sight. In the creation story of the Book of Genesis, for instance, they are given power over the rest of the earth, but not over one another (Genesis 1:27–31).

- It is based on the nation's own experience as slaves in Egypt. The history of the Jews gave them sympathy with the underdog.

- And it is based on God's law (see, for example, Deuteronomy 24:14–22 and Chapter 22 in this book).

Later, as Jewish society got more wealthy under the Kings of Israel and Judah, the gap between rich and poor got wider. The poor were oppressed and exploited just as they were in other countries. God's law was ignored.

So the Old Testament prophets spoke up for the poor and oppressed. They demanded care for the poor as part of true religion. A good example of this is a passage from the Book of the prophet Isaiah:

All around the world, and in our own country, there are people in need. We see the desperate plight of refugees on TV and in the newspapers. There are many reasons for poverty, but the Bible's teaching is clear. God cares about the poor, and those who want to please God must care for them too—not in theory, but with generous practical help.

> **The kind of fasting I want is this:
> Remove the chains of oppression and the yoke of injustice, and let the oppressed go free. Share your food with the hungry and open your homes to the homeless poor. Give clothes to those who have nothing to wear, and do not refuse to help your own relatives.**
>
> **Then my favour will shine on you like the morning sun, and your wounds will be quickly healed. I will always be with you to save you; my presence will protect you on every side. When you pray, I will answer you. When you call to me, I will respond.**
>
> **If you put an end to oppression, to every kind of gesture of contempt, and to every evil word; if you give food to the hungry and satisfy those who are in need, then the darkness around you will turn to the brightness of noon.**
>
> **Isaiah 58:6–10**

The Old Testament historians, too, in writing down the history of their people, chose stories from the past which they thought would help men and women—especially powerful ones—to live in the way God wanted. These were often about how to treat the poor.

The story of **Naboth's Vineyard** in 1 Kings 21 is a good example. King Ahab of Israel is persuaded by his power-crazed wife Jezebel to arrange the death of Naboth, a man much poorer than himself, so that he can take Naboth's land. But God sends Elijah the prophet to pronounce terrible judgement on Ahab. Not even kings are above God's justice.

When the Christian church began, it kept the Jewish Scriptures. They are now the 'Old Testament' of the Christian Bible—part of the way Christians believe God still speaks to them. So one of the religious reasons Christians care about the poor is because they have inherited the teaching about social justice in the Old Testament.

New Testament teaching

The poor have a special place in the life and teaching of Jesus himself. Luke's Gospel, particularly, shows Jesus sharing the life of the poor and identifying with them. Luke tells us that Mary and Joseph were temporarily homeless when Jesus was born. A manger where the animals fed had to serve as his cradle. The angels announce his birth, not to the rich but to shepherds, who are the first to visit him. When Mary and Joseph go to Jerusalem to have Jesus circumcized, the sacrifice they offer to God is the one the Torah set aside for poor people—two young pigeons. (All who could afford to were supposed to offer a lamb: see Leviticus 12:8.)

The teaching of John the Baptist in preparation for Jesus' adult ministry, echoes the social concern of the Old Testament prophets. (See Luke 3:10–14.)

Jesus' own teaching was about the **Kingdom of God**. In his day, many believed that their wealth was a sign of God's blessing and an assurance of their place in the coming Kingdom.

Jesus' message shocked them. The really important people in the Kingdom, he said, are not the respectable and the wealthy. They are the outcasts of society: the sinners, lepers, tax gatherers and prostitutes—and above all the poor:

> **Happy are you poor;
> The Kingdom of God is yours!
> Happy are you who are hungry now;
> You will be filled.**
>
> **Luke 6:20–21**

This theme is repeated frequently in the Gospels. When a rich man asks Jesus what he should do to 'receive eternal life', Jesus tells him to sell everything he has, give the money to the poor, and follow him (Mark 10:17–22).

Those who follow Jesus are to live simple lives, not worrying about possessions but trusting in God to provide for their basic needs. No one can love both God and money, Jesus said (Matthew 6:19–34). *They are to serve the poor*—and the Gospels imply that if people refuse to do this, then God will punish them. The parable of the Rich Man and Lazarus from Luke was probably included in the Gospel because Luke thought it was a good example of the sort of thing that Jesus said (see Luke 16:19–31).

The Parable of the Sheep and the Goats in Matthew's Gospel (25:31–46) implies that Jesus' oneness with the poor—his **identification** and **solidarity** with them—is so complete that when people serve the poor, they are really serving Jesus—even if they do not realize it. Here too, whether people go to heaven or hell seems to depend on how they have behaved towards those in need.

So the second religious reason why Christians think

it is their duty to serve the poor is because Jesus teaches them to in the Gospels. They do it 'in obedience to Christ', because what Christ says is the most important way they have of knowing what is the right thing to do.

After Jesus' death and resurrection, the early church carried on the teaching of Jesus and tried to live up to it. In the New Testament letters the first leaders encourage and instruct the new Christians about serving the poor. Two good examples are James 2:1–19 and 1 John 3:17–18. If you read between the lines, you will discover that life in the early church was not always easy. Some Christians apparently needed to be persuaded that they really did have to do something to help the poor!

So, we could sum up all we have said so far by saying that **Christians serve the poor because the Bible tells them to**.

Follow-up

Questions

1 Give two religious reasons why Christians serve the poor.

2 What stories from the Old Testament could you use to illustrate Christian teaching about serving the poor?

3 Why did the writers of the Old Testament think that care for the poor was part of true religion?

4 What do you understand by the term 'Jesus' identification with the poor'? Use examples in your answer.

5 Explain how Jesus' teaching on the poor and the Kingdom of God differed from the attitude of the people of his time.

For discussion

Jesus told the Rich Man to sell all he had, give the money to the poor, and follow him.

(a) Do you think this could ever be a realistic option for Christians today?

(b) In what ways do you think a Christian might try to be obedient to the spirit of Jesus' teaching about poverty?

Activity

The story of Naboth's vineyard is in 1 Kings 21. Prepare a short drama piece based on the story. You will need the following characters: Naboth, Jezebel, Ahab, Elijah, the angry mob, two scoundrels.

Most of us are probably aware that there is a great deal of poverty in the world. Television news frequently brings us pictures of starving people. It was the experience of seeing such pictures on TV in 1984 which led Bob Geldof, the former lead singer with the Boomtown Rats, to set up the charity 'Band Aid'. Band Aid raised £8 million through its hit single 'Do they know it's Christmas?' at the end of that year: a huge success. The money was sent to provide relief to people starving in the Horn of Africa.

> **WHAT ARE THE CAUSES OF WORLD POVERTY?**

> **HOW WIDESPREAD IS IT?**

> **WHAT HAS CHRISTIANITY GOT TO SAY ABOUT IT ALL?**

Band Aid developed into 'Live Aid' and a host of spin-offs like Comic Relief and Red Nose Day began. Geldof's idea of using the media to touch people's consciences had caught on. The result is that people growing up today are probably more conscious of the divisions between the world's rich and poor countries than they were in previous generations. Frequently this expresses itself in real concern and action.

In this chapter we are going to take a brief look at these questions. World poverty is a huge topic. Whole books could be written about it. We can only summarize the information here.

Rich North, poor South

You may have seen a map like this before. It shows the world divided into rich countries above the line and the materially poor countries beneath it. The rich countries are often called the North and the poorer countries the South. Until recently it was usual to talk about the poorer countries as 'Third World nations' and the rich countries as belonging to the 'First World'. But these names have gone out of fashion today for two reasons:

- The terms 'First' and 'Third' World can give the impression that the 'First World' is somehow better or more important than the 'Third World'.

- Communist countries were supposed to be the 'Second World'. The collapse of Soviet communism at the beginning of the 1990s means that this way of dividing up the world is now out-of-date.

So we shall use the more modern terms and talk about the North and the South. If you look at the map you will see that this is quite an accurate description. Only a

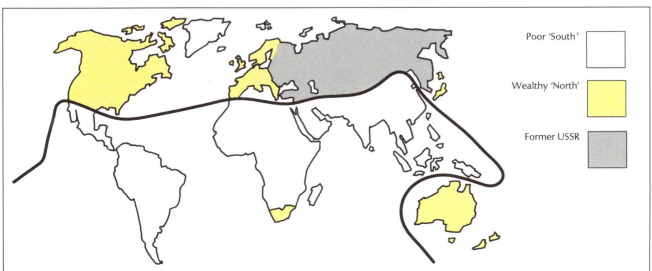

Poor 'South'

Wealthy 'North'

Former USSR

few of the world's rich countries are in the southern hemisphere: so for our purposes we shall count Australia, for example, as belonging to the North.

Sometimes the countries of the South are also called the **developing nations**.

Let's have a look at a few figures:

- Only 25% of the world's population live in the North, but they have 80% of the world's money.

- Only about half the people living in the South have the chance of formal education.

- In the North you can expect to live, on average, for about 70 years. Average life expectancy in the South is 50 years. One of the reasons it is so low is because a great many die as babies and children in the South. Frequently they die from diseases which we know how to cure and which are made worse by poverty.

- At any given time, a quarter of the people living in the South will be hungry.

THE BRANDT REPORT, 1980

Today we are more aware than we once were of the shocking differences between North and South because of the 1980 Brandt Report. Willy Brandt, for a long time Chancellor (Prime Minister) of West Germany, in his later years spent some time as the chairman of an international commission set up to examine what the world community could do about the problems of the developing nations. The Brandt Report—'North-South: A Programme for Survival'—set down the Commission's findings.

But the Brandt Report did more than raise public awareness in the North about the sufferings of people living in the South. Until it was published, most people thought that help for the developing nations was largely a matter of sending money or food to keep people alive during emergencies.

The Brandt Report helped people to realize the limitations of emergency aid. For any lasting change you have to attack the roots of the problem—the causes of poverty. By giving people in the South the means to improve their economic and social conditions the world community could do a great deal to strike at the roots of world poverty.

The Brandt Report said that the international community could do more to help the South. Funds could be provided to develop agriculture. Better fertilizers and irrigation were needed to grow more food, and better crop storage

would help to guard against times of famine. (The impact of natural disasters is made very much worse by the poverty of the countries they hit.) Given funding, the developing nations would be able to increase food production and so improve their internal economies. Today this kind of international effort is encouraged through the Food and Agriculture Organization and the World Health Organization of the United Nations.

The Brandt Report also called for changes in the world's banking and financial organization. Since most of the money and all the major banks were in the North, countries in the South had to rely on banks in the North to lend them money. And the banking system was fixed so that the rich countries got even richer at the expense of the poor, who could never pay back their debts. This situation needed reform.

Although the Brandt Report made people in the North more aware of the needs of developing nations, huge problems still remain today. Only a tiny part of the money spent by governments in the North goes to help the people of the South. In fact, we in the North receive many times more money from the South than we give to it in aid! The countries of the South are still extremely poor: many have huge debts to northern banks: babies, children and adults die unnecessarily of starvation and curable diseases.

It's not our fault !

We have been looking at some unpleasant facts in this chapter. It is not a very comfortable thing to admit that we in the North are rich while other people are starving to death—even worse, that we are rich *because* other people suffer. It is hard to accept: and because it is so hard, we sometimes try to find alternative reasons for the poverty in the world—reasons that do not threaten us or our standard of living.

Let's look at two of the ideas we sometimes use to help us not to feel so bad about world poverty, and see if they stand up:

Idea one

" **It's all to do with the population explosion. There are too many people in developing countries and they have too many children. There is not enough food for them all, so it's their own fault if they starve.**

It is certainly true that the world's population is increasing—and t is also true that it is increasing fastest in the South. But before we leap to any conclusions it is worth examining the situation more closely:

- One of the major reasons people have large families in poor countries is *because they are so poor*. Let's try to explore this by using an example. If you are a Southern farmer you need labour to work your land: most farming machinery is too expensive. But labour is very expensive too, so you have children.

  In this way you provide for your labour needs and some protection against the time when you become too feeble to work yourself. There is a good chance that some of your children will die before growing up, so you have to have a number of them to make sure that things will be all right.

- People in rich countries can afford to practise birth control: they don't need to have children. So the populations of these countries are declining, or rising only slowly. But these are still the countries which consume most of the world's food !

- The countries with most people per square mile are in the North, not the South.

- Even though the world's population is increasing,

the world probably still produces enough food to feed everybody adequately.

So the idea that world poverty is all to do with people in the South having too many children is not as convincing as it seems when you begin to examine it. There may well be a world population problem. But in the South the problem is a *result* of poverty. Many people believe that the real answer therefore lies in a better distribution of wealth. (See also Chapter 28.)

Idea two

" **It's nothing to do with us. We should look after our own people, not keep sending money abroad. It's not our fault they are poor: they must learn to look after themselves.**

It's true that the blame for the poverty of the countries in the South does not rest with us *as individuals*. None of us has deliberately set out to starve a Southern baby to death, and we did not ask to be born into rich countries.

But in another sense what is happening is 'our' fault—because *as a community* those who live in the North benefit from the sufferings of people in the South.

For instance, the reason many Southern countries have got into debt with Northern banks is because Northern firms encourage them to give up their traditional patterns of farming and instead start producing a few specialized crops for sale to us.

This is called 'cash cropping'. It works reasonably well until the price of the crop falls—which is caused by the same Northern firms shopping around to see where they can get the cheapest deals. The Southern countries' economies go bust as a result.

The Southern governments then have to borrow money from the only place where they can get it: the North again ! In simple terms this means that our cheap coffee, sugar, tea, cloth and a host of other things we enjoy are only possible because other people are living in a poverty we would never accept for ourselves. If we drink coffee or wear clothes—or any number of other things we take for granted—we cannot really say 'It's nothing to do with us.' It clearly is.

Christians believe that there is another reason why we cannot really say 'it is nothing to do with us'. It is a fundamental Christian belief that all people are made in the image of God and are infinitely valuable (see Chapter 5.) Therefore Christians believe it is wrong for people to be indifferent to one another: the suffering of one person, no matter how far away, should affect us all. If we *are* indifferent to one another, we are failing God and failing to be truly human—and in that case we certainly can be blamed as individuals.

In St Luke's Gospel, Jesus tells a terrifying story about this:

 Read Luke 16:19–31

Christian action

Christians feel that it is part of their religious duty to help the poor. For Christians living in the North, this means helping in some way to improve the conditions of those in the South. So a number of those Christian charities have been set up as **development agencies**. Christian Aid and CAFOD are two of these.

These Ghanaian women are part of a village group supported by Christian Aid through the Food for Hunger Campaign. Helping people to support themselves is far better than hand-outs.

CHRISTIAN AID

Christian Aid grew out of the work undertaken by the Protestant churches of Britain after the Second World War to help refugees in Europe. In its early days it was called 'The Department of Inter-Church Aid and Refugee Service,' but it changed its name in 1964 as its work grew and it began to focus on aid outside Europe—which by now had largely recovered from the effects of the war.

Christian Aid has always been an ecumenical organization and is supported today by more than 40 different denominations of Christians in the UK. Christian Aid is probably best known for its 'Christian Aid Week'. For seven days in May, church members from all over the country make door-to-door collections for the world's poor.

Overall, Christian Aid raised over £20 million in the financial year 1990–91—and received a further £11 million in government grants to help with its work. It claims that 85% of this money goes directly to help the needy, with only 15% being spent on administration.

Christian Aid's 'Statement of Commitment' (opposite) sums up its aims:

In penitence and hope we commit ourselves to strengthen the poor against injustice.

The majority of the world's people have scarcely enough to keep them alive. They have little or no say in what happens to them.

Unlike the strong they cannot protect or further their own interests.

We cannot be content to alleviate their suffering. It must be brought to an end.

We must act strategically to strengthen the arm of the poor until they can stand up to those who so often act against them and have the power to determine their own development under God.

This CAFOD worker in Zambia is engaged in home-based health care for AIDS patients. The 18-year-old mother and her 11-month-old baby are both HIV positive.

We believe this commitment, above all to a strategy for justice, is required of us by our Christian faith, which also requires us to look beyond a world that is fair to a Kingdom that is more fair; beyond the power of the strong to strength made perfect in weakness; beyond justice to forgiveness and reconciliation.

CAFOD

CAFOD is a Roman Catholic organization. Its initials stand for 'The Catholic Fund for Overseas Development,' and it was set up by the Catholic bishops of England and Wales in 1962. It has aims very similar to those of Christian Aid, and the two charities work very closely together in many areas today. Although it has full-time staff, CAFOD has no members. The idea is that CAFOD is supposed to be the Catholic Church living out one part of its faith. So every Catholic in England and Wales is a part of CAFOD, which uses the Catholic organizations which already exist—especially parishes and schools—to put its message across and to raise funds.

CAFOD makes particular use of the practice of deliberately going without food (or fasting), which is strongly rooted in Catholic tradition and which is linked particularly to prayer (see Matthew 6:6 and 17–18). The first Friday in October and the second Friday in Lent are set aside by Catholics in England and Wales as Family Fast Days.

These are used as special days of prayer for the poor, when those who are fit and healthy eat little or nothing in order to feel something of the suffering experienced by the world's hungry all the time. The money which would have been used to buy food on these days is then donated to CAFOD and used in its projects around the world.

Education is an essential part of the work of CAFOD and Christian Aid. Some of this takes place in the Southern countries as part of the projects they run in partnership with the people of the South. But their workers say that perhaps even more important is their educational work in the countries of the North, which is aimed at raising the awareness of the rich about the problems of poverty, correcting some prejudiced ideas, and helping Christians to realize their responsibilities. An important area of co-operation between CAFOD and Christian Aid is in the production of educational materials.

Follow-up

1 Describe two major differences between the living standards of people living in the North and South.

2 (a) What was the Brandt Report?
(b) Summarize two of its recommendations in your own words.

3 Describe in your own words the work of either Christian Aid or CAFOD.

4 'Give a man a fish and you will feed him for a day: teach him how to fish and he will feed himself for life.' Explain the meaning of this saying and its relevance for the work of the development agencies.

5 Explain the reasons why a Christian would find Jesus' story of the Rich Man and Lazarus relevant to a discussion of the economic divisions between North and South.

For discussion

'Population growth does not cause poverty: poverty causes population growth.' Discuss this in groups and say whether or not you agree with it.

Activity

Design a poster, write a poem or prepare a school liturgy on the theme 'Our Divided World'.

The past 150 years have seen great changes in the world. Some of these changes have been exciting and wonderful. But some have been very worrying.

Industrialization and advances in travel and communication have brought great benefits, but also new problems for society. Many of these have to do with the differences between rich and poor:

- The gap between rich countries and poor countries has got wider and wider.

- Huge amounts of money have been spent on modern weapons.

- There has been a lot of friction between workers and owners in industry.

- Unemployment has risen in the developed countries.

Because problems like these raise questions for the whole of society we call them **social questions**.

There has been a strong emphasis on social teaching in the Catholic and Protestant churches since the end of the nineteenth century. All through this period, they have tried to work out how the Christian commitment to the poor should be carried out in the modern world.

The Roman Catholic Church

Roman Catholics are encouraged by the Church to think about social questions and to take their responsibilities to the poor very seriously. In 1987 Pope John Paul II published an encyclical called *Sollicitudo Rei Socialis* ('Social Concern'). Here are some of the most important issues he raised.

Causes of poverty in the modern world

There are several new and worrying causes of poverty:

- The world markets work in favour of the rich and powerful: profits are not shared equally. This causes homelessness and unemployment in rich countries, while poor countries cannot develop their economies properly and their people are kept in poverty.

- International debt has crippled the economies of many countries in the Southern hemisphere (often called 'Third World' countries.) They have had to borrow so much money from banks in developed nations that nearly all the wealth they create now has to go to paying back interest. There is nothing left for the people. Developed nations take much more from poorer countries in the form of debt repayment than they give in aid.

- For most of the time since the Second World War the world has been divided into two 'blocs' with capitalist countries on one hand and communist countries on the other. This has meant four things:
  - the attention of world leaders has been focussed on the Cold War and not on the problem of world poverty;
  - huge amounts of money have been spent on armaments which could have been used to relieve poverty;
  - the rich countries have given aid to the poor countries to get them on their side in the Cold War and not to help them properly (this has often taken the form of supplying weapons);
  - when wars have happened there have been large numbers of refugees adding to all the other problems; war has also caused famine.

- There have been problems to do with rises and falls in population. But sometimes the measures taken to deal with these have been brutal and wrong. They have denied people's human rights and forced people to use methods of controlling birth which the Church cannot accept (see Chapter 10).

We can summarize all of this by saying that all the long-term problems of poverty in today's world are *avoidable* ones. There is enough food in the world for everyone. The money spent on weapons could easily provide clothes, housing and medical treatment for the entire world population. Natural disasters such as floods or famines cause temporary poverty, but could be dealt with relatively quickly if we could organize things better.

So what is wrong with us? Why can we not get it together and sort things out?

According to the Catholic Church the answer to this question is that many of our ways of thinking have been wrong. Put simply, poverty has been caused by sin. People have been thinking of development simply in terms of profits or political power without taking into account issues of morality and human rights or the way God intends the world to be. Because individual people have thought like this (many Christians included), trade and politics have gone wrong and people have suffered and died as a result. In *Sollicitudo Rei Socialis* Pope John Paul calls the institutions of trade the *structures of sin*. The Church teaches that these must be changed in favour of the poor.

The way forward

All of this can seem like gloomy reading. But Catholics can point to great signs of hope and love. People today, especially young people, are probably more aware of the problem of poverty than they have been at any other time this century. Although China is still communist, the cold war is over. The United Nations organization has promoted development and education in poor countries and has suggested minimum levels of aid which the rich countries ought to be providing. And there is the teaching of the Church itself, which has been very influential in bringing some of these changes about.

The Catholic Church teaches that Christians have a duty to inform themselves about the problem of poverty and to pray, think and act to protect the poor in everything they do. The Church calls this 'having an **option for the Poor**'. By changing their own hearts Christians can begin to change the individual sins which build up into the 'structures of sin' we see in trade and politics and which cause so much suffering. In many Catholic parishes *Justice and Peace Groups* have been set up to help with this. There Catholics can meet together to discuss the Church's teaching and decide what they should do about it. And by supporting CAFOD (see Chapter 27) and similar organizations in other countries every Catholic is involved in this aspect of the Church's mission.

Above all, the Mass is the inspiration for Catholics as they think about social questions. At the Mass the people bring the world's goods to the altar. These are bread and wine which people have made from the things God gave them. Everybody has paid something towards their cost: they belong to everybody equally. On the altar Catholics believe these are transformed into the Body and Blood of Christ who shares himself in love with all. So for Catholics the Mass is a *sharing meal* at which people share with one another and God shares himself with them. But the Mass is not just spmething to be done on Sundays and then forgotten. Living out the meaning of the Mass in the world means sharing there as well.

MODERN CATHOLIC SOCIAL TEACHING

◆ **Pope Leo XIII**   *Modern Catholic social teaching really began in 1891 with Pope Leo XIII's encyclical 'Rerum Novarum' ('About New Things'). The Industrial Revolution had produced a new type of capitalism and the Pope was worried by the terrible conditions which had resulted for many of the poor. He wrote that in this new system:*

'Workers have been surrendered, isolated and helpless, to the hard-heartedness of employers and the greed of unchecked competition . . .a small number of very rich men have been able to lay upon the teeming masses of the labouring poor a yoke little better than slavery itself.'

◆ **Pope Pius XI**   *In 1931 Pope Pius XI issued the encyclical 'Quadragesimo Anno' ('Forty Years After', because it came forty years after 'Rerum Novarum'). 'Quadragesimo Anno' was especially concerned with the way rich countries were using their economic power to exploit poorer countries.*

◆ **Pope John XXIII**   *John XXIII was Pope from 1958 until 1963. He carried on the tradition of social teaching in two encyclicals: 'Mater et Magistra' ('Mother and Teacher') and 'Pacem in Terris' ('Peace on Earth'), published in 1961 and 1963. Like Pius XI, Pope John wanted to see a balance restored between the rich and poor. In 'Mater et Magistra' he suggested that more should be done to improve the conditions of farming communities, and that workers in profitable industries should have proper shares in the wealth they have helped to create. In 'Pacem in Terris' he called attention to the horrors of the arms race. 'Nuclear weapons,' he said, 'must be banned.'*

◆ **Vatican II**   *John XXIII called the Second Vatican Council (see Chapter 3). The Council summed up* the Church's social teaching in the introduction to one of its most important declarations, 'Gaudium et Spes' (The Pastoral Constitution of the Church in the Modern World). It says:

'The joys and the hopes, the griefs and the anxieties of the people of this age, especially those who are poor or in any way afflicted, these too are the joys and hopes, the griefs and anxieties of the followers of Christ.'

◆ **Pope Paul VI**   After Vatican II, Pope Paul VI continued the tradition of social teaching in his encyclical 'Populorum Progressio' ('The Development of Peoples'), 1967. Pope Paul pointed out that God intended the world for everybody but there was great inequality in the way resources were distributed. Huge amounts of money were being spent on modern weapons when countless millions were starving. Christians had a moral duty to think about these things and act to change them.

Pope Paul set up a new department in the administration of the Church, called the Pontifical Commission for Justice and Peace ('Iustitia et Pax'). This Commission is still at work today. Pope Paul said that its job was

'To bring to the whole of God's People the full knowledge of the part expected of them at the present time, so as to further the progress of poorer peoples, to encourage social justice among nations, and to offer to less developed nations the means whereby they can further their own progress.'

▮ The work of the Protestant churches

In Chapter 26 we saw that the Bible calls all Christians to serve the poor. Living this out can provide a practical way for Christians of different denominations to work together and learn from one another as they struggle to improve society and help those in need. Now we shall explore examples of Christian action for the poor from among the Protestant communities and churches.

The Salvation Army

The Salvation Army began in London in 1865. Its founder was a Methodist minister named William Booth.

The London of 1865 was a terrible place to be poor. Homelessness, prostitution, disease and drunkenness were common. Many 'respectable' people at the time closed their eyes to these problems. They told themselves—and one another— that the poor were poor through their own fault. They thought they were idle, ignorant and depraved—that they did not deserve any help.

But William Booth was different. He was not sentimental. He knew that many people, sunk in the despair of poverty, destroyed themselves with alcohol and turned to crime. But his honesty and his Christian faith would not allow him to take any easy way out: after all, Jesus had not walked away from sinners. People were still people, whatever they had done. 'They are all men,' he wrote. 'All with a spark of God in them, which can never be wholly obscured while life exists.'

Booth believed that Christianity demanded care for the poor even when others said they did not deserve it. He believed that a Christian country could never simply turn its back on people, saying, 'It's all their own fault.' Society had a duty to provide even for its most careless members. 'If any social scheme is to be comprehensive and practical,' he said, 'it must provide for the drunkard and the harlot . . .the improvident and out of work.'

In this way the Salvation Army began as an attempt to live out the Bible's call to serve the poor in nineteenth-century London. Booth and his helpers felt that many of the people they were trying to help were put off Christianity by the solemnity and difficult language of traditional church services. Many of the poor had never really heard the Gospel preached— and, like all Christians, Booth believed that people needed to accept the Gospel message if they were going to be really happy and free.

Booth's answer to this problem was to set up his organization in a way which was deliberately very different from the existing Christian churches. The poor found these too hard to relate to—but they knew about soldiers, uniforms and marching bands. So Booth took these ideas from the military, and in 1878 the Salvation Army adopted the form in which is still exists today. Its ministers are called officers, and have ranks like those in the army—Booth himself was its first General.

Each officer is trained in theology and field work for two years. Ordinary members are called 'soldiers', the

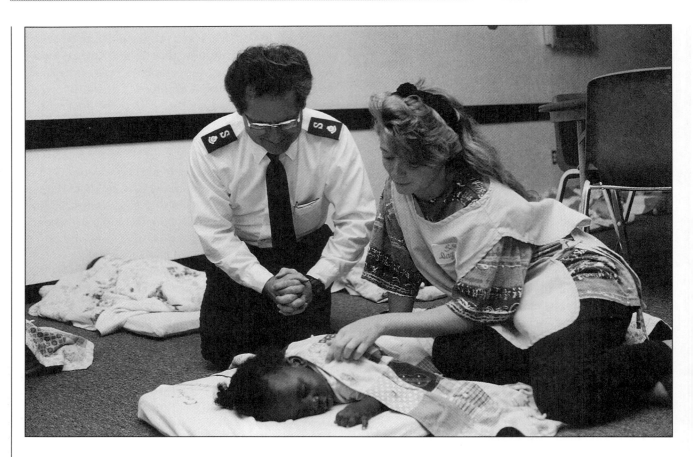

declaration of faith signed by each new member is called the 'Articles of War', and the meeting-house for worship is called a 'Citadel'.

The worship of the Salvation Army is centred on reading the Bible, preaching and music, which is accompanied on instruments played by the Corps members—especially brass instruments. Services are regularly held in the open air, where the sound of a brass band can still attract a crowd today, just as it did in London in the 1870s.

The Salvation Army has worked with alcoholics since its foundation, and is a teetotal organization: Booth and his followers had seen the damage done by drink and were convinced that only an absolute ban on alcohol would result in long-term release.

Today, the Salvation Army has grown to be an international organization with headquarters in over 80 countries, about 25,000 officers and a membership of more than $2^1/_2$ million. It operates more than 3,600 social institutions. It is Britain's sixth largest charity, running food outlets and hostels for the homeless in inner cities, drop-in centres for the young unemployed, and alcohol counselling and

From the very beginning the Salvation Army has worked to help the neediest people, feeding the hungry, housing the homeless, showing the love of Christ in practical ways. It still does so today.

rehabilitation centres.

Is its work still needed today? Perhaps we could reflect on the fact that in 1904 census figures showed an average of 2,000 people sleeping rough in London each night. Things seemed to get better after the First World War. But today, in the 1990s, the Salvation Army estimates that the number of street homeless in London is . . . 2,000.

The Church of England

We have seen that William Booth began the Salvation Army partly because he thought that the familiar Christian churches were failing to bring the Gospel message to the poor in London. And he may very well have been right.

In England in the nineteenth century, most people who went to church were the reasonably well-off middle class. The national church, the Church of England, had for years been organized in a system of parishes which dated back to the time before the

St Francis of Assisi

Catholics and many other Christians look to the saints to provide them with examples of how to live the Christian life. One of the saints who is remembered for his love of the poor is St Francis of Assisi (1181–1226).

Francis was born into a very rich merchant family. As a young man he spent money freely and generally had a good time.

Francis' life changed dramatically when he was twenty-one. After spending a few months as a prisoner-of-war in a nearby town he returned to Assisi ill and demoralized. It took him some while to get better, and during this time he became convinced that there must be more to life.

He tried to return to his old habits, but they did not seem so much fun any more. He'd been a Christian of a kind, but now he spent more and more time in prayer, thinking about the things of God. Slowly he became convinced that God was calling him to serve the poor.

After a pilgrimage to Rome he gave up his old ways completely, and spent his time caring for the lepers who hung around outside the walls of Assisi, washing their sores and feeding them. He also rebuilt some broken-down old churches in the nearby countryside with his own hands. His father beat him, locked him up and then disowned him, completely astonished and horrified by what Francis was doing. But Francis did not care. He asked the Bishop of Assisi to protect him, gave everything he had back to his father (including the clothes he was wearing!) and carried on as before, living rough, caring for lepers and rebuilding churches.

One day Francis was listening to the Gospel at Mass in one of the churches he had rebuilt when some words of Jesus struck home. In the reading, Jesus was telling the disciples to leave everything behind and preach the coming of God's Kingdom (Matthew 10:7–19).

At once Francis knew what he had to do. God was calling him to live with the poorest of the poor, to share their life completely and to preach the Gospel. And that is exactly what he did. He gave away what few remaining possessions he had and spent the rest of his life teaching, preaching and caring for those in poverty like his own.

At first many people thought he was mad, although some kind souls gave him enough scraps to keep him from starving. But soon his obvious holiness attracted others to join him: some as brothers (friars) sharing his life, some as nuns serving the poor in constant prayer, and some as married people living out a simple version of his 'rule' in the world. Today the Franciscans are the biggest religious order in the world.

Industrial Revolution—a time when most people lived in the countryside. During the Industrial Revolution, when people began to move into the towns to find work in the new factories and railways, the Church of England was slow to catch up. It remained strong in the countryside, but it suffered losses among the new urban working class, who largely lost the habit of going to church. By the time new city parishes were opened up, much of the damage had already been done. The Church of England had become a largely middle- and upper-class organization.

But this did not mean that the Church of England lost its sense of mission to the poor. During the late nineteenth and twentieth centuries, the Anglo-Catholic and Evangelical movements (though strongly opposed to one another in ideas to do with faith and worship) both worked hard in slum parishes. In this way a strong tradition of teaching about social justice grew up in Anglicanism—and this is a tradition which still continues today. Let's look at two important examples from the recent past.

BIAS TO THE POOR and FAITH IN THE CITY

David Sheppard became the Anglican Bishop of Liverpool in 1975 after spending twenty years working in parish ministry in East London. A former England cricketer, public schoolboy and a Cambridge graduate, Bishop David had a relatively privileged upbringing. Yet his experiences working in some of the most deprived areas of England and his reflections of the meaning of the Bible's message have made him the most famous champion of the poor in the Church of England today. This is partly through his work in Liverpool, but for most people outside the city is is through his book 'Bias to the Poor' which was published in 1983 and quickly became one of the best-selling religious books of the 1980s.

In his book, Bishop David argued that the Bible message of Christianity shows a strong bias in favour of the poor. Christians in Britain, he said, need to look hard at British society, where there is a great deal of poverty, racism and injustice; they must work for change. While Bishop David was writing 'Bias to the Poor' serious rioting broke out in Toxteth, a particularly deprived area of Liverpool and part of his diocese. The riots seemed to underline the urgency of what he had to say.

Bishop David works closely with the Roman Catholic Archbishop of Liverpool, Derek Warlock. Together they have been outspoken in defence of the poor and in criticizing government policies. This has not always made them popular with politicians, but is a good example of how Christians from different traditions can work together on a project and learn from one another's insights.

'Bias to the Poor' was a very influential book, but at the end of the day it was just one man's work. The sorts of issues that Bishop David raised were taken up by the Church of England as a whole in 1983, when the Archbishop of Canterbury appointed a Commission to look at the problems of the inner cities.

The Commission published its report in 1985. It was called 'Faith in the City—a call for Action by Church and Nation'. Once again, the report criticized government policies. It said, among other things, that not enough was being done to create jobs, that unemployment and child benefits were too small, and that more provision should be made for the homeless. It implied that the government was dragging its feet on some much-needed reforms of the legal system and criticized much of the thinking behind its economic policies.

The report also made recommendations about how the Church of England could be more effective in its work in the inner cities, for instance, by looking at ways in which the Church itself could be involved in job creation schemes. It urged Christians to continue to question the morality of a system of economics which appeared to be making the rich richer and the poor poorer.

Today, Anglican parishes in better-off areas contribute a proportion of their annual income to congregations in the inner cities and other deprived areas.

Mother Teresa of Calcutta

Like Saint Francis, Mother Teresa came to her way of life gradually. She was born in Yugoslavia and spent a long time as a nun and schoolteacher in India. In 1946, however, she felt that God was asking more of her.

She got permission from her Order to teach children in the worst slums in Calcutta. Many had never had any education. But there was worse to come. In the dustbins and filthy streets she saw children and adults dying, their bodies gnawed at by the rats even while they were still alive. In this way she began her life work: the care of the dying and the rescue of abandoned children.

Like Francis, she has attracted others to join in her work, and now there are houses of the Sisters of Charity in many countries of the world. Their mother house is still in the disused Hindu temple in Calcutta, given to Mother Teresa in the early days. Eating the simplest food and with no possessions of their own, the Brothers and Sisters care for the dying, run hospitals for lepers, and do what they can to feed the hungry.

In 1976 Mother Teresa won the Nobel Peace Prize. 'Our love of the poor' she says, 'comes from our love of Jesus. We try to serve him in the poorest of the poor.'

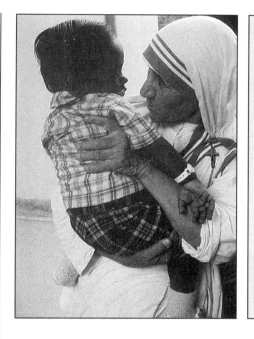

Mother Teresa has become world famous for her work in the slums of Calcutta. Countless others, unknown, reach out in selfless love to those in need.

Follow-up

Questions

1 What do Catholics mean by 'the Option for the Poor'?

2 Outline the teaching of the Catholic Church on the causes of poverty.

3 St Francis of Assisi showed his love for the poor by living in poverty himself. Mother Teresa and her Brothers and Sisters do the same today.
(a) What good do you think lives like this do to the rest of us?
(b) Do you think anything other than this is needed to help the poor? Explain your answer by referring to the teaching of the Catholic Church.

4 In what ways might a Catholic parish try to serve the poor?

5 Quick answer questions:
(a) Who founded the Salvation Army?
(b) Why does it have a rule forbidding alcohol?
(c) How many people were estimated to be living rough in London in 1904, and how has this changed today?
(d) What was 'Bias to the Poor' and when was it published?
(e) What was 'Faith in the City' and when was it published?

6 Explain why Booth felt the need to give his organization a structure which was different from that of the existing churches, and how he achieved this.

7 Explain the effect of the Industrial Revolution on the relationship between the Church of England and the working class. You may find that using diagrams will help you.

8 Explain why both 'Bias to the Poor' and 'Faith in the City' attracted criticism from some politicians.

For discussion

'Charity begins at home. We shouldn't be sending money abroad when we have got people in need here.' In your opinion, how should a Christian respond to this statement?

'If you are going to be serious about Christianity, then you can't help it affecting your politics.' What do you think?

Activity

Copy out and learn the quotation from the Vatican II document *Gaudium et Spes* from this chapter.

Draw up a table of the major events in Catholic social teaching since the 1890s. We have done the first one for you:

Title	English translation of title	Who issued it	Date
Rerum Novarum	'About New things'	Pope Leo XIII	1891

Collect some newspaper cuttings, magazine pictures or other published material which you think could be used to argue that Britain is still an unjust society. Present these as a classroom wall display, set alongside some appropriate Bible quotations about justice and concern for the poor (Chapter 26 will help you). What does your display tell you about being a Christian in Britain today?

Children have always been especially vulnerable, and there are many organizations set up to help them in different ways. Here we look at two of the largest children's 'charities': The Children's Society, founded by the Church of England, and NCH Action for Children, founded by the Methodist Church, both in response to the needs of homeless children.

The Children's Society

The Children's Society (like NCH Action for Children, see page 140) was founded in London in the last century. With 30,000 homeless children in the capital in 1881, it is not surprising that such organizations were needed. The poverty and squalor described in the novels of Charles Dickens were fact, not fiction.

The Children's Society began with the work of Edward Rudolf, a civil servant who taught at a Sunday school. Worried when two of his pupils started missing lessons, he went to look for them. He found them begging. Rudolf was determined to find homes for them and for others like them. He founded the Waifs and Strays, which later became known as The Church of England Children's Society or simply The Children's Society.

Today, The Children's Society runs over 100 projects in England and Wales:

- 50 **Family Centres** provide support for young families in areas where family life is under pressure.

The Children's Society

A Safe House

'You don't have time to feel anything—you get caught up just trying to survive . . . I have now been on the streets on and off since I was nine years old.'

Alex is now seventeen. She arrived at The Children's Society's Safe House in Leeds: one of their refuges for runaways.

'The Safe House is the place where I got my first hug. In Safe Houses you know you are going to be listened to. When I was five, I told a schoolteacher what was happening. She told me not to make up dirty stories. So I kept my mouth shut.'

Safe Houses provide counselling, care and support for people like Alex. They help them to be healed from their experiences. The Leeds project leader Mary Clarke says that the young people are usually in turmoil when they arrive.

'They ask a lot of questions about their safety. It is important they understand we are nothing to do with the police or social services . . . Sometimes they are literally starving when they arrive and the first thing they need is a meal. Or they might want a bath.'

Although the location is kept secret to protect the young people, the Leeds Safe House is in an ordinary street. This prevents it feeling like an institution. It has room for eight runaways at any one time. In the eight months after it first opened, it helped fifty young people under seventeen.

London Community Work Project

'In the hotel where we used to stay the cockroaches would be crawling all over the bed and up on the windows.'

This was said by a child who was being helped by The Children's Society's Community Work Project in London.

In London in 1981, 4650 families lived in temporary accommodation, mainly in bed and breakfast hotels. In 1991, the figure had risen to over 34,000 households, including 30,000 children. The rising trend continues.

The London Community Work Project co-operates with other agencies to help the homeless and to make others aware of the growing problem. When refugees arrived in London from such places as Somalia and Eritrea, where they faced persecution and war, the Project helped to ensure that they had access to education and to local health and advice services. It is also active in Tower Hamlets, where over half the families live below the poverty line.

The Children's Society provides safe houses for vulnerable people who have run away from home.

- **Residential Units** helped 285 children in 1992. The Society prefers to help young people in their families and in the local community, but the Residential Units meet cases of exceptional need.

- **Ordinary housing projects** provide ordinary homes for young people with disabilities, so that they can lead a full life in the community. This is also achieved through the **Homefinding Scheme**, which finds them good homes.

- **Leaving Care** projects help young people to adjust to their new situation when they have left local authority care. It is estimated that 40% of those sleeping rough in London have been in the care of the local authorities. Under the Children's Act of 1989, the law says support must be given to such people, but not all local authorities have provided it.

- **Legal advice** is given to represent children's interest in court, often particularly needed in divorce proceedings.

- **Street work projects**. We have already looked at the case of Alex and the Leeds Safe House. There are 98,000 incidents every year. Sadly, some runaways will drift into crime and prostitution if they are not helped.

- Other work includes the London Community Work Project (see box); helping young people who are
  - in trouble with the police
  - or have become addicted to drugs, alcohol or gambling
  - or have been sexually abused
  - or are suffering from trauma following their parent's divorce
  - or have severe emotional problems.

The Children's Society stresses that it is not enough to deal with the effects of such problems. It is also essential to deal with the causes; to try to prevent such problems occurring in the first place.

WHERE DOES THE MONEY COME FROM?

It cost £25.4 million to run the work of The Children's Society from March 1991 to March 1992. Of that money, 5.6% was spent on vital administration.

£14,654,000 came from voluntary giving, from these sources:

- ◆ Door-to-door collections during Children's Society Week 1991:   £545,383

- ◆ Christmas Link: a paper chain contest, hosted by Roy Castle: £93,000

  (The longest chain, made by four schools in Plymouth, was over three kilometres long!)

- ◆ Donations from the BBC's 'Children in Need' Appeal: £400,000

◆ *Charity boxes, which the
Society gives to people
to fill in their homes:*   £1,623,000

◆ *Legacies (people giving
money in their
wills):*   £6,074,000

◆ *149 Children's Society
shops, run by
volunteers:*   £1,000,000

Other fundraising events included:

◆ *Collections at Christmas Christingle services*

◆ *A sponsored 'knit in', promoted by **Prima**
magazine, whose readers knitted jumpers
which were then sold. Littlewoods donated the
prizes.*

◆ *Covenants (a legal term: when someone
promises to give a certain amount regularly, the
charity also receives the tax the giver would
normally have paid on that sum)*

◆ *Pay-roll giving (made from monthly pay and
given directly to a charity)*

◆ *An 'American tea party' at a Blackpool hotel*

◆ *A clergyman playing the complete organ works
of J.S. Bach to raise funds for the Society.*

*The Children's Society was also the nominated
charity of the Children's World chain and of the
Daily Mail Ideal Home Exhibition.*

The rest of the money came from:

◆ *central and local
government*   £8,883,000

◆ *investments*   £1,526,000

*The figures sound vast, but the Society still needs
more, and also asks for the prayers of its
supporters. It ended the year £298,000 in the red,
while the needs of young people and the
demands on its resources continue to grow.*

The National Children's Home
(NCH Action For Children)

The National Children's Home was founded in 1869 by
the Reverend Thomas Bowman Stephenson, a
Methodist minister who went on to become President
of the Methodist Conference. Stephenson was
appalled that thousands of children in London were
homeless, hungry and poor. He and two of his
colleagues leased a cottage in Lambeth, which
became the first Children's Home.

The National Children's Home, now named NCH
Action For Children, today remains part of the
Methodist Church. These are some of its principles:

● The recognition of the worth and value of each
individual. Each individual and his or her family have
the capacity to grow in love and to develop their
potential.

● The need to improve social conditions and to
challenge injustice.

● The NCH's work reflects the work of Jesus, who
loved people who were on the fringes of society or
excluded from it.

● The NCH's work embraces all in need, regardless of
their ethnic origin, religious beliefs or other
distinctions.

In 1992, the NCH's budget was 50 million. It helped
over 16,000 children through over 200 projects. More
than half of these projects aim to keep families
together.

In 1992, the projects included:

● 73 community-based **Family Centres**, which
provided support for young families, including
single-parent families, who faced problems. They
offered them a place to talk through their difficulties
helping them to stay together and to grow together.

● 8 **Centres for sexually abused children**, who are
given counselling, psychotherapy and other help.

● 10 **Counselling Projects** for young people with
problems such as homelessness, debt and drug
abuse.

● 25 **Inter-dependence Projects**, to provide support
for young people leaving care.

● 7 **Conciliation Services**, which assist couples who

Fiona and Kate

Fiona and Kate are just two of the people helped by the NCH in 1992.

Fiona

Fiona was fourteen. She and her four younger brothers and sisters were sexually abused by her father for a number of years. She missed school and frequently ran away from home. When she was in care, her father's ill-treatment of the family became known. He was sent to prison for ten years.

She blamed herself for splitting up the family. Her mother was desperately upset: she had not known what was going on, and Fiona's reaction to her was one of anger. Fiona's younger brother developed a speech problem and was not talking.

The NCH helped the children and their mother to become closer: to be reconciled. They all received individual counselling. Fiona and her mother also met together with a counsellor, and the whole family met as a group so that they could learn to overcome the stress on the family's life that was caused by the abuse.

Kate

Kate had been in local authority care since she was ten. Her parents had physically abused her and had then abandoned her. She had tried to live with a number of foster families, but could not settle.

The NCH's Eastbourne Community Support Service helped her to achieve her aim of living independently. The project's initial assessment period enabled Kate and the Service to get to know each other. Kate agreed on a placement in approved lodgings, with people around who could help when she needed them. This worked out well, and she was given a four month tenancy in an NCH bedsit.

She learned how to run a home (coping on your own with laundry, cooking and cleaning is not easy at first!). NCH staff helped her to come to terms with the way her parents had treated her, and to understand why she had problems with foster families.

At the end of her tenancy, Kate moved into a bedsit owned by a private sector landlord. The NCH staff continued to support her. She went on to attend a local college, and continued to use the NCH's drop-in facility for friendship and support.

---

divorce to remain on good terms. This helps them, and also allows their children to stay in touch with both their parents.

- 4 **Homefinding Services** which help with adoption. Nearly all the children who have found homes in this way have been neglected or ill-treated, and over half of them have suffered sexual abuse.

- 5 **Respite Care Projects**. These provide short-term facilities for looking after children with special needs, to give their parents a break. (Carers need to be cared for, too.)

- 26 **Community Projects**, often in the poorer areas of the country, which help young people and young families to identify their needs and develop ways of meeting them. Many of these projects work with the local Methodist churches.

- **Overseas projects** in Jamaica, the Eastern Caribbean and Zimbabwe.

Follow-up

Questions

1 Select at least **five** projects run by *either* The Children's Society *or* NCH Action For Children. Explain what these projects do.

2 Look again at the section, 'Where does the money come from?'

You will see that the Children's Society's work cost £25.4 million from March 1991 to March 1992. Suppose everyone in Britain had given the Society just fifty pence a year. That would have raised the money, and more.

The figures in question three show the need is still great. Poverty, starvation and need continue to afflict millions in the world. The charities cannot do everything that needs to be done.

The government raises taxes. These help the

needy in many ways, funding the Health Service, unemployment and supplementary benefit, and so on. In 1992, the government gave £2 billion in aid to developing countries. This money came from taxation.

So, the tax we pay goes in part to help others. We are not allowed by law to keep all our money. It is not all ours to do with as we like.

Carefully read View A and View B. Which do you agree with? If you do not agree with either, why do you disagree, and what do you think?

VIEW A

'Charities should not be necessary. They help, and that's important, but they don't meet all the need. They just don't have enough money. As long as there's no other system, people should keep supporting them. But it would be much better if the government paid the bills for the work charities do now. The government can raise money far more easily than charities can, because it collects taxes. And the government's got more money than charities, so it can do much more too. We could even put up taxes and spend the extra tax revenue on wiping out famine and putting an end to poverty. After all, it's more important that the poor should be fed than that other people should be allowed to keep all their money.'

VIEW B

'The government shouldn't fund any more "charity" type work than it does at the moment. It's up to the individual how much he or she should give. If people don't want to give very much, or even if they don't want to give anything at all, that may be wrong, but it's their choice. You can say that people should give more, but you can't make them. Maybe people with large salaries should be persuaded to live a bit more simply, and cut down on luxuries like a big expensive car when a small cheap one will do. They could give the difference away. They might decide to have a different bank account in which they could put a fair amount of money each month, and give it out as the appeals come up on television. Some people might decide to give away a hundred pounds a month, if they can spare that much. Lots of us could make savings to help others. But you can't force people to give. It has to be up to them.'

3 Think about the following points:

- When the Children's Society was founded in 1881, there were 20,000 homeless children in London.
  In 1991, 30,000 children spent Christmas in a hostel or in bed and breakfast accommodation for the homeless. Some 43,000 children in the United Kingdom run away every year.

- In Jesus' time, many people thought that if you were ill or disabled, it was either because you had sinned or your parents had sinned. It was a punishment for doing wrong. Jesus utterly rejected this idea. (See John 9: 1–41.)

- Today, many people say that if you are poor or homeless, it is your own fault. It is the result of laziness or stupidity.

Now answer this question, giving your reasons in full: 'If people are poor or homeless, it's because they deserve it. It's their own fault.' Is this true?

Activities

- Why does Christianity say Christians should support work like that of the Children's Society and the NCH Action For Children?
  In small groups, work out as many reasons as you can think of. Then report back to the rest of the class.

- In this exercise, your group is the school's new charities committee. You need to come up with some fund-raising activities to raise money for the charity you decide to sponsor. You need to raise as much money as possible, and also to make sure that the charity's work has a high profile in the rest of the school. You also have to try not to offend anyone in the way you raise the money!
  What did you come up with?

Mental handicap

Many people today are either physically or mentally disabled.

The largest group of disabled people in the UK are those who have a learning disability or mental handicap—over a million people.

The work of MENCAP

MENCAP—the Royal Society for Mentally Handicapped Children and Adults—is the largest organization in the UK committed to learning disability issues. In this chapter, we interview three of MENCAP's staff:

- Brian McGinnis, the Special Adviser

- Robert Hunter, the National Development Officer for the Gateway Clubs

- Keith Burgess, the IT and Communications Manager.

Before we start the interview, it is important to make it clear that there is a difference between mental *handicap* and mental *illness*:

'Mental illness' is a blanket term which covers a range of illnesses which affect the mind. These illnesses range from depression to schizophrenia and dementia; they can be treated by drugs and also by psychotherapy.

What do we mean by 'mental handicap'?

Brian McGinnis: It's a combination of lower intelligence—though it's hard to measure intelligence—and lower social skills. In most cases, it strikes people from birth or shortly afterwards, when the brain hasn't fully developed. People with learning disabilities range from those who will go to an ordinary school, get paid employment, marry and have children to people who can't speak, are doubly incontinent, have limited sight and hearing and maybe can't walk.

What is MENCAP for?

Brian McGinnis: It's to support families and individuals with learning disabilities. We educate the public, influence people who take decisions about the lives of people with learning disabilities, and provide direct services.

We were founded in 1946 by parents who had children with learning disabilities. In those days, such children were completely excluded from education: they went to junior training centres and the parents wanted schools for them. There was also the parents' worry, which is still around today: 'What happens when I die? Who'll look after my son or daughter?' We have nearly 400 homes. The residential care work takes the largest amount of our money. Of an annual turnover now over £50 million, about £46 million represents payment for the services we provide, by central and local government. Most of that is for residential services.

Robert Hunter: We also have 700 affiliated Gateway clubs and projects. They have about 40,000 members, 20,000 volunteer helpers and fifteen full time staff. The clubs vary, but they're for social activities and education for leisure. They concentrate on sport and art. There are some specialist clubs: we have water sport clubs in Bristol for swimming, canoeing and so on.

We have a number of junior clubs with links with special needs schools. We play specialized sports like unihoc—hockey that's been adapted for people with learning disabilities. It has simplified rules. We take part in an international football competition in Geneva every year, and there are regional swimming events. There's an element of competition in it but we do send mixed ability teams over. The most important form of competition is competing with yourself.

You use the words 'learning disability' rather than 'handicapped' or 'disabled'. How important is it to use the 'correct' term to describe people?

Robert Hunter: The *most* important thing is that, like the rest of us, they have names! Using 'correct' language can be confusing. People want to avoid giving offence, but 'correct' language just isn't precise enough.

Keith Burgess: I find the language thing a bit irritating, because at the end of the day we're still trying to help the same group of people. The immense debate going on about using the right terms seems to take an awful lot of energy, which could be much better used in helping the people themselves!

How do you help families who have mentally handicapped children?

Brian McGinnis: I think most parents have built up a picture of the son or daughter they want.

Educational success, sporting prowess, physical beauty, endearing personality, that sort of thing. A lot of those expectations are radically changed. So parents need to adjust to the reality of the child they've actually got, as opposed to the one for whom they've been planning and daydreaming.

When a child's born with a disability, you can't give a lecture on what's going to happen in the next forty years. You can give clues as to the way things might go. We put parents in touch with other parents so they can talk to each other about the way forward. We advise people on how to make the best use of social security, education, leisure, social services and the health service. The regulations surrounding these things are complicated. So we give advice to parents so they can get what they need when they need it.

Robert Hunter: The first trauma is learning that your child is disabled. We provide counselling and support to help parents come to terms with that, and put them in touch with *local* support groups. It's more personal if it's someone who lives down the road in your area.

Keith Burgess: I do know one couple who had a mentally handicapped child, and the problems that raised destroyed their marriage in about three years. The older child suffered from his mother's lack of time: she had to concentrate on the child with the disability.

Brian McGinnis: One of the mothers we've worked with has a grown-up daughter who's just begun in residential care. She says she had much more trouble with her non-handicapped children than with her handicapped daughter.

So having a mentally handicapped child can be a positive, enriching experience ?

Brian McGinnis: Yes. One of our colleagues here has adopted two handicapped youngsters. They're both in their teens now. He says you can get to play sandcastles on the beach for years after parents with 'normal' children would have given up ! You have children who are far more dependent on you. So you're really wanted and needed, rather than being pushed aside as the years pass.

You can't generalize, and to say that all people with disabilities are little angels is silly. But with a lot of them, there is something rather special and appealing about their simple approach to life. They often have an uncomplicated attitude to other people: they're willing to welcome them, when lots of us are defensive about them. You get some 'mentally handicapped' people who are very direct, very approachable, very caring.

Robert Hunter: Parents are sometimes anxious that they shouldn't do things that are risky or difficult. If some of the parents saw some of the things they do in Gateway clubs, they'd have a fit ! It's interesting that you get some people who become really lively and interesting in a Gateway club.

Yet the minute mum and dad arrive to take them home, there's a complete reversal to dependence. You know they're saying, 'I'd better act a bit differently, because they expect something different.' You can educate parents out of this, sometimes by shock tactics. You know, 'What do you mean, you went abseiling at the weekend ?' We don't, of course, take silly risks.

Do you think it's better to care for people in their families rather than in residential care ?

Brian McGinnis: It's better to care for people in their families when they're at the age at which the rest of us expect to be in our families. It's not necessarily the same when you're twenty, thirty, forty or fifty. You expect to have a home of your own, and not to live with mum and dad. That's what the society's residential care is about.

The homes are for small groups: three to six people in a house with staff to help. The members of staff might be someone who calls occasionally, or, more commonly, someone who is on the premises all the time. And there's one-to-one if you need one-to-one.

Keith Burgess: The houses would be in the community, because we're not trying to separate people from normal life.

Robert Hunter: A woman on one of our holidays recently turned round to her mum and said, 'I'm twenty-three, I want to have my own flat.' If people are properly cared for, these are the sort of experiences they can have.

Moving on: the law allows for foetuses to be aborted because they are handicapped. What are your views on that ?

Brian McGinnis: The law allows abortion after the normal twenty-four week limit if a foetus is handicapped. It's a personal view, but I'm unhappy about what that says. It seems to be devaluing people with disabilities.

There's a frame of mind which moves from saying, 'You abort the child who would have been handicapped,' to saying, 'The child who needs a lot of medical care to keep him or her alive really doesn't deserve that medical care.' You can then slide into asking, 'If somebody is going to cost an awful lot of money in childhood and adult life, can we really afford that as a society?' I don't think anyone automatically makes the jump, but you can slide from one to the other. That's a real worry.

You're Christians, although MENCAP itself is not a religious organization. Why do you think God allows people to be born with handicaps?

Robert Hunter: If God created, God created well. After a long time of working with people with disabilities, I felt it was as if God was saying to me, 'Stop making an issue out of this. This is a person, you're a person.'

Brian McGinnis: It seems to me that we all fall so far short of the ideal, physically, mentally, morally or whatever, that it doesn't make much sense to draw a strange distinction between people who fail in a moral sense and people who fall short in some physical or mental way.

There was a man called Nick* who had a severe learning difficulty in the L'Arche Community in Lambeth. He was also a victim of advancing senile dementia. They were sitting in a group talking about what peace meant. Nick was a man of very few words, but he drew a picture of Christ on the cross with the moon and stars under one arm, and the sun under another.

When he was asked to explain, he said, 'Christ died to give us peace.' And that was from somebody who was severely handicapped, who might have been thought not to have understood much of the conversation that was going on around him. The drawing he'd done was not just about peace for human beings. It was that early Christian vision of Christ's death bringing peace to the universe.

* For the story of Nick, see Therese Vantor, *Nick: Man of the Heart.*

The biggest group of those with learning disability is people born with Down's syndrome.

Physical handicap

So far, we have looked at mental disability. Here we are going to explore the work of two people who have been involved with those who have physical handicaps.

Physical handicap may be a great disadvantage but people like Mary Verghese have proved it need be no barrier to great achievement.

Mary Verghese

Mary Verghese, a devout member of the Orthodox Syrian Church, was born in 1925. She qualified as a doctor at the Vellore Christian Medical College, India. In 1954, shortly after completing her training, she was badly injured in a car crash. Her spinal cord was severely damaged, and she was left a paraplegic (her legs and lower abdomen were paralysed, and all feeling in them was lost).

She was determined, however, not to surrender. Confined to a wheelchair, and encouraged by her colleague Dr Paul Brand, she began to specialize in surgery on people's hands and feet. This was not easy work: the operations were delicate and required great skill. Added to that were the heat of the day and the problem of operating on people from a wheelchair.

She soon began on another branch of surgery: making eyebrows for people who had lost them when suffering from leprosy. This was more than simple cosmetic surgery. Employers were often suspicious of people who had been lepers, even though there was no danger of infection, simply because people are so afraid of the disease. If you had no eyebrows, it was a sure sign that you had been a leper. So the operation made it less easy to discriminate against them in employment.

This sort of concern for people's dignity runs through Mary Verghese's work. Disabled people should be treated as human beings, not simply as objects of pity. There is a danger of seeing the disability and not the person. Mary Verghese avoided this danger. She worked to restore to the disabled a sense of their own worth, and to help them live life to the full.

Visiting the Royal Perth Hospital in Australia, she was greatly impressed by the rehabilitation programmes run there for the disabled. These concentrated on physical fitness: for example, strong arms can help to compensate for paralysed legs. Sport was vital in all this, and the Paralympics were very popular! Dr Verghese wanted to get this kind of programme going in Vellore, but lack of money made it impossible for a time.

In 1960, she was awarded a grant by the World Rehabilitation Fund. This was for a course at the Institute of Physical Medicine and Rehabilitation at New York University. During the course—in which she learnt to drive, in the New York traffic!—she improved her ability to educate and rehabilitate the disabled.

While she was away, and to her delight, the Vellore hospital had constructed their centre for rehabilitation. Physiotherapists were now employed, and the centre trained medical students for its work. Dr Verghese was made the Head of the Department in 1963. Under her leadership, new apparatus was designed, at a price the poor could afford. Lightweight ramps were built to enable wheelchairs to go up steps. 'Pickers', pincers on the end of lightweight rods, enabled paraplegics to get things down from high shelves. Sport meetings were started.

The department moved to new premises in 1966, paid for by a Canadian donor. The Rehabilitation Institute, as it was now called, was opened by the Indian Minister of Health. Disabled people were able to come for six months or more residential help in peaceful surroundings. New job skills were taught: embroidery, carpentry, book-binding, teaching and so on. They could now earn their own living.

People were taught to become mobile, even if they had lost the use of all their limbs. They were taught how to move around their homes by practising in mock-ups of typical Indian homes, built for that purpose in the Institute. Sport, especially swimming, was very important in helping to increase people's mobility.

Dr Mary Verghese is now confined to bed by ill-health. Yet she continues to work. She is greatly involved in a project to build a Christian Mission to the Physically Handicapped in Vellore. This will be a residential home for those disabled men and women who require this type of care. She has received honours from the Indian Medical Council, and in 1972 she received the highly-prized Padmire Shri Award from the Indian government.

Leonard Cheshire

Leonard Cheshire was born in 1917 in Cheshire. He read Law at Merton College, Oxford. At Oxford, he gained a reputation as a bit of a lad: he enjoyed gambling, drinking and driving fast cars. He was a pilot in the Second World War, and a very distinguished one: he was Wing Commander of the Dam Busters Squadron, and flew on a hundred bombing raids. He was awarded the Victoria Cross, the highest military honour, for bravery.

In 1945, he witnessed the destruction of the Japanese city Nagasaki by the Americans' atomic bomb. Another Japanese city, Hiroshima, had already been destroyed by a similar weapon. The bomb on Nagasaki killed 40,000 people. Cheshire, like many others, believed this action was justified, terrible though it was—because it brought the war to an end. (Hitler had been defeated some months before, but Japan did not surrender until a few days after the destruction of Nagasaki.) Cheshire felt that many more people would have died if the war had continued.

He tried a number of jobs after the war, but with limited success. He and some of his friends soon set up a home for ex-servicemen who had no family. The first attempt failed. Their second attempt was at a house called Le Court, in Liss, Hampshire.

Cheshire came to hear that Arthur Dykes, one of those who had worked on their first scheme, was dying in hospital of cancer. He agreed to find Dykes a home. When he was unable to do so, he decided to nurse Dykes himself. He had no experience of nursing, but he was willing to learn. Dykes was a devout Roman Catholic, and died peacefully three months after Cheshire started to look after him.

The atomic bomb had made a great impression on Cheshire, who felt that there must be something better for human beings than to wage war. He had begun to wonder whether there was anything in religion. It had certainly helped Dykes, who had died without fear.

In 1954 Leonard Cheshire's Christmas message was broadcast by the BBC. Here some of the patients at Le Court—the people he cared for—watch him make the recording.

Cheshire read a book on the faith that his friend had read during his illness. His conviction grew that Christianity was true, that it did indeed answer the questions of life. In 1948, Cheshire became a Roman Catholic.

By now, Cheshire felt he had a vocation (a calling) from God to look after those who were ill. The local hospitals got word that he was willing to look after those for whom they had no room. He was soon looking after forty people: some were seriously ill or dying, others were frail or elderly. For a long time, Cheshire worked with them on his own at Le Court, then others joined him.

In 1950, the doctors warned him that he had to rest, or he would become seriously ill through overwork. He left Le Court reluctantly, but felt that the others there could look after the guests better than he could.

He took a job with Vickers Armstrong, a company involved in aircraft manufacture. When Michael, a young man who was an epileptic, asked him for help, Cheshire invited him to share his cottage. No one would give Michael lodgings because of his disability. Then he met Hilda, who was also disabled. He decided a second Home was needed. With the help of local volunteers, some from the Royal Navy airfield nearby, he organized the conversion of a number of huts on the edge of the Vickers' airfield.

St Theresa's, the new Home, was soon full. Le Court and St Theresa's became known as the Cheshire Homes, and the Cheshire Foundation Homes for the Sick began as a charity. They were open to people of any religious belief, or of none.

Overwork took its toll. Cheshire spent two years in hospital recovering from tuberculosis. While he was there, he directed two projects. The first was Group Captain Cheshire's Mission, which spread the Christian message from a bus which travelled around the country. The second was a series of pilgrimages to Lourdes.

Lourdes is a town in France where a young girl called Bernadette had a vision of a lady, who was later identified as the Virgin Mary. Many people who could not be cured by medicine visited the shrine at Lourdes: they still do today. The remarkable thing is that many of them are completely cured by the time they leave. It does not happen every time, but the extraordinary thing is that it happens at all.

Cheshire married Sue Ryder in 1959. They set up the Ryder-Cheshire Foundation, with the aim of coming up with new ideas to combat suffering. (It is now know as 'The Mission for the Relief of Suffering'.)

By the end of 1959, fifteen Cheshire Homes had been established in Britain, six in India, one in Malaya and one in Nigeria. Some specialized in looking after the mentally ill, severely disabled children, orphans or people with tuberculosis. In 1993, there were 85 Homes in the UK and 185 in 50 countries overseas. 37 UK Family Support Services provide day-to-day care in their own homes for people with disabilities.

Cheshire stressed that those in the Homes should have time to themselves and should be involved in the Homes' day-to-day running. It is vitally important not to patronize people who are being cared for.

In 1992, Cheshire became confined to a wheelchair with motor neurone disease. He saw it as a blessing, as part of God's plan, as he could now speak not of 'you, the disabled', but of 'we, the disabled'.

Leonard Cheshire died in July 1992.

Follow-up

Questions

1 In what ways might bringing up a handicapped child be difficult for a family?
How can organizations like MENCAP help?
Answer in detail.

2 Why were the Cheshire Homes started?

3 Write a couple of paragraphs to explain what the Cheshire Homes do.

For discussion

'People with learning difficulties have nothing to offer and nothing to teach others. They are simply a burden.' How would you react to someone who said this?

'If God existed, he would not allow people to be born with handicaps.'
What might be a Christian answer to this statement? (See the chapter on 'The Problem of Pain' to help you.)

'It's best to care for mentally handicapped people in their family homes.'
Do you agree?

Why might someone choose to work with the disabled? Is is the sort of work you would want to do?

Do you have to be physically and mentally fit to enjoy life?

'It is important not to patronize people who are helped by charities.'
Why might someone say this?
What sort of things could charities or ordinary people do to help achieve it?

Activity

Find out about a project in your area which helps people with either physical or mental disabilities.

Write your own notes on the work of Mary Verghese. How does she put Christian teaching into practice?

Further reading:

Wheelchair Surgeon: The Story of Mary Verghese by Joan Clifford (Faith in Action series, published by the Religious and Moral Education Press).

Life is not easy. Probably all of us are lonely, unhappy or depressed at one time or another. Sadly, some people reach the point when they feel they can no longer cope. Or they feel they place too great a burden on those close to them. Suicide seems to offer a way out. Death appears to be better than life. Our lives are our own: surely we have the right to die if we choose?

Or do we?

A great many people think not. They would point out:

- Suicide is selfish: it causes a great deal of unhappiness to the people left behind. The grief that people suffer when someone they love has died is often much greater following a suicide. It may be coupled with anger: 'How could he do it to us?' 'Didn't she think about us at all?'

Many who attempt suicide do not really want to die. It is a cry for help. The Samaritans were set up to act as an emergency line for those who felt suicidal. They are always open and ready to listen. Telephone calls and visits are kept completely confidential: the specially trained volunteers are not allowed to discuss their work. They have helped many who would otherwise now be dead.

- Things might well get better, however black they look at the time. Holding on might be very hard and painful, but will be better in the long run. Suicide may take some courage, but it takes more courage to go on living. It may seem that there is nothing to live for, but there will be in the future.

- People who are very depressed are not in a position to make a sensible, rational decision. If they could see things clearly, they would not want to die. Society must protect them from themselves.

These things could be said by someone of any faith or none. They would agree that people who are depressed or unhappy need help, whether from the love of family, friends or others, or from doctors, psychiatrists and psychotherapists (who are trained to help people with mental problems).

What does Christianity say about suicide?

Christians believe that human beings are of infinite value because they have been created by God. Even the strongest human love is less than God's love for each one of us. People in distress need help and deserve compassion. Yet life is sacred because it comes from God. This is why most Christians would say that suicide is wrong. Christian thinkers or theologians make the following points:

- God created us and Jesus' death saved us. Suicide throws God's gift back in his face. It is a rejection of all God has done for us.

- We are not given complete charge over our own lives. God loves us and cares for us—he is in charge at the end. (Suicide therefore rejects this *sovereignty* of God.)

- One of the Ten Commandments is 'Thou shalt not kill.' This applies to suicide as well.

- Despair, which leads to suicide, is a denial of hope. Despair says, 'This is the end: there is nothing else.' It is a denial of God.

- Christianity teaches that suicide is wrong. But the days are gone when suicides were denied a Christian burial. There is more understanding today about mental illness. And suicide is not always

Roman Catholic teaching

The Roman Catholic position on euthanasia is stated in the 'Declaration on Euthanasia' (*Jura et Bona*) issued by the Sacred Congregation of the Doctrine of the Faith in 1980. Here is an outline of its teaching:

The starting-point is that every person is created by God and offered Christ's salvation. Killing an innocent person is never acceptable, whether he or she be an embryo, foetus, infant, adult, old person or someone who is dying. Any attempt on an innocent person's life is opposing God's love for that person.

God calls human beings to preserve their lives and to live as Christians (except when they may have to sacrifice themselves for others). So suicide and euthanasia are wrong. Suicide denies that we have duties to others in society, to our neighbours. It is different from self-sacrifice, which is directed towards other people.

People who commit suicide are not always responsible for their actions. Suffering can lead people to make mistakes, not just in the case of suicide but also in asking for euthanasia. It is best to understand this as a crying out for love and for help.

Circumstances like long illness and old age can actually help people to face death, even though death is frightening.

When faced with a patient who is terminally ill, doctors

- should not give anything with the deliberate intention of killing the patient;

- but they *may* give pain relief, even if as a *side effect* of this life is shortened, as long as the patient does not become so confused that he or she cannot prepare properly for death. (This point re-states the teaching of Pope Pius XII.)

carefully planned. It is often done in the heat of the moment, when it is very hard to think clearly and behave rationally.

- There is a difference between suicide and self-sacrifice. For example, if you work with people who are dying of an infectious disease, and you know that doing so may kill you, this is not suicide. Nor is giving your life for another.

▓ Euthanasia

The word 'euthanasia' comes from two Greek words meaning 'good (easy) death'. It raises many of the same moral problems as suicide. However, euthanasia involves someone else, who either performs the killing or provides the means of death (which generally means drugs). There are two types of euthanasia:

- **Compulsory euthanasia** is when other people decide when a person's life is going to end. This might be his or her relatives, a doctor or even society as a whole. It is sometimes called 'mercy killing' when it applies to people with terrible illnesses, such as severely handicapped children.

The most extreme example of compulsory euthanasia was when the Nazis carried out a programme of killing the mentally and physically handicapped in the Third Reich.

- **Voluntary euthanasia** means that the person him or herself asks to die. Some believe that patients who are dying of an incurable and painful disease should be allowed to ask a doctor to help them to die. Perhaps they could sign a legal document asking for this, and witnessed by one or more persons who had no connection with the case. The doctor could then provide a lethal drug for the person to give him or herself, or the doctor could do it for them. Views like these are put forward by the Voluntary Euthanasia Society.

Some Christians believe that euthanasia should be allowed, because it is kinder in some circumstances to let people die than to make them carry on living.

But most Christians do not accept this. The Roman Catholic Church condemns euthanasia absolutely (see below). The Church of England's 1975 report 'On Dying Well' and the Methodist Conference's statement in 1974 both oppose euthanasia. Christians are not alone in this: in 1950 the World Medical Association declared

Care for the dying

The first **hospices** were founded at the beginning of this century. They care for people who are dying from terminal diseases. Some offer home care, others offer care in a separate unit or ward. Those who are dying and their families are helped to face death, and to accept it with dignity.

People who are dying are encouraged by hospices to be as fulfilled as possible physically, mentally and spiritually. Their relatives are offered advice, counselling and support, and are helped after the death.

Most hospices are Christian foundations, and some of them rely entirely on voluntary donations.

Their care for the dying—the control of pain and the emphasis on allowing people to die with dignity—provides a stark contrast with a society which prefers not to think about death, or unthinkingly embraces euthanasia as an easy solution.

Helen House in Oxford is one of many hospices with a Christian foundation.
Unusually, it specializes in care for children and their families.

euthanasia unethical and there are other examples. The following points could be made against euthanasia by both Christians and non-Christians:

- It would work against the relationship of trust between a doctor and a patient. It would also be unfair to doctors whose brief is to save life to allow them to kill a patient. Even if they did not have to do so themselves, they might well feel uncomfortable working with colleagues who did.

- It would be difficult to know whether a legal document signed by a patient was really what the patient wanted. The patient might have changed his or her mind, or have been put under pressure by uncaring relatives, or may not have been thinking clearly when it was signed.

- It could be the thin edge of the wedge. This is especially true of compulsory euthanasia. If it were allowed for some things, how long would it be before it became allowed for others? When would it reach the stage of the Nazis' programme?

Christians who oppose euthanasia do so because of their belief that human beings are God's creation and that life is sacred. If that makes suicide wrong, it also makes euthanasia wrong. It breaks the commandment, 'Thou shalt not kill.' People have a duty to help others when they suffer, but not at any price. Killing someone who is ill is still murder, and it is 'playing God' to say who may live and who shall die.

It might be objected that if all this is true, we should use every possible means to keep people alive. But there is a difference between causing death by not giving the treatment that would make someone well and withholding treatment during the last stages of a terminal illness, when it could not cure the patient anyway.

Follow-up

Questions

1 What is
(a) suicide
(b) euthanasia?

2 Why do most Christians oppose suicide and euthanasia? (Ensure you indicate clearly the Roman Catholic teaching.)

Activity

Try to invite a volunteer from your local branch of the Samaritans to speak to your group about the organization's work. (It would be best to find their address in the telephone book and write to them.)

Motion for a class debate:
'This house believes that people should have the right to die when they please.'

What is a hospice? Find out about the work of a hospice in your area.

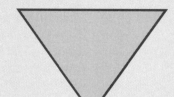

PART FIVE

World Issues

32 War 1: The United Nations

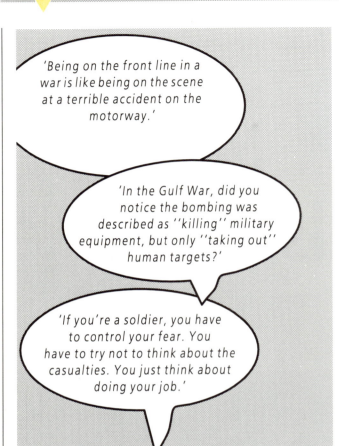

'Being on the front line in a war is like being on the scene at a terrible accident on the motorway.'

'In the Gulf War, did you notice the bombing was described as "killing" military equipment, but only "taking out" human targets?'

'If you're a soldier, you have to control your fear. You have to try not to think about the casualties. You just think about doing your job.'

These three statements about war provide food for thought. These chapters look at some of the issues war raises, and some of the ways in which governments and people have responded to them.

The United Nations

The United Nations was set up after the Second World War. Its purposes were:

- to promote international peace and security, and 'to save succeeding generations from the scourge of war';

- to develop friendly relations between countries;

- to work to solve international economic, social, cultural and humanitarian problems;

- to promote respect for human rights.

The United Nations has six major bodies:

1. The Security Council, which has fifteen countries as its members. The US, the UK, Russia, China and France are the 'permanent members'. The other ten members are elected by the General Assembly (see below). Each member has one vote. Its decisions have to be agreed by nine out of the fifteen members. However, any one of the five permanent members can veto (throw out) decisions on 'substantive (major) matters'. Every member country of the United Nations agrees to carry out the Security Council's decisions.

If an argument between countries leads to war, the Security Council may either

- insist on a cease-fire;
  or:

- carry out collective military action. This might mean sending UN observers or UN peace-keeping troops to help reduce tension. The Security Council authorized the use of force against Iraq in the Gulf War (1991).

If a country's interests are being discussed, it will be invited to join the discussion, but it will have no vote.

2. The General Assembly, which debates world issues.

Each member country has one vote. Major decisions, such as recommendations on peace and security, or on expelling or suspending a member state, need a two-thirds majority to be passed. Other decisions need a simple majority (more than half the vote).

The idea behind the General Assembly is that arguing through disputes between countries helps them to come to a peaceful agreement. The General Assembly cannot usually force member states to do anything, but it can put pressure on them. After all, its recommendations are seen to express world opinion. However, if the Security Council cannot agree when war threatens, the General Assembly can take action.

The General Assembly drew up the United Nations Declaration on Human Rights (see Chapter 5). It has also encouraged aid and development programmes, anti-racist campaigns, and has negotiated treaties.

3. The Secretariat. When the UN was set up, it was intended to maintain peace in the world. This needed an international civil service—people who would be loyal to the whole international community rather than to one country. The Secretariat is headed by the Secretary General of the United Nations.

It carries out the day-to-day work of the UN:

- it mediates (acts as a go-between) in international disputes;

- it administers peace keeping operations;

- it monitors human rights.

4. The Economic and Social Council. Poverty and poor standards of living breed unrest and are a major cause of war. The Economic and Social Council co-ordinates the UN's social work and development work.

5. The Trusteeship Council helps countries who are gaining independence from foreign rule. The anger of colonized people against their foreign rulers is another cause of war. The Trusteeship Council aims to ensure such countries gain their independence peacefully.

6. The International Court of Justice. Countries have their own laws, but disputes between countries can cause unrest and even war. The International Court of Justice tries to establish and enforce *international* law.

Other bodies attached to the UN include:
- the World Health Organization (WHO)
- the Office of the UN High Commissioner for Refugees
- the General Agreement on Tariffs and Trade (GATT)

The UN has sponsored a number of treaties:
- the ban on developing weapons in space (1967)
- the ban on spreading the availability of nuclear weapons (1968)
- the ban on deploying nuclear weapons on the ocean floor (1971)
- the ban on biochemical warfare (1975).

It has been involved in a number of peacekeeping operations:

- In **Cyprus**, in 1964, the Greek and Turkish Cypriot communities appeared to be heading for civil war. The Security Council authorized a peacekeeping force, and 3,000 British troops on the island became 'UN policemen'. Canada, Sweden, Ireland and Finland contributed other troops.

- In the **Middle East** a peace-keeping force was deployed by the UN after the war between Israel and its neighbours in 1973. The United Nations led the peace talks after the collapse of **Yugoslavia** in

One of the most important roles of the United Nations is that of peace keeping. This UN vehicle driven by British troops cruises through Vitez in the Bosnian war zone.

Helping the victims of war

War continues to destroy the lives of millions. The **Geneva Conventions** and the **Red Cross** aim to help the victims of war.

The first of the Geneva Conventions was signed in 1864. The countries who signed them agree to the Conventions' terms:

- Civilians are neutral and must be treated humanely.

- Those who are wounded in war must also be treated humanely.

- Prisoners-of-war may not be physically or mentally tortured. Threats or force (coercion) may not be used against them.

- Hostage taking, deportations (removing people from their land), torture, collective punishment, and discrimination on the grounds of race, religion, nationality or politics are banned.

The conventions recognized that modern warfare makes it less easy to distinguish between the home front and the war front. However, they try to protect civilians who are threatened by bombing. They also insist that ships bearing the Red Cross emblem and doctors and nurses should be regarded as neutral.

The full name of the Red Cross is the International Movement of the Red Cross and Red Crescent. (The cross is the symbol of Christianity; the crescent is the symbol of Islam—both faiths lay strong emphasis on caring for the weak.) The Red Cross was founded in 1863 by Jean Henri Dunant, a Swiss humanitarian.

It was set up to help the victims of war, and to provide them with medical care. It also aims to carry out the terms of the Geneva Conventions. In peacetime, it helps refugees and those suffering as a result of natural disasters, trains people in first aid, and teaches them how to ensure their water supply is clean. Polluted water can cause many illnesses. It also ensures that enough blood is available for transfusions.

the early 1990s. UN troops tried to ensure the safe passage of aid to hundreds of thousands of people who were without food or medical supplies.

- UN troops also did their best to protect aid supplies in **Somalia** in 1992/3: the country had deteriorated into a state of mob rule while its people starved.

F o l l o w - u p

Questions

1 In what ways does the United Nations try to stop wars?

2 (a) Outline the work of the International Movement of the Red Cross and Red Crescent.
(b) Outline the terms of the Geneva Conventions.

3 Read this chapter again, carefully. Select some reasons to answer the question, 'What causes war?'

Activity

One of the most vivid ways we have of communicating human experience is through poetry. You may have read some poems about war. The list below gives a few suggestions to get you started. You should be able to find them in a library. (If you need help, ask the librarian!) As you read them, think about what the writer is trying to say. What are your reactions?

Wilfred Owen: 'Exposure'; 'Futility'; 'The Send Off'.

In what ways do people suffer during a war?
Watch the news this week or read the papers to help you with your answer. Prepare a short talk for the rest of your group.

In 1992, the United Kingdom spent:

- £23.5 billion on defence
- £2.3 billion on overseas aid
- £30 billion on health
- £7.9 billion on education

There have been more than 127 wars since 1945.

 'It is impossible to conceive of a just war in a nuclear age.'

Pope John XXIII

The bomb and the Cold War

The Japanese city of Hiroshima was destroyed by a nuclear bomb on 6 August 1945. The bomb weighed two kilograms and was not much bigger than a cricket ball. 140,000 people died in the explosion. Years later, people from the area were still dying from the after-effects of radiation, and many women bore stillborn or grossly deformed babies. The city of Nagasaki was destroyed by a nuclear bomb three days after Hiroshima. The Japanese surrendered, ending the Second World War.

The Hiroshima bomb had the explosive force of thirteen thousand tons of dynamite. By today's standards, it was tiny. One United States Titan II missile has the explosive force of ten million tons of dynamite. At one point in the 1980s, it was estimated that the Soviet and American nuclear arsenals combined had the equivalent power of over eleven thousand million tons of dynamite.

Figures like these are so vast that they are hard to take in. Why on earth were such weapons thought to be needed? Do we still need them today?

After the Second World War, a Soviet advance into Europe appeared likely. The USSR had not withdrawn from the countries it occupied during the war. There was a good deal to suggest that it wanted to expand its communist empire further. Soviet communists saw their system as one that should form a blueprint for a new world order. The Soviet Premier Khruschev said, 'We will bury you' to the people of the West. Other Soviet premiers seemed to agree with him.

The Western alliance of NATO (North Atlantic Treaty Organization) opted for a policy of deterrence. Nuclear weapons were built and targeted on cities and major military centres of the USSR. The aim was to

Shadow-painting at a CND demo in Barrow, where Trident is made. Shadow-paintings echo the silhouettes left by victims at Hiroshima and Nagasaki.

UNILATERAL DISARMAMENT—ARGUMENTS FOR:

1.   If a nuclear war broke out, millions of people—perhaps the whole population of the planet—would die. The balance of nature would be destroyed, perhaps for ever. Any war in which nuclear weapons were used could easily become an all-out war. (Christians would add that it would be undoing God's work in creating the world and humankind.)

Nuclear weapons are so evil that we must disarm. It is evil even to possess them.

2.   The Cold War is over. So we no longer need a deterrent. Who are we supposed to be deterring?

In any case, deterrence is immoral. We would have to be prepared to carry out the threat. Otherwise it would not be a threat! But we could never carry it out, because it would mean killing so many people. And most of them would be civilians, not the people who started the war.

3   If we have nuclear weapons, we would be a target in a nuclear war. The opponent would want to strike first, to 'knock out' our nuclear weapons. If we get rid of them, we stop being a target.

4.   Nuclear weapons do not defend you against a nuclear attack. There is no defence against that.

5.   If Britain got rid of its nuclear weapons, it would set a good example and start the ball rolling. Other countries would follow.

6.   Britain has its own nuclear deterrent, which is independent of the Americans' forces. We do not need it. We only have it because it kids us into thinking we are still a world power.

7.   If you limit the number of weapons, you limit the risk of war. And nuclear weapons are a waste of money, which could be spent on overseas aid, helping the poor, improving education and so on.

8.   Nuclear weapons could be set off by mistake, such as computer error.

9.   Most countries, including most European countries, manage perfectly well without their own nuclear weapons. We don't need them, either.

UNILATERAL DISARMAMENT—ARGUMENTS AGAINST:

1.   You cannot disinvent nuclear weapons. We simply have to make sure they are not used.

2.   The Cold War may be over, but we do not know what is around the corner. We may need deterrence against someone else in the future.

Deterrence can be based on bluff! Nobody would be stupid enough to try to call the bluff. Deterrence has prevented a world war since 1945.

3.   The opponent would not strike first, because he would be afraid of the possible retaliation. Even if he missed one nuclear missile (and many of them are in submarines, anyway), the possible retaliation would still be massive.

4.   Deterrence prevents a nuclear attack.

5.   It would be nice to think others would follow our example, but it doesn't take human nature into account.

6.   We are bound by treaties we have made with other countries to do our fair share. We are part of NATO, and should not act on our own.

7.   Before the Second World War, the 'appeasers' thought having fewer weapons would limit the risk of war. They were wrong. And it's a mistake to think that because money is earmarked to be spent on x, it would also be available for y.

8.   Setting nuclear weapons off by mistake is so unlikely as to be practically impossible.

9.   If we disarm, we run the risk of knowledge about nuclear weapons spreading to other countries who want them, like Iraq. This would make disarming terribly dangerous.

frighten the Soviet Union so that it would not attack the West. If the Soviets invaded the West, or if they used their nuclear weapons, they would be completely destroyed. The threat was of 'mutually assured destruction'. If one side improved its military capability, the other side felt it had to do so too. Otherwise it could not be defended. Stockpiles of nuclear weapons increased massively. So did spending on arms. This build-up is known as the **arms race**.

The period when deterrence was used against the Soviet Union was called the **Cold War**. It lasted until the late 1980s, when Soviet Premier Mikhail Gorbachev worked with the US President Ronald Reagan to decrease the stockpiles of nuclear weapons and to end the distrust between the superpowers. The Union of Soviet Socialist Republics has now itself been dismantled.

Many believe that deterrence during the Cold War prevented a third world war, although there was a very close shave during the Cuban Missile Crisis of 1962. Most countries today do not have nuclear weapons. Those that do include the USA, Russia, the UK, France and China. Are they still needed?

▓ Getting rid of nuclear weapons

The Campaign for Nuclear Disarmament (CND) argues that we do not need nuclear weapons, and we never did. Many Christians agree with this, and some are members of a branch of Christian CND.

Should Britain get rid of its nuclear weapons?

To answer this question, we need to define some key words and ideas, and then look at the arguments for and against.

Weapons of mass destruction include nuclear weapons, chemical weapons such as gas, and biological weapons ('germ warfare'). Biological weapons are completely banned by international treaties. CND is against all weapons of mass destruction.

'Conventional' weapons are those which are not weapons of mass destruction—tanks, machine guns, and so on.

Disarmament means 'getting rid of weapons', especially of mass destruction. There are two forms of disarmament:

● **Multilateral disarmament**. This means that both or all sides agree to disarm at the same time, and probably at the same rate.

(Multilateral disarmament is supported by the encyclical (letter) of Pope John XXIII, *Pacem in Terris*, which also said the arms race should end, and that nuclear weapons should be banned.)

● **Unilateral disarmament** means that one side disarms first, encouraging the others to follow.

(The Labour Party had a policy of unilateral disarmament during most of the 1980s. Unilateral disarmament was also supported by a Church of England report in 1982 called *The Church and the Bomb*. The report was, however, rejected by the General Synod—the 'parliament' of the Church of England—which favoured multilateral disarmament.)

▓ Follow-up

Questions

1 Define:
the Cold War
the arms race
weapons of mass destruction
conventional weapons
disarmament
multilateral disarmament
unilateral disarmament.

2 What did
(a) the Church of England, and
(b) Pope John XXIII
say about nuclear weapons?

3 When have nuclear weapons been used in war?

For discussion

Look at what is said about the just war in Chapter 34. Could a nuclear war ever be a just war? Explain your answer.

Activity

Organize a class debate on the motion: 'Unilateral disarmament is the only sensible option for Britain.'

34 War 3: Christian Attitudes

Christian attitudes to war have generally fallen into one of three groups—the ideas of
- the Crusade
- the just war
- pacifism (see Chapter 36)

▨ The Crusade

A Crusade is a 'Holy War'. The Book of Exodus in the Old Testament tells how Israel escaped from slavery in Egypt when Moses was the nation's leader. (This escape took place in about 1280 BC.) The celebratory Song of Moses begins like this:

 Then Moses and the Israelites sang this song to the Lord: 'I will sing to the Lord, because he has won a glorious victory; he has thrown the horses and their riders into the sea. The Lord is my strong defender; he is the one who has saved me. He is my God, and I will praise him, my father's God, and I will sing about his greatness. The Lord is a warrior; the Lord is his name.'

Exodus 15:1–3

Christians today are not proud of the ancient Crusades against the Muslims in the Holy Land. This engraving is intended to show the clemency of St Louis (about AD 1219) in sparing the lives of women and children.

Some scholars suggest this is the oldest piece of poetry in the whole Bible: perhaps as early as the thirteenth century BC. Notice that God is described as a warrior. This was one of the major ways in which the ancient Israelites thought of God. He was called 'the God of hosts' ('armies'). They believed that the God of hosts had given them rules about how to fight the **holy war**. God was thought to be in the midst of their armies as an unseen supreme commander. The people they conquered—men, women and children—were to be completely exterminated. The victims of the war, and the booty, were to be consecrated or dedicated to God, as though they were his property. Anyone who kept some of the spoil would be stoned to death. The Israelites believed this was what God wanted.

Two examples of the holy war from the Old Testament are the battle of Jericho and Gideon's victory over the Midianites.

📖 **Read Joshua 6:15–21; 7:10–26 Judges 7:9–21**

Roman Catholic teaching

This is a summary from *Gaudium et Spes* (The Pastoral Constitution on the Church in the Modern World), issued by the Second Vatican Council in 1965:

- There will never be a truly human world for everyone until all devote themselves to peace.

- Peace is more than the absence of war. Peace is 'the effect of righteousness': the fruit of the right ordering of things. People should never quench their thirst for an ever more just society. They must therefore love one another, and respect one another's dignity.

- Modern weapons allow human beings to be more savage today than at any time in history. So agreements between nations to limit war must be honoured, and further agreements must be sought. People should be allowed to be conscientious objectors in time of war, so long as they accept some other form of community service.

- As a last resort, and provided that other efforts at peace have failed, nations cannot be denied the right to self defence. But they may not dominate another nation: they may only defend themselves. When military personnel carry out their duty properly, they should think of themselves as protecting their fellow citizens' security and freedom. They should also remember that their intention in going to war is to win peace.

- The church condemns total warfare by the use of weapons of mass destruction, such as nuclear weapons. Destroying whole cities or vast areas of land is a crime against God and against humanity, which deserves absolute condemnation.

- The arms race or the possession of large stocks of weapons may deter would-be aggressors. However, it is no lasting answer. As long as money is squandered on arms, we cannot give adequate aid to those in the world who are suffering. We must therefore seek other ways of overcoming conflict.

- We must aim to ban war by international agreement. [This aim is supported by the World Council of Churches.] Therefore, people must work towards ending the arms race and start to disarm. This is best done on both sides rather than by one side alone (unilaterally).

- Many politicians seek peace and wish to limit the threat of war. Yet politicians will be encouraged in their efforts by public opinion. People must therefore be educated, so that they realise how vital the effort for peace is.

- Causes of war must be rooted out. These include injustice (especially when the poor are exploited by the rich and the powerful), the desire for power, contempt for others, envy, distrust, pride and selfishness.

It all sounds rather bloodthirsty! Some Christians believe the accounts are historically accurate: God expected his followers to exterminate his enemies (including the children) and then to burn their city to the ground. But this does not seem to fit with the God of love whom Jesus taught people to call 'Father'. And perhaps these stories tell us more about the beliefs of the people of the time than they do about God.

In terms of actual history, Joshua was an Israelite leader some time during the thirteenth century BC. He became a popular hero. Gideon was a judge, an Israelite leader appointed for his charismatic qualities, who seems to have driven the Midianites out of Israel in the twelfth century BC.

The idea of holy war has from time to time appeared in Christian history as 'crusades'.

There are four beliefs behind crusades:

1. The reason for the war is a holy one.
2. God will guide and lead the armies.
3. The crusaders are on God's side: the enemy are against God.
4. The war must be carried on to the bitter end.

The World Council of Churches

The Seventh Assembly of the World Council of Churches was held in 1991. The majority of the delegates there agreed with the Lebanese Archbishop Aram Keshishian that the Gulf War of 1991 was 'neither holy nor just.' The General Secretary of the Middle Eastern Council of Churches was asked at the World Council of Churches whose side God was on in the Gulf War. He replied, 'God is on the side of those who are suffering.'

The World Council of Churches opposed Saddam Hussein's invasion of Kuwait in 1990. Yet it called for an immediate ceasefire. It was acceptable to use sanctions against Iraq, but not war.

> **I no longer believe in an omnipotent [all powerful], macho, warrior God who rescues all good guys and punishes all bad guys. Rather, I rely on the compassionate God who weeps with us for life in the midst of the cruel destruction of life.**
>
> **Chung Hyun Kyung, Professor of Theology at Ewha Women's University, Seoul, quoted in the documents of the seventh assembly of the World Council of Churches, 1991.**

jihad (Arabic for 'struggle' or 'war'). *Jihad* is the duty of the Muslim to defend Islam, to ensure that it is spread, and if necessary to fight for it. *Jihad* can take the form of physical violence. The Prophet Muhammad was told by God that he could attack some Jews and Christians who had betrayed him. He could fight them until they submitted to the authority of Islam. They did not have to become Muslims, but had to accept Islamic rule.

Today, few Christians or Muslims today would say that war is a good thing. Christian hymns like 'Onward, Christian soldiers' and 'Soldiers of Christ, arise' are not telling Christians to take up arms. Imagery taken from war is used to describe the spiritual struggle: Christians' struggle against sin and evil, in themselves and in the world in general. Even Christians who allow that war is sometimes necessary or unavoidable, never think it good. Similarly, Muslims today tend to concentrate on the idea of *jihad* as the spiritual struggle of the individual to be true to Islam and to develop the faith in his or her own life.

Distrust and fear have caused a great deal of harm in the past between Christians and Muslims. They are now trying to bridge the gap: to learn to understand one another, rather than be enemies. They want not just to respect the similarities between the faiths, but also the differences. The World Council of Churches and the Roman Catholic Church both support these aims.

The Crusades themselves were a series of wars undertaken by Christians in the eleventh, twelfth and thirteenth centuries AD. They mainly centred on the Holy Land of Palestine (Israel). The capital city of Jerusalem had been ruled by Muslims since AD 637, and by Turkish Muslims since 1071. The Crusaders, with the church's support, wanted to recover the holy places in the Holy Land from the Muslim 'infidels'.

The Christian rulers were also worried that the Turks would continue to expand their empire until they became a direct threat. And, on an even more worldly view, they wanted better trade routes to the East.

The Crusades were spurred on by the Popes, who promised eternal life to all Christians who fell in battle. Some of the Crusades were successful. They did manage to capture Jerusalem, but they lost it again. There were eight Crusades in all. Most Christians today deeply regret these wars in the name of Christ, as they regret their treatment of the Jews and Muslims at this time.

The Muslims of the time accepted the doctrine of

The just war

War can never be good—indeed, it is wrong—but it might sometimes be less wrong than refusing to go to war. The 'just war' idea is one Christian view of war. If a war is said to be just, it is on the side of justice, which ultimately comes from God.

The just war theory has its historical roots in the late Roman Empire. Under the Emperor Constantine, at the end of the third century AD, Christianity became the Empire's official religion. Christians began to serve in the army, and a Christian view of war began to develop. St Augustine (354–430), for example, said Christian love meant people had a duty to defend an innocent neighbour from attack.

By the end of the Middle Ages, a series of rules or conditions for a Just War had been drawn up. This owed much to the work of the Christian philosopher and Dominican friar, St Thomas Aquinas (about 1225–74).

The work of an Army chaplain

Priests or ministers who work in the armed forces are called chaplains. They may have a rank, but are usually addressed as 'padre', the Spanish word for 'father'. Chaplains do not carry guns and do not fight.

The chaplains are fully involved in the work of the people to whom they minister. They go where the forces go. In the Second World War, many went with captured troops into prisoner of war camps. Being involved in the forces' life makes them more approachable.

The people chaplains serve are not always churchgoers, yet their work is recognized by the armed forces as important to Christians and non-Christians alike. They are needed to comfort the dying in wartime, but their work is much wider than that.

The Reverend Paul Carter is the Anglican chaplain with the Army Training Regiment at Bassingbourn.

We take seventeen to twenty-four year olds, and they come here for ten weeks. I see them for six forty minute periods for what's called 'Character Training'.

Most of the young men know nothing about the Bible, so I teach them how to look up a Gospel, how to look up a chapter and verse, so they can find their way around the Bible themselves. In the final period I talk about death. These men are going to be confronted with that.

Many of our seventeen and eighteen year olds are away from home for the first time, so I partly have to fill the place of a parent! Some come to see me because of problems with their parents,

Army chaplains do not fight, but they are on the battlefield with the troops. Here soldiers kneel in prayer before battle in the Gulf War.

because they think they've got their girlfriends pregnant, because of problems with the law, because they want to get married and aren't sure if they can do that in the army, because of medical problems. And there are the pastoral duties among the staff here: we've had some sad marriage break-ups, so I've tried to help those people. I do baptisms, but not many weddings because the recruits aren't here long enough.

Every Sunday we have a Eucharist. A good 30% of the recruits are in church for the first time in their lives, so we use the modern service. We use traditional and modern hymns, and I try to make my sermons interesting and visual. In the Eucharist, I explain to them what we believe is going on when we take bread and wine as a sacrament of Our Lord.

Depending on the nature of the conflict, our role in war is to work alongside the doctor at the

regimental aid post. That's the first line of first aid, two or three hundred metres behind the front line. There are padres at each of the medical units. We're there to provide comfort and to help: we're given medical training. And I have to deal with the dead: documenting them and burying them.

The just war theory is the only way I can justify what a modern army does. I believe the armed forces are an extension of the police force. They're seeking to maintain law and order, but on an international level. The army is the servant of our political masters, so it's essential that everyone in a democracy ensures that our politicians are making wise decisions. War in a fallen world is sometimes the lesser of two evils.

The just war idea has become more complex now. The problem of involving civilians is more difficult. I suspect an enemy would ensure their military hardware was as civilianized as possible. And today, how do you draw the distinction between a combatant and a non-combatant? Are British Aerospace workers involved in the armed conflict if they make the kit we use? Our military commanders are taught about the *proportionate* use of force, and they're taught it very seriously. It's the duty of bishops and other Christian leaders to say, 'No, that use of military hardware in that situation is unacceptable,' and it would be my duty to say to our commanders that that is the stance we take. Bishop Bell had the courage to do this in the Second World War.'

The conditions for a war to be called a just war:

- War must be declared by a proper authority, such as a government. A rebellion by citizens is not enough.

- The cause must be just: there must be a good reason for the war. It is not just to start a war to expand an empire.

- The intention of the war must be to do good and to overcome evil. This rules out revenge, ambition and nationalism.

- War must be a last resort. Everything else should be tried first (which means extensive negotiations must be attempted.) If a country is attacked in a minor way, it should not automatically declare war on the aggressor.

- The good a war will do must outweigh the harm. Is it worth the loss of life?

- It must be possible to win. War should never be a futile gesture. If success looks unlikely, war should not be started.

- The methods used must be just. Force should be in proportion to the situation. Excessive cruelty is not acceptable.

Follow-up

Questions

1 What further causes of war may be identified from this chapter?

2 (a) Explain the idea of the holy war, in the Old Testament.
(b) Summarise three passages from the Old Testament which illustrate the holy war.
(c) What were the Crusades?

3 (a) What does it mean to call a war a 'just war'?
(b) Outline the conditions for a just war.

4 Outline the teaching of the Roman Catholic Church on war. (Remember to quote the document's full title.)

5 Outline the work of an army chaplain.

For discusssion

Consider the following situations, and explain why they would be against the conditions of the just war:

- war against an immeasurably more powerful opponent

- 'war' declared by an animal liberation front against shops who sell fur coats

- refusing to talk with the enemy

- shooting prisoners of war

- the German invasion of Poland in 1939

- bombing civilians in order to demoralize the population

- the 'war' of the IRA against the British.

Make a list of all the war films you can remember seeing. Do you think that films like these can have an effect on the way we think about war? Discuss this in groups and report back to the rest of the class.

The Lord gives strength to his people, and blesses them with peace.

Psalm 29:11

 A Child is born to us!
A son is given to us!
And he will be our ruler.
He will be called, 'Wonderful Counsellor,'
'Mighty God,' 'Eternal Father,'
'Prince of peace.'

The description of the Messiah from Isaiah 9:6

 Live in peace with one another.

Jesus, in Mark 9:50

 Blessed are the peacemakers, for they shall be called sons of God.

Jesus, in Matthew 5:9

Peace is what I leave with you; it is my own peace that I give you.

Jesus, in John 14:27

It was late that Sunday evening, [the night Jesus rose from the dead] and the disciples were gathered together behind locked doors, because they were afraid of the Jewish authorities. Then Jesus came and stood among them. 'Peace be with you,' he said. After saying this, he showed them his hands and his side. The disciples were filled with joy at seeing the Lord. Jesus said to them again, 'Peace be with you. As the Father sent me, so I send you . . .'

John 20:19–21

And God's peace, which is far beyond human understanding, will keep your hearts and minds safe in union with Christ Jesus.

Paul, in Philippians 4:7

 May God, our source of peace, be with all of you.'

Paul, in Romans 15:33

All Christians want peace, but not all Christians are pacifists. The Bible calls God 'the God of Peace' and Jesus 'the Prince of Peace'. The Old Testament looked forward to the time when the Messiah would arrive: the prophet Micah said this would be a time of peace.

Paul says that people who have been put right with God through faith 'have peace with God through our Lord Jesus Christ' (Romans 5:1).

So, peace means more than 'not being in a war'. Christianity teaches that Jesus' work makes people at peace with God, and will enable them to have peace in themselves. Peace must also be worked for in society. Social justice—getting rid of injustice, hunger and wrong treatment of other people—is also vital for peace.

Christians who accept the idea of a just war say that the aim of such a war is to bring peace. Some Christians reject war completely: they are pacifists. Pacifists believe in *Pacifism*. Pacifism completely rejects violence: pacifists will not fight in wars, and try to find other, non-violent ways to solve conflict between people.

A reign of peace

 Read Micah 4:1–4

The prophet Micah taught in the eighth century BC in Judah, the southern Israelite kingdom. (The first three verses of this passage are also found in the book of the prophet Isaiah. Isaiah lived at about the same as Micah, and worked in Israel, the northern Israelite kingdom. It is not certain whether the passage was written by Isaiah or by Micah, or even by someone else whose name we do not know.)

The passage gives a picture of what the world will be like when it is ruled by God. The Gospels say that Jesus announced the beginning of God's rule: the kingdom of God had come. They also say that he taught the kingdom of God would arrive finally and completely at the end of time, when Jesus would return.

The passage from Micah shows that the Kingdom of God will be a time of complete peace:

- The mountain where the Temple stood, Mount Zion—the holiest place in the world for the Jews— would become the holiest place in the world for all the nations, not just for the Jews.

  The early Christians believed this was a symbol of what had happened in the church, God's new community. People from all nations could become Christians. They no longer needed to be Jews to be

London, January 1991—when thousands of marchers took part in a 'stop the war' demonstration. Many Christians are pacifists, rejecting war completely.

God's people. For Christians, the holiest thing in the world is not the Temple, but Jesus himself. So early Christians thought 'the mountain where the Temple stands' was a symbol for Jesus.

- The nations will go to Mount Zion to learn God's ways. God will settle their disputes.

- There will be no more nationalism and no more war: 'They will hammer their swords into ploughs and their spears into pruning knives' (Micah 4:3). The Kingdom of God brings complete peace.

The Prince of Peace

Many of the Jews in Jesus' time thought the Messiah would be a warrior, a Jewish king who would lead their armies and drive the Romans from their land. Would Jesus be like this?

Before he began his work or ministry, Jesus went into the desert in Judea. There, he was tempted by the Devil.

 Read Matthew 4:1–11

In each of the three temptations, the Devil tries to tempt Jesus to use his power in the wrong way.

- 'If you are God's Son, order these stones to turn into bread.'

    Jesus refuses to use his power for himself. And making sure people have food is not enough. They need more than that. Jesus quotes from Deuteronomy: 'Man cannot live on bread alone, but needs every word that God speaks.'

- 'If you are God's Son, throw yourself down.'

    Jesus is being tempted to be a superman, to dazzle people with miracles so that they follow him. Yet he refuses to do miracles for this reason. He quotes again from Deuteronomy: 'Do not put the Lord your God to the test.'

- 'All this I will give you, if you kneel down and worship me.'

    Jesus is tempted to become a political Messiah, the sort of Messiah many Jews expected. In his reply, he quotes for a third time from Deuteronomy: 'Worship the Lord your God and serve only him!'

So, Jesus rejects the temptations to misuse his power. He will not be a political Messiah who will bring bloodshed. People who think the Messiah will bring war are completely wrong.

Christian pacifists

Some Christians are pacifists. It seems that the early church was mainly pacifist. Very few Christians joined any army until the Emperor Constantine was converted to Christianity at the beginning of the fourth century AD. After that, Christianity became the religion of the Roman Empire, and Christians joined the army.

Christian pacifists today say violence is never acceptable. They say it breaks the commandment, 'Thou shalt not kill.' It is against the Christian idea of love. They point to a number of passages in the Gospels, which they say support their views:

Look up Matthew 5:38–46 and Luke 22:35–53. Jesus at the Last Supper tells his disciples that things have reached a crisis. He uses the symbol of buying a sword to get the point across. They misunderstand him, and think he expects them to fight. When they draw their swords in the Garden of Gethsemane, he orders them to stop fighting, and heals the high priest's slave, who has been injured.

Some pacifists in times of war have become **conscientious objectors**. This means that their consciences refuse to let them take up arms. In the United Kingdom, conscientious objectors did not have to fight in the First or Second World Wars. However, they were required to do something else instead, such as helping with the medical care at home or with the troops, or joining the fire brigade. In many countries, conscientious objection is illegal.

(Not all conscientious objectors are pacifists. Some object to a particular war because they think it is unjust.)

Members of *The Religious Society of Friends* (sometimes called 'Quakers') are pacifist. The Friends started with the work of George Fox in the seventeenth century in England.

In 1660, a 'declaration' was given by the Friends to King Charles II. It read:

> **We utterly deny all outward wars and strife, and fightings with outward weapons, for any end, or under any pretence whatever; this is our testimony to the whole world. The Spirt of Christ by which we are guided is not**

A famous pacifist

Donald Soper (now Lord Soper) was born in Wandsworth in 1903. He was president of the Methodist Conference, and for forty-two years was the superintendent of the Methodist West London Mission. He has preached the Gospel on London's Tower Hill for sixty years, and from Speaker's Corner in London's Hyde Park for forty years.

Lord Soper's pacifism led him to be banned from broadcasting during the Second World War. He believes it is possible for human beings to become perfect, and he sees Jesus' Sermon on the Mount as the blueprint for any decent human society. People will be able to act in a responsible way if their environment and society encourage them to. Society needs to be changed before people as a whole can change.

Lord Soper is a socialist who supports many of the ideas of the Labour Party. He declared that it was not possible to be a Christian and a Conservative.

Violence, he says, is always wrong. It does not create a new beginning, and does not solve problems. Given the methods of modern warfare, pacifism is the only possible option.

Lord Soper, the famous Methodist pacifist, hands a wooden cross to a security official at the Ministry of Defence, as part of a peaceful protest against the Government's nuclear policy.

changeable, so as once to command us from a thing as evil, and again to move unto it; and we certainly know, and testify to the world that the Spirit of Christ, which leads us into all truth, will never move us to fight and war against any man with outward weapons, neither for the Kingdom of Christ, nor for the kingdoms of this world.

The Quaker Peace Testimony means the way that the Friends bear witness to peace. It is not a document or a creed that all Friends have to accept. It refers to this work of 'bearing witness,' which the Friends have done throughout their history. The way to overcome conflict is to appeal to the 'something of God' in everyone, not to fight them or to threaten them with punishment. God reaches out through people to touch 'that of God' in others. Love, telling the truth, co-operation, non-violence, imagination and laughter are all 'weapons' which do not destroy, but heal. War is always the most damaging option because the damage it leaves is permanent.

Many Friends were conscientious objectors in the First and Second World Wars, when the Quaker Ambulance Unit was active. Friends have joined protests against nuclear and other weapons. They have worked for disarmament and oppose the arms trade because the more weapons there are, the more likely they are to be used. If injustice and poverty are not overcome, there will be no peace. There are Friends' offices at the United Nations and at the European Community. These encourage different nations and people to talk to and learn from each other.

Bearing witness to peace should not just be done in wartime, but in everyday life.

Follow-up

Questions

1 Summarize
(a) Micah 4:1–4
(b) Matthew 4:1–11
Explain what each of these passages is saying about peace.

2 Learn the second part of Micah 4:3 and one other quotation from the Bible about peace.

3 What are conscientious objectors?

4 (a) What is pacifism?
(b) Explain briefly what Lord Soper says about pacifism.
(c) What is the Quaker Peace Testimony?
Answer in as much detail as you can.

5 If you had to define the word 'peace' in one sentence, what would you say?

For discussion

'Blessed are the peacemakers.'

In the Gulf War in 1991:

- The 216 tomahawk cruise missiles fired by 19 January 1991 cost 280 million US dollars. That is the same as the total price of food aid to Ethiopia for six months.

- One Tornado jet cost 21 million, the same as Save the Children's Sudan budget for one year.

- The five Tornado fighters lost by 23 January cost 105 million. That was enough to buy a month's food for the twenty million Africans who were likely to starve in 1991.

Should Christians be pacifists?

Activity

There are many traditional symbols for peace. Some of these are religious, some are not. Use as many as you can think of to design a wall display on the theme of peace.

36 Patriotism

Patriotism means 'the loyal support of one's country'. A **patriot** is someone who loyally supports their country.

Is it a good thing to be proud of your country? Or is patriotism 'the last refuge of a scoundrel', as Dr Samuel Johnson put it?

A football hooligan might get drunk and beat people up, yet say he's proud to be British.

Jimmy Savile does a great deal of hospital charity work, yet he also says he is proud to be British.

So perhaps we can say that patriotism can be good if it leads people to want the best for their fellow countrymen and countrywomen, but bad if it does not.

Nationalism

Patriotism can lead to **nationalism**—the idea that the nation's good is one of the most important aims of politics. Nationalism can have a positive effect: it can encourage oppressed people to want freedom from their distant colonial masters. However, nationalism can lead to problems. Governments all round the world often try to justify unfair or immoral laws by appealing to people's love of their country. 'It's best for Britain!'

Nationalism can lead people to hate foreigners (the word for this is 'xenophobia') and it can lead to racism. Some nationalists think that whatever their country does is right. Nationalism can cause war. It can also support **terrorism**: the use of violence for political purposes.

THE IRA

The Irish Republican Army is a nationalist organization which wants the British to withdraw from Northern Ireland. The United Kingdom held on to the six counties of Ulster (Northern Ireland) when the rest of the country was given its independence in 1922. It did so because the majority of the population in the six counties were Protestants who did not want to become part of Ireland. For many years after 1922 the Catholic minority in Ulster suffered considerable hardship

Girls from a local Roman Catholic school at Greysteel in Northern Ireland show their grief during a funeral for five Catholics killed by Ulster Freedom Fighter gunmen. Terrorism fuelled by nationalism brings grief to both sides in the situation.

Mahatma Gandhi

Mohandas K. Gandhi (1869-1948) was a leader of the Indian nationalist movement. He was a great Hindu teacher who became known as Mahatma: 'great soul'. Not only did he lead India to independence from the British, but he influenced many, including Martin Luther King.

When he was eighteen, Gandhi studied law in London, and became a lawyer in Bombay and later in an Indian law firm in South Africa. He experienced South African racism at first hand, and this led him to become a major figure in the movement against racism on behalf of the South African Indian community.

He developed *satyagraha* ('steadfastness in truth'): the theory and practise of non-violent resistance. He once said, 'The law of suffering will work, just as the law of gravitation will work, whether we accept it or not.' Refusing to retaliate or to use violence would eventually defeat any opponent.

In 1920 he became a leader of the Indian National Congress, which adopted a policy of non-cooperation with the British. The Congress undertook protest marches against unfair British policies (such as the 1930 tax on salt), and boycotted British goods. Gandhi himself was repeatedly imprisoned by the British. He spent the years from 1942-1944 in gaol for demanding that the British leave India.

He campaigned to improve the status of the lowest class in Indian society, the 'untouchables'; he favoured a simple lifestyle for Indians and did not want India to become an industrial nation.

He worked tirelessly to achieve reconciliation between the Indian Hindu majority and the Muslim minority. Yet he failed to prevent the Muslims from creating the separate Islamic state of Pakistan after India was granted independence.

He was assassinated by a Hindu extremist in Delhi on 30 January 1948.

Gandhi arrives at 10 Downing Street for a meeting with Ramsay MacDonald in 1931, a time when he was leading non-violent protest marches against the policies of the British Government who then ruled India.

and discrimination at the hands of the majority. This is still the case today.

Most Roman Catholics in Ireland and Northern Ireland are moderate republicans: they think Ulster should eventually become part of the Irish Republic but do not support the violent actions of the IRA, preferring to work with the British government to this end. In Ulster, peaceful republican parties such as the SDLP receive far more support than the IRA or its political wing, Sinn Fein.

Members of the IRA claim to be Roman Catholics, but the Pope pleaded with them to stop the violence, and the Irish Roman Catholic hierarchy repeatedly condemns the IRA's atrocities. It is not possible to see how one can be a Christian—Roman Catholic or Protestant—and a terrorist.

In August 1994, the IRA announced the cessation of its 'military operations'. Protestant paramilitary groups have also ended their violent campaigns.

Terrorism

Terrorist groups are generally secret or semi-secret organizations. They use violence to try to achieve their ends. This is often directed against civilians: bombing pubs, shooting members of the public, or blowing up airliners are intended to make people so frightened or sickened by the terrorist group that they bring pressure on the government to give the terrorists what they want. The security forces—the troops and the police—in Northern Ireland faced attack by the IRA. However, terrorism may strengthen rather than weaken the public's morale. People become so outraged that they unite to oppose the terrorists, rather than give in to them.

In some countries, banned political groups take up arms. (See on the ANC in Chapter 20). They are often called 'terrorists' by the government, but 'freedom fighters' or 'guerrillas' by their supporters. Some of these groups genuinely want freedom for their country, whereas others simply want to set up another oppressive, totalitarian regime. 'Terrorism' is sometimes used to describe all political violence, such as the 'state terrorism' of Nazi Germany.

Fortunately terrorism is not the only way of

opposing a government or a particular government policy. There is also **non-violent protest**. In a democracy, the most obvious example of non-violent protest against a government is to vote against them in elections. Democratic governments are answerable to the people at the ballot box.

Other forms of non-violent protest might include:

- **Drawing attention to the issue**, for example by writing to an MP or to the media, by organizing peaceful demonstrations or boycotts. (A boycott is a refusal to have anything to do with something: many people boycotted imported South African goods as a protest against apartheid.)

- **Civil disobedience**: breaking the law in a non-violent way to bring pressure on the authorities to act. Examples of civil disobedience might include sit-ins, disrupting traffic by lying down in the road, or refusing to pay a percentage of tax that would be spent on weapons. CND supporters, though not CND itself, often used civil disobedience as part of their campaigning. It is also the method favoured by pacifists to oppose corrupt government policies: it was used by Martin Luther King (see Chapter 19) and by Gandhi.

Follow-up

Questions

1 Explain what is meant by:
   (a) patriotism
   (b) nationalism
   (c) terrorism
   (d) non-violent protest and civil disobedience.

2 The terrorists in Israel in Jesus' day were the Zealots, who undertook armed resistance against the Romans, and believed that the Messiah would be a military leader and the king of the Jews. Some of Jesus' disciples were Zealots. They saw themselves as freedom fighters.

Look up Matthew 26:47–53, the account of Jesus' arrest. Quote Jesus' words in verse 52, which show that he opposed the Zealots' ideas. How might this quotation be relevant today?

3 Outline the work of either Martin Luther King (see Chapter 19) or Mahatma Gandhi.

4 The idea that a government or a country can do wrong is not a new one. Neither is it a new idea that people should oppose a country that does wrong.

The Old Testament story of Jonah is about God's condemnation of a cruel, warring people, and how Jonah tried to wriggle out of his responsibility to preach against them. You may know the story already.

The book of Jonah probably dates from about the fifth century BC, although it is difficult to be certain. The story has its amusing side, but it also has a serious point.

Either read the whole book, or, if you do not have time for that, read chapters 1, 3 and 4.

For discussion

'You can be proud of your family, but it would be silly if that led you to hate other people's families!'

Does this statement have anything to say about patriotism or nationalism?

Do you agree with the statement?

Activity

Try to see the film *Gandhi*. (Most video libraries stock it.)

37 Sexism

Sexism (like racism) is about prejudice and discrimination. But this time the issue is gender.

Sexism is the attitude that one sex is in some way better than the other—usually that men are better than women. This has its roots in sexual *stereotyping*, where women are seen solely as mothers and as the object of male sexual desire.

Let's look at a more subtle example of stereotyping. The fact that women are able to be mothers leads many people to think that there are some jobs which are more 'naturally' suited to women than they are to men. These jobs are ones which use the same sorts of skills that are supposed to come naturally to a mother. Nursing, primary school teaching and child care are three examples.

Do you think that some jobs are more suitable for women than they are for men? Are there some which are unsuitable for a woman? Why do you think you think like this?

It may not seem very harmful to believe that nursing is a good job for some women. It might even be true that there are some genuine differences between the sexes which come from the fact that men are biologically designed to be fathers whereas women are designed to be mothers. But for many women today this sort of thinking seems dangerous—especially when it is expressed by men.

Why is sexual stereotyping dangerous?

The reason why many women (and increasing numbers of men) think that sexual stereotyping even of a very mild sort is dangerous is that it denies women the power to choose what to do with their own lives. If society as a whole looks on women merely as potential wives and mothers, then those women who want some other role will find it difficult. The way society is organized will not take account of the fact that many women are not content with what have previously been seen as women's 'traditional' roles. Obstacles will be put in their way which men do not encounter, and women will find it difficult to get on.

Many people think we can see something like this going on today in the world of work.

In 1975 the **Sex Discrimination Act** was passed by Parliament in the UK. This made it illegal for an employer to discriminate against job applicants on the grounds of their sex: equal opportunities must be given to men and to women. The Act also says that once employers have appointed people, they must provide women and men with equal opportunities for training and promotion.

NOTE: The 1975 Act made some exceptions to its general ruling. One of these, for instance, said that women should not work underground in mines. Another exception was made for ministers of religion.

But despite the 1975 Act, there are still far fewer women in Britain in 'top jobs' than there are men. Here are some possible reasons:

- The system of employment takes little account of women's need to take a break from work for child-bearing. Most companies give between three and four months off for maternity leave. A minimum of thirteen weeks is required by law. If a woman takes a longer break from work to bring up children, she frequently loses some or all her previous seniority when she returns. Her knowledge and skills may have become out-of-date. She may lack confidence and need retraining. All these factors may discourage women from seeking promotion.

- Some employers may be deliberately unwilling to promote young women to senior positions because they are afraid that they will leave the job to have children. They may think that from the company's point of view, money spent in training these women does not represent a sound investment—and maternity leave itself is expensive for the employer, who has to find a temporary trained replacement. The employer may well find an excuse to get round the 1975 Act and give the promotion to a man.

- Many women experience occasional difficulties in trying to look after children *and* working—particularly if a child is ill. Employers may be reluctant to appoint a woman to a post if they think that she will be taking time off work to look after her family.

If you look carefully at the points opposite you will see that they all stem from the a belief that women are essentially mothers first and employees second. A male-dominated society is not very good at working out ways in which it might be possible to be both at once. So what measures do you think could be taken to improve the number of women in senior positions at work ?

Changing attitudes

The movement to give women a better deal in society is called the **feminist movement**, or sometimes just 'The Women's Movement'. Feminism is an extremely broad set of ideas, and feminist thinkers and writers often disagree with one another about how to go about things. But all feminists would agree that women have had a raw deal in the past and continue to have a raw deal today.

In order to achieve changes, feminists say that people's attitudes towards women need to change—and that means particularly, men's attitudes.

Are some occupations really more 'suitable' for women than others. or is that sexual stereotyping?

Feminist writers argue that throughout history, Western society has been largely dominated by men who made the rules (it has been a *patriarchal* society). Things have begun to change, but only very slowly. In Britain, for instance:

- A woman could not divorce her husband until 1857.

- The first woman doctor did not qualify until 1865.

- Women were not allowed to vote until 1918: and then they had to be over thirty years old. Women did not vote on the same terms as men until 1928.

- A woman was not elected prime minister until 1979.

But perhaps it has been the development and widespread use of reliable contraception methods during the last half of the twentieth century which has led to increasing choice for women and the increasing popularity of the feminist movement. For the first time in history, women can now have sexual relationships without the responsibilities of motherhood.

The language we use

Feminist thinkers point out that our attitudes towards women are often expressed in the language we use for quite ordinary things—traditional language which we have inherited from the past. For example, we often say 'mankind' or even 'man' when we mean the human race—people. Or we might say 'When a baby is born, he...' as though all babies were boys. Feminists argue that this sort of language reinforces a low view of women, simply by making assumptions.

The all-male preserve

Many feminists also argue that men try to preserve what they think of as their superiority over women through organizations such as all-male clubs and societies. Some of these have a large number of men who have senior positions in industry and the professions. Feminists argue that the attitudes expressed towards women at their meetings tend to reinforce prejudices and stereotypes.

Christianity and feminism

Christianity has its roots in Old Testament Judaism and grew up in the classical traditions of the Roman Empire. Both of these were societies in which men had the dominant role—they were patriarchal societies.

We can see this reflected pretty clearly in the Bible. For instance, the Old Testament gives laws about how a man could divorce his wife if he wanted to, but it does not say anything about allowing a woman to divorce her husband (Deuteronomy 24:1). And the laws about the punishment for rape seem to imply that an unmarried woman is her father's property—a man who rapes an unmarried woman has to pay her father compensation. He also has to marry her: she apparently gets no choice in the matter (Deuteronomy 22: 28–29). In contrast to this, the punishment for raping a married or betrothed woman was death.

In general we could say that the view of women in Old Testament Law was as part of a man's property. But it is worth noting that in the history books of the Old Testament we read of many extremely powerful and influential women, some heroes, some villains: Deborah (Judges 4–5), Delilah (Judges 16), Jezebel

(1 Kings 16–21), Esther, and Ruth are examples. The last two have Old Testament books of their own.

A patriarchal view of women reappears in some parts of the New Testament, particularly in the letters the early Christian leaders wrote to their churches. Here is a famous example:

> **In every church service I want the men to pray...women should learn in silence and all humility. I do not allow them to teach or to have authority over men: they must keep quiet. For Adam was created first, and then Eve...it was the woman who was deceived and broke God's law. But a woman will be saved through having children, if she perseveres in faith and love and holiness, with modesty.**
>
> **1 Timothy 2:8–15**

When we look at the long history of the church after New Testament times we often find Christian thinkers having this same patriarchal attitude towards women. One of the early church's great theologians and bishops, St Clement of Alexandria said: 'Every woman should be overwhelmed with shame at the thought that she is a woman.'

The sixteenth century Protestant reformer Martin Luther declared that it was a woman's role to 'remain at home, sit still, keep house and bring up children'.

As in the quotation from 1 Timothy above, people often justified these attitudes by saying that according to the Book of Genesis, it was the woman Eve who first introduced sin into the world. This was supposed to show how weak women were.

Because of all this, some feminist thinkers believe that Christianity has itself been a major cause of injustice towards women. These feminists would argue that even Jesus himself was guilty of sexism. Here are two major reasons why:

- Jesus called God 'Father'. But God is a spirit: God cannot be either male or female. By calling God 'Father' Jesus was making men out to be more like God than women were. This has continued in the way the church has taught people to worship: God is always called 'he' for instance, and fellow-Christians used often to be referred to simply as 'brothers' and not 'brothers and sisters'.

- Jesus did not choose any women to be among his closest disciples. All the twelve apostles were men.

This opened the way for later generations of Christian leaders to claim that only men could be leaders in the church, and to use that power to keep women down.

Many feminists believe that the church still denies women their rights: especially the Roman Catholic Church with its teaching on abortion and contraception (see Chapter 10) and with its emphasis on family life and the dignity of motherhood. (In this view, Catholic devotion to Mary the mother of Jesus is seen as a way that the church encourages people to see women solely in terms of motherhood: it maintains a harmful stereotype.)

For all these reasons, some feminists reject Christianity altogether.

Are they right: is Christianity too sexist to survive? Many Christian women would say this is going too far. They would describe themselves as Christian feminists.

Christian feminists

Christian feminism accepts that the history of the church has often been a sorry tale of injustice towards women. But they find hope and inspiration *in the Bible itself*:

- The Book of Genesis makes it clear that women and men are both made 'in the image of God' (Genesis 1:27).

- Jesus did not in fact share the poor view of women which was common among men of his time. Although the apostles were all men, nonetheless he was friends with women. (See especially Luke 10:38–42. Here Mary is seen as a disciple, sitting at Jesus' feet. Jesus says that she is doing better than her sister Martha, who is busy with the stereotyped female occupation of housework. Don't get confused—this is not the Mary who was Jesus' mother.) And the women disciples were the first to witness the resurrection—the male apostles would not believe them to begin with (Luke 24:1–11).

- Several times in the Old Testament, God is pictured in female terms (see for example Isaiah 49:15–16). So it is not against Christian tradition to think of God as Mother. Christian feminists would say that the church needs to explore and recover the feminine side of God.

- Throughout the Bible, God is seen as the one who sets free the oppressed and raises up the humble. The struggle for their liberation is something which God cares about: and it is expressed most clearly in the New Testament by a woman—in the Magnificat or 'Song of Mary' spoken by Jesus' mother in Luke 1:46–55. This struggle for liberation is women's struggle too.

- The patriarchal society which surrounded early Christianity obviously influenced some of the writings in the New Testament. It has continued to do so throughout church history—and the church too readily just accepted things as they were, and even propped them up. *But Christianity has a radical message about men and women which the church itself is only just beginning to listen to.*

This message is found in the New Testament: Galatians 3:27–28 puts it in a nutshell.

> **You were baptized into union with Christ, and now you are clothed, so to speak, with the life of Christ himself. So there is no difference between Jews and Gentiles, between slaves and free men, between men and women; you are all one in union with Christ Jesus.**

Many Christian women see the movement for a greater emphasis on the feminine side of God and for a better understanding of what the Bible has to say about women as a sign of God's Holy Spirit at work in the church. God is calling the church to work for change; and that means to change the Christian church itself, as well as to work for change in society at large.

Women's ordination

For nearly 2,000 years ordained Christian ministers were nearly all men. Many people see this fact as one of the most shocking examples of how Christianity has helped to maintain the idea that leadership always has to be male—that it is always men who make the rules.

During the twentieth century, however, a movement for the ordination of women to the Christian ministry has gathered momentum from the sort of thinking we have described above. Today nearly

In 1988 Anglican church leaders at the Lambeth Conference voted in favour of the consecration of women bishops. But the vital vote to ordain women as priests was not formally passed by Synod until 1992.

all the mainstream Protestant churches ordain women as ministers or priests. In Britain, the Church of England finally voted to do this in 1992 after a long and sometimes bitter discussion.

However, not all Christians have been convinced that this is really the right way forward. In particular, the Roman Catholic and Eastern Orthodox churches have serious reservations about the ordination of women. They both continue the traditional practice of accepting only men as candidates for the priesthood and deaconate. And within the Protestant church some are concerned that to ordain women to the ministry contradicts too much of what the Bible says.

THE ROMAN CATHOLIC VIEW

In 1976 the Catholic Church set out its teaching about women's ordination in its 'Declaration on the Admission of Women to the Ministerial Priesthood.' This is a summary of what it said:

◆ Women's roles have changed in modern times. Many people think that the Catholic Church ought to ordain women as priests.

◆ Some heretical Christian groups tried this in the early centuries of the church, but the experiment did not last. Christianity as a whole always stuck to the tradition which had been passed down from Jesus and the apostles.

◆ Jesus certainly broke with the tradition of his time in the way he treated women. He was accompanied by women on his travels, and honoured his mother Mary. So he was not afraid of shocking people or of contradicting their cultural assumptions. But despite this it remains a fact that he chose only men to be apostles. (Catholic Christians believe that bishops, priests and deacons get their authority from the apostles.)

◆ Although women priests were common in the pagan world of early Christianity, and although women were praised and valued by Christian writers, there was never any question of ordaining women to the Christian priesthood—despite the fact that the church had made other startling changes, like admitting Gentiles to the church without making them become Jews first (Jesus himself and all the apostles had been Jews).

◆ At the Mass the priest represents Christ himself. The priest is a sign of Christ who was and is a man. The church is the bride of Christ, and Christ is the bridegroom. When the actions of Christ are represented at the Mass, the role of Christ must be taken by a man. This does not mean that men are better than women. But it means that there is a difference in their roles.

◆ There are many good reasons on a human level why the church might want to ordain women to the priesthood. But the priesthood does not belong to the church: it belongs to Christ. Nobody—man or woman—has a right to be a priest: priesthood is a particular life of service. Men and women are equal because they are God's children.

In 1994, Pope John Paul II stated that the Roman Catholic Church does not have the authority to admit women to the priesthood.

Dangerous ideas ?

Some Christians feel that there are considerable dangers in feminism, despite its many obvious good points. They would say that feminism is about the *power* of women, that it sees the relationship between the sexes largely in terms of power. But Christianity is about love, and the relationship between the sexes is expressed in love through marriage.

Many feminists give enthusiastic support to ideas such as abortion on demand and some feminist writers think that marriage and family life are traps from which women must free themselves. These are ideas which seem to contradict much of Christian teaching, and some Christians would argue that feminism has done harm to family life and to women themselves. They would say that the movement for the ordination of women has sometimes been too close to radical feminism for comfort. They would add that by keeping with tradition and ordaining only men, the church would be reminding society that women and men have different vocations but are equal in the sight of God.

Follow-up

Questions

1 What is sexism?

2 Give an example of how sexual discrimination might be practised in the world of work.

3 Give two reasons why Christianity might be seen as:
   (a) encouraging sexism
   (b) discouraging sexism.

4 What were the main provisions of the 1975 Sex Discrimination Act?

5 Why does the Catholic Church accept only men as candidates for the priesthood?

Activity

Invite a woman minister to come to talk to your class about her ministry.

Spring

**Nothing is so beautiful as Spring—
When weeds, in wheels, shoot long and
    lovely and lush;
Thrush's eggs look little low heavens, and
    thrush
Through the echoing timber does so rise and
    wring
The ear, it strikes like lightnings to hear him
    sing;
The glassy peartree leaves and blooms, they
    brush
The descending blue; that blue is all in a rush
With richness; the racing lambs too have fair
    their fling.**

**What is all this juice and all this joy?
A strain of the earth's sweet being in the
    beginning
In Eden garden.—Have, get, before it cloy,
Before it cloud, Christ, lord, and sour with
    sinning,
Innocent mind and Mayday in girl and boy,
Most, O maid's child, thy choice and worthy
    the winning.**

                      Gerard Manley Hopkins

Gerard Manley Hopkins (1844–89) was a priest as well as a poet. In the first verse of this poem he celebrates the beauty of the natural world at springtime. In the second verse he says that this beauty comes from God's creation of the world—'in the beginning in Eden garden'. And in the last line he implies that Christ chose it and died for it (Jesus is the 'maid's child').

Now read the poem carefully again, looking especially at the fourth and fifth lines of the second verse. Here Hopkins introduces a darker note: the beauty of the created world which God loves so much can 'cloud and sour with sinning'. Hopkins was probably not thinking of any particular sin which could destroy the beauty of the world or the pleasure we take in it. He probably meant that any sin can harden our hearts and make us blind to the beauty of God.

But today a new dimension has been added to our appreciation of this poem. We are all very much aware of the things people have done which now threaten not only the beauty of nature, but perhaps the very existence of the natural world as we know it.

Sometimes people have done these things because they did not realize what they were doing. At other times their actions have been more blameworthy. So today our polluted and exhausted world looks very much as though it has 'clouded and soured with sinning'. We can if we like see Hopkins' poem as a prophecy for our times.

In his poem 'Spring' Hopkins was following in a long tradition of Christian spiritual writers who emphasized the love of God seen in the creation of nature. This tradition is often said to have begun with St Francis of Assisi (see Chapter 28). Francis spent a great deal of his life in the countryside. He loved the natural world, which reminded him of different aspects of God: and he is said to have had a particular empathy with animals and birds, taming a fierce wolf on one occasion and preaching to the birds on another.

Towards the end of his life Francis wrote a hymn in his own native Italian which summed up some of what he felt. It is called the 'Canticle of the Sun'. Here it is in translation:

**❝ O most high, almighty and good Lord
God,
To you be praise, glory, honour and blessing.
Praise to you, my Lord, for all your creatures,
Especially for Brother Sun
Who brings us the day and the light:
How beautiful he is, and with what splendour he
shines.
Praise to you, my Lord, for Sister Moon,
and for the stars so bright in the heavens.,
Praise to you, my Lord, for Sister Water,
So precious, so clean and so humble.
Praise to you, my Lord, for Sister Earth, who
sustains us
and delights us with her many fruits and her
coloured flowers and the grass.
Praise to you, my Lord, for Sister Death,
Who will come to embrace each one of us.**

The well-known hymn 'All creatures of our God and King' is a version of the 'Canticle of the Sun'.

Some uncomfortable facts

In order to survive, we need water, food, air, energy sources, homes and medicines. We get all of these from the world's natural resources. But the world's resources are limited. Some are in danger of running out, while others have been so badly damaged by our industrial society that their very existence is threatened.

We want to appreciate the beauty and order of the world and to care for its wildlife. We want to pass this great pleasure on to our children as part of what it means to be fully human. But great areas of natural beauty have been spoiled as we have pursued our other needs and desires. Some species of animals have become extinct, and others are threatened. Other animals are plentiful, but suffer cruelty at the hands of men and women.

Here is a brief list of some specific concerns:

- The great rainforests of the world are disappearing at a rate of about 100 acres a minute. If this were allowed to carry on they would all disappear over the next fifty years. Yet these forests provide oxygen through photosynthesis and are immensely rich in animal life. They also provide many of the plants which are used in the production of new medicines.

  Many of the rainforest countries—Brazil, for example—have heavy foreign debts (see Chapters 27 and 28). They say they need the money from the deforestation programmes to pay off their loans.

- The nuclear power industry produces large amounts of radioactive waste which is very difficult to get rid of. Some of it—the kind that is stored at special sites like Sellafield in Cumbria—will stay radioactive for millions of years. Other less radioactive waste is dumped at sea. All of it has to be transported, and future generations will have to deal with it.

  Human error and incompetence in the nuclear industry has already caused big problems: the

It is all too easy to destroy the delicate balance of the created world. After the Exon Valdez oil-spill off the coast of Alaska, a massive clean-up programme began. But our best efforts can sometimes make things worse.

This is what 'factory farming' can mean: pens so tiny that these pigs cannot lie down or turn round. Animals pay the price when people demand cheap food. The Bible shows God's love for people—but animals are God's creation too.

nuclear disaster at Chernobyl in 1985 released a radioactive cloud over northern Europe and has left much of the area surrounding the power plant uninhabitable.

● The sulphur oxides produced in Britain's power stations fall as acid rain on the forests of Germany and kill the trees. In Sweden acid rain poisons the lakes, thousands of which now have no fish. British law allows this to happen.

● Intensive farming methods inflict conditions on pigs, calves and other animals which many people find disturbing. These practices are perfectly legal and result from the demands we make for cheap food.

And so the list goes on. In recent years a huge 'Green' or 'Environmental Movement' has grown up as people have become more and more concerned about the damage being done to our world. 'Environmentally friendly' products are on sale in every supermarket.

Many Geography, Religious Education and Science textbooks written in recent years have tried to raise students' awareness of the issues involved in care for the environment. In Britain, the National Curriculum followed in schools has a distinctly 'green flavour'.

And if you have ever watched children's television with a younger brother or sister you may have noticed that it isn't very long before there is something about the environment. All this means that people growing up today are probably more conscious of environmental issues than at any time in the past.

▋ The Bible and the natural world

Christianity shares with Islam and Judaism the idea that the world is *God's creation*. It is not part of God. Nor did the universe just happen by accident one day. Rather it is filled with purpose and meaning, and reflects God's goodness.

How can we take proper care of the world? It is common sense to plant at least one tree for every one we cut down. Christians believe God has given people the responsibility of looking after the world and all its resources.

We can see these ideas very clearly in the Bible, and particularly in the Old Testament.

 The world and all that is in it belongs to the LORD:
the earth and all who live on it are his.
He built it on the deep waters beneath the earth and laid its foundations in the ocean depths.

Psalm 24:1–2

 O Lord, our God,
your greatness is seen in all the world . . .
When I look at the sky, which you have made, at the moon and the stars, which you set in their places—
what is man, that you think of him?
Yet you made him inferior only to yourself . . .
You appointed him ruler over everything you made;
You placed him over all creation.

Psalm 8:1, 3–6 (see, too, Psalm 19:1–5)

Texts like these are among the oldest parts of the Bible. Many of them were written at a time when the people of Israel were tempted to adopt the religions of the countries around them, especially the religion of the Canaanites, whose country they had largely taken over.

Now one of the interesting things about Canaanite religion is that it was very much concerned with trying to get what you wanted from the natural world. There were different gods for different natural phenomena—and by worshipping them you hoped to get a good harvest, for instance.

This was very different from the religion of Israel. The Old Testament prophets and writers repeatedly insisted that the natural world belonged to one God, who was the creator of everything. God had put men and women in charge: but the ruler of everything was God. We have seen this in Psalm 8 above, and we see it again in the Creation story in the Book of Genesis:

 Read Genesis 1:26–31

But being in charge of the world does not mean people can do what they like with it and try to get as much out of it as they can, for two reasons:

● Trying to manipulate the world for one's own advantage was a characteristic of *pagan religion*, as

we have seen. The Israelites' attitude was to be different: it was to be one of humble awe before God's creation—the sort of attitude expressed in the Psalms.

● The idea that you can do what you like with something you rule over is quite contrary to what the Bible teaches about what human rulers should be like. They are to be God's stewards or deputies who are looking after things for him. They are meant to rule fairly, as God himself rules, and obey his laws of justice.

We can sum this up by saying that the Bible teaches that people's attitudes towards the natural world should be one of *good stewardship*.

We can see the idea of good stewardship behind the laws of the Old Testament which deal with farming and the treatment of farm animals. In particular, the owner was not allowed to prevent a farm animal from eating some of the crop while it was working (Deuteronomy 25:4) and farmers were not allowed to go back over their fields once they had been harvested. Anything which remained unpicked was left for the poor (Deuteronomy 24:19–22). In this way the people were reminded:

● that the world and its animals belonged to God;

● that they should not exploit nature ruthlessly;

● that they should be generous towards the needs of others.

 How relevant do you think these three principles are to our modern environmental problems?

Christians today

Christians today have become very aware of environmental issues, just as everybody else has. This has led to an increasing realization that the Bible with its idea of 'good stewardship', has something to offer the Green Movement—and indeed, the world. So in churches today it is quite common to hear prayers offered for a better use of the world's resources. It is also an issue on which Christians campaign with members of other religions.

Environmental issues have recently received direct notice in the official teaching of the various Christian denominations. In particular, a meeting (*Synod*) of the Roman Catholic bishops in 1971 issued a report entitled 'Justice in the World' (*Convenientes ex Universo*).

Among other issues, the bishops drew attention to the problems associated with environmental pollution caused by rich nations which need more and more resources and energy, but then dump their waste. They said that people in the rich countries should be prepared to accept a less material way of life, and to waste less, if the planet was to survive.

But the question remains—for Christians as for everyone else—how do we put this into practice

- as individuals

- as a nation

- as a world community?

Follow-up

Questions

1 Give one example of industrial pollution and one of the exhausting of the world's resources.

2 How might a Christian use the Bible's teaching to argue against
(a) intensive farming and
(b) nuclear dumping?

3 In your own words, describe what Christians mean by 'good stewardship'. Explain its relevance for environmental issues.

For discussion

What steps do you think need to be taken to protect the rainforests, taking into account the poverty of many of the countries in which they stand?

'It is sometimes said that this is a Christian country. But when I read my Bible it seems to me that we our treatment of the environment owes more to paganism than to Christianity.' Do you agree? Give your reasons, using what is said about Bible history in this chapter.

Activity

Write a 'Canticle of the Sun' of your own for today's world.

Bible References

Old Testament

Genesis
chapters 1–3	17–18, 107
1:26–31	184
1:27	29, 68, 177
1:27–31	122
2:23–24	44
2:24	47
9:6	76

Exodus
15:1–3	160
20:1–17	18–19
20:8–11	115
20:12	41
20:14	44
21:24	25

Leviticus
12:8	123
19:18	13, 25
19:33–34	90
20:10	44
24:19–20	71
24:20	25

Deuteronomy
5:18	44
5:21	109
6:4–5	13
19:15–21	80
22:28–29	176
24:1	176
24:1–4	24, 45
24:4	184
24:14–22	107, 122
24:19–22	184

Joshua
6:15–21	160–161
7:10–26	160–161

Judges
chapters 4–5	176
7:19–21	160–161
chapter 16	176

Ruth (book of)
	176

2 Samuel
chapters 11–12	442 Kings
chapters 16–21	176
chapter 21	123, 124

Esther (book of)
	176

Psalms
8:1, 3–6	184
19:1–5	184
24:1–2	184
29:11	165
139:13, 15	68

Proverbs
6:6–11	116

Isaiah
9:6	165
49:15–16	68, 177
58:6–10	122–123

Amos
8:4–6	106–107

Jonah (book of)
	173

Micah
4:1–4	165–166

New Testament

Matthew
4:1–11	167
chapters 5–7	22–28
5:9	165
5:38–39	71, 76
5:38–46	167
5:43–44	76
6:6	130
6:9	42
6:17–18	130
6:19–34	123
7:3–5	103
10:7–19	135
11:19	115
16:18–19	20
18:22–35	75
22:39	32
25:31–46	32, 40, 123
26:47–53	173

Mark
2:27–28	115–116
3:35	42
6:6–12	19
6:31	115
9:50	165
10:2–12	45
10:9	49
10:11–12	24
10:17–22	123
10:17–31	107
10:43–45	105
12:28–34	13

Luke
1:46–55	177
3:10–14	123
6:20–21	123
7:1–10	90
10:25–37	32, 90
10:38–42	177
12:6	68
12:13–21	109
14:15–24	103
14:16–24	115
15:11–32	74
16:18	24
16:19–31	123, 128
20:19–26	81
22:35–53	167
23:32–43	74
24:1–11	177

John
2:1–11	115
7:53–8:11	80
8:3–11	45
9:1–41	142
9:3	37
14:16–17:26	19
14:27	165
15:12–13	42
19:25–27	42
20:19–21	165

Acts
5:29	82
11:1–18	91

Romans
5:1	165
7:14–25	87
chapters 12–14	83
13:1	15
15:33	165

1 Corinthians
7:3–5	54
chapter 13	16

Galatians
3:26–29	91–92
3:27–28	177
5:16–26	21

Ephesians
4:25–32	40
5:28–33	46

Philippians
4:7	165

Colossians
1:24	38
3:11	92
3:20–21	41
3:23	106

2 Thessalonians
3:6–13	111

1 Timothy
2:8–15	176
5:8	41
6:6–10	109

Philemon (Paul's letter)
	15

James
2:1–19	124
2:17	32

1 John
3:17–18	124
4:7–21	14

Index

Acknowledgments

The authors would like to express their thanks to those colleagues who have helped with research material for this book: Frank Beran, Nigel Spooner, Fr David Lloyd and especially Helen Knox. We also thank those others whose help has been invaluable: David Cameron and Amnesty International, Gerry Doyle and the Church of England's Children's Society, The Rev. William Lynn and NCH Action For Children, Brian McGinnis, Robert Hunter and Keith Burgess of MENCAP, Sally Miller, Marigold S. Bentley of The Religious Society of Friends, Michael and Norma Morrison, Ronald Barclay, Archbishop Desmond Tutu, and Padre Paul Carter.

The primary source for the chapter on Mary Verghese is Joan Clifford's *Wheelchair Surgeon*, published by RMEP, and we are grateful to Mrs Clifford for her co-operation.

Quotations

Except where otherwise stated, Bible text is reproduced from the *Good News Bible*, copyright © American Bible Society, New York, 1966, 1971 and 4th edition 1976, published by the Bible Societies/HarperCollins.

Page 47: *In Touch*, copyright © IFES.

Page 47: *The Alternative Service Book 1980*, copyright © The Central Board of Finance of the Church of England, reproduced with permission.

Page 49: *The Marriage Rite*, copyright © 1970 Liturgy Commission Bishops' Conference of England and Wales.

Addresses

Amnesty International (British Section),
99–119 Roseberry Avenue,
London EC1R 4RE

Adfam National,
First Floor, Chapel House,
18 Hatton Place,
London EC1N 8ND

The Standing Conference on Drug Abuse,
1–4 Hatton Place,
London EC1N 8ND

The Children's Society,
Edward Rudolf House, Margery Street,
London WC1X 0JL

NCH Action For Children,
85 Highbury Park,
London N5 1UD

Photographs

Amnesty International: 32
Camera Press: David Hoffman, 117; Anthony Marshall, 168
Children's Society: 139
Christian Aid/Elaine Duigenan: 128
CND/Martin Jones: 157
DAS Photo: 14, 69
David Hoffman: 82, 113, 120
Helen House, Oxford: 151
Home Office Prison Service: 73, 74–75
Hulton Deutsch: 147, 170
Image Bank: 7
Keston Institute: 48
Carol Lee: 129
Lion Publishing: David Alexander, 23, 39;
   David Townsend, front cover and 36, 115
Lupe Cunha Photography: 29, 57, 145, cover (below, right)
Mary Evans Picture Library: 10–11, 17, 160
NCH Action For Children: 9, 110
Press Association/Topham: 30, 34–35, 86, 94, 98, 99, 106 (right), 121, 155, 166, 171, 178, cover (below, left; above, left)
Rex Features: 77, 122, 137, 163
Salvation Army: 134
The Samaritans: 149
Science Photo Library: 53, 62, 153, 181, 182
Skjold Photographs: 19, 26, 41, 106 (left), 146, 183
Zefa Picture Library: 40, 44, 47, 51, 65 (both), 175

Illustrations

Ivan Hissey: 8, 61, 101, 125 (above)
Lion Publishing: 3, 20, 50, 64, 70, 92, 96, 105, 109, 114, 125 (map), 154
Tony Cantale Graphics: 91